The Kohlberg Legacy for the
Helping Professions

The Kohlberg Legacy for the Helping Professions

Lisa Kuhmerker
with Uwe Gielen and Richard L. Hayes

Doxa Books
Birmingham, Alabama

Library of Congress Cataloging-in-Publication Data

Kuhmerker, Lisa.
 The Kohlberg legacy for the helping professions / Lisa Kuhmerker; with Uwe Gielen and Richard L. Hayes.
 Includes bibliographical references and index.
 ISBN 0-9637034-1-2
 1. Kohlberg, Lawrence, 1927-1987. 2. Moral development. 3. Moral education. I. Gielen, Uwe. II. Hayes, Richard L. (Richard Lee), 1946- . III. Title.
BF109.K6K84 1991   90-25862
155.2'32—dc20   CIP

Contents

Dedication to Lawrence Kohlberg

First and foremost, the authors wish to express their indebtedness to Lawrence Kohlberg, whose theories, mentorship, and professional example reached, touched, and changed each of us in innumerable ways. He was generous with his time and friendship, and he helped to shape the thinking about moral issues for hundreds of us through the Center for Moral Education, the Association for Moral Education, and through the vast network of informal connections he sustained through the years. What we learned from him created a common bond among us and has made each of us better professionals in our own fields.

LAWRENCE KOHLBERG AND HIS COLLEAGUES AT THE CENTER FOR MORAL EDUCATION, HARVARD UNIVERSITY

From the left: Clark Power, Mordecai Nisan, Dan Candee, Michael Murphy, Lawrence Kohlberg, James Fowler, Carol Gilligan, Robert Selman, and Fritz Oser

Preface

Lisa Kuhmerker

The goal of this volume is to provide a road map for viewing the breadth and significance of Lawrence Kohlberg's work. It is designed for the student and practitioner seeking a single volume describing Kohlberg's theory and research and its applications to education, counseling, and clinical practice.

Lawrence Kohlberg transformed the way a generation of psychologists and educators think about moral development. Until the middle of the twentieth century it was generally assumed that morality was a consequence of cultural transmission, an accumulation of "inputs" that hopefully, eventually, would lead to moral behavior. Psychoanalysis identified the kind of impediments that could distort moral development; other traditions viewed moral development as a process of maturation in which the environment provided the necessary nourishment for the natural and gradual unfolding of the organism. Kohlberg's insistence that moral psychology focus on ethical principles of justice, and not just on adjustment to cultural norms, brought classical philosophical concerns back into a comprehensive reanalysis of moral development in the mid-twentieth century.

Moral development was not widely studied or debated during the first half of the twentieth century, in part because it was considered so individual as to defy systematic analysis. Educators could exhort, model desirable behavior, remove impediments to "natural" development, and then hope for the best. Kohlberg revolutionized our thinking by demonstrating that moral development is "cognitive-developmental," and that the child from an early age is a natural moral

1

philosopher who takes an active role in constructing his or her moral reality.

Kohlberg demonstrated that there was an underlying structure to the way human beings reason about moral issues and that these structures are recognizable and sequential ways of making meaning. He and his associates found such parallels in reasoning from person to person and across cultures that he characterized these sequential ways of making meaning as invariant, universal, and irreversible stages.

Furthermore, over a period of twenty years, Kohlberg and his associates developed and refined assessment strategies that could identify and chart changes in the structure of reasoning about moral issues. With this tool it became possible to measure change before and after an educational intervention, and this provided a tremendous impetus to educational research.

The focus on reasoning about principles of justice also served to "lift figure from ground"; raising questions about what other factors might be critical to moral development. Researchers asked themselves if other aspects of moral development might be "staged" and/or assessed though strategies similar to the ones Kohlberg employed in his study of moral reasoning.

Almost every college psychology text for the past twenty-five years has described Kohlberg's stage concept, and it is with this aspect of his work that today's practitioner is most familiar. But it has not been easy to move from this introduction to an exploration of the ways in which Kohlbergian theory and research may be relevant to the educator, counselor, and clinician in the 1990s and beyond.

While the original research into moral reasoning focused on ten-to-sixteen-year olds, Kohlberg's longitudinal studies, and the work of other researchers, revealed that adult reasoning about moral issues could also be characterized in terms of stages and that adult development could be fostered by the challenges of adult life and arrested by its stresses. This has had a profound influence on counseling, pastoral care, clinical practice, and programs in corrective institutions.

During the last ten years of his life, Kohlberg had a direct influence on education that involved not only the application of his stage model but affirmed that a democratic school structure could foster, not only individual moral development, but also the development of group norms about fairness and commitment.

A vast body of literature on moral development mushroomed during the last twenty-five years, some building on Kohlbergian theory and research, some critical of it, but almost all of it incorporating some aspects of the cognitive-developmental model. In its annual bibliography of new books and articles, the *Moral Education Forum* has averaged three hundred titles each year, and its annual Annotated Bibliography of Doctoral Dissertations ranges from sixty to ninety titles. At least 75 percent of all the studies and articles make reference to Kohlberg's work.

Some of these publications are highly relevant for today. Some are outdated, in part because Kohlberg was always "bootstrapping" himself toward more comprehensive ways of viewing moral reasoning and its relation to moral behavior. Often there was a long time gap between research in progress and its publication. The inner circle of colleagues and friends—of whom there might be five, six, seven, or eight hundred—were already building on revised concepts, while the work of serious scholars or researchers "in the hinterlands" might be outdated before it left the typewriter.

Because the authors of this volume each have more than twenty years of involvement in the field of moral development, have had long-standing personal contact with Kohlberg himself and with colleagues in the Association for Moral Education, we have been able to sift through this vast literature to provide the reader with an uncluttered and comprehensive overview of Kohlberg's work in the fields of moral development theory, research, and education.

Our primary goal is to present Kohlberg's work clearly, so that the practitioner can be helped in his or her professional activity. With a few exceptions, we do not focus on Kohlberg's critics. The annotated list of suggested readings for chapters 2 - 4 guides the reader to some of these critical evaluations. The bibliography at the end of the volume encompasses every one of the references by Kohlberg and his associates. Selected references by other authors are included. A doctoral student or researcher will find in this volume all the information he or she needs to decide whether or not Kohlberg's work is relevant to a projected research topic. The educator or counselor can see clearly whether or not the work of Kohlberg and his associates has relevance for his or her particular role in the helping profession.

* * *

In October 1985, Lawrence Kohlberg gave a lecture on his conception of supreme morality to the Institute of Morology in Tokyo, Japan. He outlined his stage theory and emphasized that the essence of the highest moral stage is a life lived according to a single ethical principle.

He opened his talk as follows: "In the belief that one's theoretical interests may be seen in better perspective, I shall start by briefly sketching how I came to be concerned about universal justice and the development of an individual's sense of justice, a question I as a moral psychologist and educator am frequently asked."

With increasing informality he then told his audience that he never claimed to be a living example of the highest stage postulated in his theory, that his high- school teachers had little reason to believe that he would turn out to be a very moral person, but that his experiences as a young adult led him to ask himself increasingly complex questions, which in turn helped to shape his moral theory.

Kohlberg's lecture serves particularly well as an opening chapter in a volume designed to introduce his work to a generation that was not part of the extensive network that shaped the thinking of philosophers, researchers, and practitioners in psychology and education starting in the 1960s. It reveals the clarity of his thinking, his integrity, humor, and the way he tried to link moral theory and moral action at every phase of his life.

From this framework for viewing the legacy of Lawrence Kohlberg, this volume moves to a systematic examination of his theory, methodology, and research findings within the context of twentieth-century philosophy and psychology. Chapter 2 introduces the famous Heinz dilemma and outlines the seven basic key terms and basic assumptions of cognitive-developmental theory as applied to the moral domain. This is followed by a description of Kohlberg's organization of universal categories of moral reasoning, his stage theory of moral reasoning, a clarification of the importance Kohlberg placed on distinguishing between rule or authority-based heteronomous thinking versus autonomous reasoning about justice issues and the place of moral reasoning in the moral domain.

Chapter 3 describes Kohlberg's twenty-year longitudinal study of American males, which began with the subject sample he used in his 1958 doctoral dissertation. The subsequent overview of research studies is divided into three primary clusters, focused on the issues that have engendered the greatest interest and controversy. These are cross-cultural research on moral reasoning, gender differences, and the relationship of moral judgment to moral action.

Kohlberg and his associates revised and refined the assessment strategies for evaluating reasoning about issues of justice over a period of twenty years. The description of the evolution of these assessment strategies shows the reader why the later strategies have greater validity and reliability and alerts the newcomer to the literature on moral development to take note of which version of the Moral Judgment Interview is used in the research designs and in the critical analysis of various studies and monographs.

Chapter 4 introduces Kohlberg's approach to the measurement of moral judgment, which culminated in the Standard Issue Moral Judgment Interview (MJI) and Scoring System. This detailed scoring system is one of Kohlberg's greatest achievements and has not been surpassed by any other methodological approach to the study of sociomoral development. Subsequently, chapter 4 discusses two alternative methods for the measurement of moral reasoning skills, Gibbs' Social Reflection Method (SRM) and Rest's Defining Issues Test (DIT), and compares the appropriateness of the MJI, SRM, and DIT for various research purposes.

Learning to score the Moral Judgment Interview requires a long and complex training period. Chapter 4 describes the rationale and the process so the practitioner can decide whether the activity, project, or research he or she may have in mind needs an instrument like the MJI and what kind of investment in terms of training, administration, scoring, and validation this can be expected to require.

The scope of this volume permits only a partial survey of Kohlbergian research projects, yet provides impressive evidence that many of Kohlberg's ideas have withstood the challenge of empirical research. An annotated list of suggested readings for chapters 2-4 guides the graduate student or potential researcher to the books, monographs, and articles that best present Kohlberg's own work and the confirmation or critique of it by the most respected specialists in moral development theory and research.

Reseachers can find references to all other books, monographs, and articles on moral development theory, research, and education in the annual bibliographies and the annual annotated list of doctoral dissertations of The Moral Education Forum. The Association for Moral Education is always ready to include the newcomer to the field into its close-knit circle of colleagues. Information about the annual conferences of the Association can be procured from its headquarters at the University of Minnesota.

Chapter 5 serves as an introduction to chapters 6 to 8 on educational interventions with which Kohlberg was involved. It puts the significance and limitations of the use of hypothetical dilemma discussions into perspective. It alerts the reader to the fact that Kohlberg had an influence on the fostering of moral development through traditional curriculum (to some degree in the elementary school, and primarily at the secondary school level) and that much of the last ten years of Kohlberg's professional life were spent in active participation in the creation of "just community" alternative school programs. Chapter 5 explores why a school might wish to transform itself into a "just community" and what the complexities of implementing such a goal might be.

Chapter 6 explores in depth the fostering of moral development through dilemma discussions. It provides samples of "classical dilemmas" and has enough "how to" information to enable the teacher to incorporate dilemma discussions into his or her curriculum.

Chapter 7 traces Kohlberg's participation in various secondary school programs, including the Cluster School in Cambridge, Massachusetts, the School-Within-A-School in Brookline, Massachusetts, the Scarsdale Alternative School in a New York suburb, and the innercity programs in New York City's Bronx and Manhattan. There is much concrete information about programs at the Scarsdale Alternative School and other programs that fostered moral development through innovative curricula within traditional subject areas.

In chapter 8, the impact of the just community experience on student development is infused with life by the inclusion of the subjective reactions to the program of two secondary school students. A dialogue between one of these students and Kohlberg is included, as are the reflections of an experienced teacher who came to her observations of "just communities" with the kind of doubts and questions the reader of this volume might have.

Chapter 9 assesses the moral culture of the school and illustrates the effort to transform the insights from the evolution of the study of the moral reasoning of individuals (MJI) to the documentation and measurement of change in group standards as a consequence of the "just community" experience. These efforts were still evolving at the time of Kohlberg's death. They have not gone through the years of refinement to which the MJI was subjected. Nevertheless, a program evaluator can use these measurements of the moral culture of a school as a starting point for assessing the effectiveness of programs in other settings.

Chapter 10 brings together Kohlberg's convictions and pronouncements on the influence, or lack of influence, of religious education on moral development. It is probably because Kohlberg focused on the structure of thinking about moral issues, rather than upon the religious content, that theologians and religious educators of widely divergent persuasions can find relevance in Kohlberg's work. This chapter focuses on the theories and search for a stage model for faith development, particularly the work of Fowler and Oser. The chapter brings together references from widely divergent sources that cast light on the way Kohlberg has been perceived from the perspectives of religious educationists. Guidelines for parents and educators who want to foster religious awareness and commitment complete the chapter.

In his postdoctoral work at the University of Chicago, Kohlberg set out to explore the integration of observations of the moral development of children and adolescents with their clinical diagnosis, treatment, and therapy. He had originally intended to be a clinical psychologist, but—as he explained in an unpublished manuscript—he decided that "more research was needed in the field of moral development before my stage concepts could be applied to practice."

Chapter 11 provides an overview of the fruitful thinking of Kohlberg on developmental issues related to clinical diagnosis and intervention. Much of this work goes back to the 1960s, but it has withstood the passage of time. Chapter 11 begins with a description of the competing counseling traditions that were current at the time Kohlberg began his work. It then focuses on the basic assumptions critical to a cognitive-structural-developmental point of view, such as that cognition is an active relating of events and that it requires cognitive conflict and exposure to higher levels of thinking.

In chapter 12, the influence of Kohlberg's critical insights on the theories of leading developmental psychologists is revealed. The direct Kohlbergian influence is most notable in the work of Robert Selman, Robert Kegan, and Gil Noam.

In chapter 13, James Rest—whose influence on the assessment of moral development is probably second only to Kohlberg himself—provides a backward and forward look at Kohlberg's stage concept and cognitive construction of social morality. This chapter can serve equally well as an introduction or summary.

We begin this volume with Lawrence Kohlberg's personal view of universal morality, and we close with another personal view of the man and his influence—the Kohlberg legacy to his friends. The closing chapter, number 14, consists of reminiscences shared at the Award Dinner of the Association for Moral Education when it honored Kohlberg in 1982. They show that even when the professor was his most absent-minded self, his full attention was on the people with whom he shared his ideas. If it had been possible, this is the way he would have wished to reach out to you—the educator, the counselor, the clinician, the practitioner who cares about the moral life.

LISA KUHMERKER
CAMBRIDGE, MASS.

PART I

MORAL DEVELOPMENT:
KOHLBERG'S THEORY, RESEARCH
FINDINGS, AND METHODOLOGY

Chapter 1

My Personal Search for Universal Morality

Lawrence Kohlberg

In the belief that one's theoretical interests may be seen in better perspective, I shall start by briefly sketching how I came to be concerned about universal justice and the development of an individual's sense of justice, a question I as a moral psychologist and educator am frequently asked. Unlike my examplars of justice, like Gandhi and Martin Luther King, I did not from an early age engage in actions stemming from a high moral ideal. Nor after having become involved in moral education have I ever seen myself as an example of the highest moral stage. Nevertheless, as I claim for all developing human beings, I have long been engaged in a search for universal justice.

This search began at the end of high school in 1945. As a moral educator I was recently asked to lecture to the staff of my old residential high school. When I arrived I saw a number of my old teachers in the audience looking at me with disbelief. They remembered me as a high-school boy who was always on probation for smoking, drinking, and visiting the girls in a nearby school. In this regard I was not vastly different from many of my school friends who felt little responsibility for rules about which we had no say. The rules I violated were to me rules of arbitrary convention rather than rules of justice or concern for the rights and welfare of other persons.

My concerns about justice were more the source of adolescent questioning of what I was later to call "conventional" morality than an active effort on my part to support the rights and welfare of others. This adolescent questioning extended to religion as well. One of my teachers sensitive to my school discontents suggested I read Dostoevsky's *Brothers Karamazov*. I found myself completely

11

immersed in the moral issues raised but particularly shared in the questioning of morality and religion of one of its characters, the brother Ivan. Ivan, talking to his brother Alyosha, points out the unending series of cruelties and injustices to the innocent, particularly children and concludes that if there is a God who governs the world where such injustices take place he would hand God back his ticket. While sympathizing with Ivan's doubting, I felt I myself could not come to any conclusions on these issues based on intellectual and school experience alone and needed to experience "real life."

As an adolescent, real life for me, outside of high school, was summer trips with friends—working on farms, road gangs, and in an airplane factory. These experiences of working and getting to know our fellow workers reaffirmed an abstract faith in American democracy I had gotten from my parents and from my reading authors like Emerson, Whitman, and Sandburg. My moral questions about the justice of my high school did not lead me to have any doubts about the justice of World War II, which I was prepared to enter upon graduation from boarding school in 1945. I reached Europe in the fall of 1945 as a member of the United States merchant marine. Having a Jewish father, what struck me was not only the wreckage of buildings and lives due to the war but getting to know the plight of the survivors of the Nazi holocaust or genocide of Jews, Gypsies, and other non-Aryans. This was not only destruction and horror but injustice such as the world had never known.

I speedily finished my term of duty in the American merchant marine and volunteered as an unpaid engineer to bring ships full of Jewish refugees illegally through the British blockade and land them in Palestine, then a British mandate. I had no moral conflicts about breaking British law which was unjust to the Jewish survivors of the holocaust from displaced persons camps with no home country to go to. So I was happy to see 2,000 refugees board our tiny ship, the Paduoah, an old Navy ice-breaker bought by the Hagenah, the Jewish defense force which later became Israel's army and navy. Our ship was captured by the British Navy as its predecessor, the Exodus, celebrated in Leon Uris' novel and movie had been.

The British Navy and Marines rammed the ships, used tear gas and steam, and clubbed their way to the steering room and the engine room and stopped the ship. Several infants died in the scuffle though the British tried to use no unnecessary violence. I, my crewmates, and the refugees were taken to a British concentration camp in Cyprus. The Hagenah helped us to escape from Cyprus to Palestine and equipped us with false papers. I and some of my crewmates stayed on a kibbutz, or collective settlement, until it was safe to leave the country with false papers and to take another ship coming from America to Europe to Palestine—a ship that became an Israeli navy ship in the 1948 war of Israel's independence against the Arab states.

My experiences with illegal immigration into Israel raised all sorts of moral questions, issues which I saw as issues of justice. Was using death and violence right or just for a political end? While the infants died and the adults went to a concentration camp, the aims of the Hagenah were political, to put international-al pressure on the British to leave Palestine. When is it permissible to be involved with violent means for supposedly just ends?

These gropings about questions of justice were intermingled with an ado-lescent hedonism and relativism about society's demands on me, be it American or Israeli society. The Israeli kibbutz represented ideals of social justice I had to admire, but was I really required to follow them, or could I live by the more familiar and easier demands of my American homeland? In the end these ques-tions became questions of ethical relativity. Was there a universal morality or was all moral choice relative, dependent on culture or on one's own personal and emo-tional choice? While words like "identity questioning" were unknown to me at the time, sorting out what I wanted to be seemed to depend on answers to some of these questions, questions which seemed to require some sort of intellectual guidance.

While attending a university was expected of someone growing up in my middle-class background, until this questioning I had had no incentive to go to a university. Faced with these questions I enrolled at the University of Chicago, which proclaimed the unexamined life not worth living and pursued eternal eth-ical issues through the great books from Plato to Dewey. Through studying John Locke, John Stuart Mill, and Thomas Jefferson I began to see universal human rights and human welfare as relative to the culture and/or the particular individual. My own moral commitment or identity made sense within the con-text of the social contract, which was the foundation of American constitution-al government. Still, I could see that philosophers like Locke and Mill did not agree with each other, and I looked for some principle that would underlie and justify all basic moral discussions. Kant's statement of the basic principle of the categorical imperative, "treat every human being as an end in himself not only as a means," seemed most fundamental. Equal respect for human dignity seemed to me the essence of justice.

My undergraduate philosophic studies had given me some tentative answers and directions to my moral questions and confirmed for me that intellectual inquiry has a profound effect on the individual's moral path. Accordingly, I wanted to go on to postgraduate work but was torn between clinical psycholo-gy, which I saw as actively helping individuals, and law school which I saw as preparation for working for social justice. I spent a summer working as an atten-dant at a mental hospital seeing from the bottom up both the needs of individu-als and the problem of social justice in that arena. This experience led me to enter psychology, where at Chicago I studied psychoanalysis under Bruno Bettleheim, humanistic psychology under Carl Rodgers, and behaviorism under Jacob Gewirtz. While learning from each, none seemed adequate to deal with the patient's moral problems and the justice pattern of the institutions.

I began to feel this more and more while spending two years as a clinical

psychology intern in a mental hospital after completing my course work. A cul-
minating incident occurred when a paranoid patient yelled to me in my office that
the chief psychiatrist was discriminating against her and persecuting her. The chief
psychiatrist came by my office, overheard her, and put her on electric shock
treatment. I protested to the chief psychiatrist that this would only confirm her
sense of injustice. When he and others did not see the point of my position, it
seemed to me time to refocus my energies.

While clinical theories attach great importance to the development of the
individual, at the time I started research work on my dissertation in 1955 very little work on children's moral development had been done. The study of moral reasoning and its development was not an established topic as stated by Brown
and Herrnstein (1975):

> When in the late 1950s and early 1960s Lawrence Kohlberg undertook to
> study moral reasoning and conduct, his choice of topic made him something
> of an "odd duck" within American psychology. The very words "moral" and
> "conduct" had a kind of No, No, Nanette period flavor to them. And social sci-
> entists were not nostalgic for that period when morality seemed to be main-
> ly a bludgeon for controlling sex and, possibly, swearing. No up-to-date
> social scientist, acquainted with psychoanalysis, behaviorism, and cultural
> anthropology used such words at all. To appreciate what Kohlberg has done
> to deepen the intellectual interest of what is, after all, a very substantial aspect
> of human psychology, one must have some sense of the tide he swam against.
> Moral reasoning, as a process, was something of which behavioral scientists
> were at least professionally unaware. . . . Terms like "attitude," "custom,"
> "norm," and "value" probably were favored because they seemed more objec-
> tive, more "uncommitted," and behavioral scientists were very anxious not to
> let their own values influence their research (though, in fact, they often did).
> In addition, behavioral scientists were almost all persuaded that cultural rel-
> ativism had been established by anthropologists' repeated discovery that a
> practice approved in one society was condemned in another. The most preva-
> lent position was, we think, that norms, customs, values, and attitudes varied
> from culture to culture and were what they were, providing no real basis for
> preferring one way of life over another (pp. 307-308).

Central to my own sense of how to approach the study of moral development was the assumption that the study must be guided by moral philosophy.
What was to count as moral or as developmental advance must start with some
philosophic definitions, assumptions, and arguments. These assumptions would
be open to question in light of empirical findings, but one could not start with the
effort to be value free.

My views that the study of development both grew out of and furthered moral
philosophy were based on John Dewey's philosophy of development and his

writings concerning the impulsive, group-conforming, and reflective stages of moral development. The first empirical work to pursue this direction was taken by the great Swiss child psychologist, Jean Piaget, in 1932. Piaget had made two great discoveries. Basic to the revolution of child psychology produced by Piaget were his interlocked assumptions or insights that the child was a philosopher and that the child's philosophy went through stages. To be a philosopher is to be concerned about space, time, causality, reality, and good and evil—by all the things that are the concerns of the grown-ups called philosophers. To go through stages is to have qualitative transformations in worldview or philosophy.

The stages that Piaget (1932) talked about were a premoral stage, a stage of heteronomous or unilateral respect for adult authorities or rules, and a morality of reciprocity and mutual respect and cooperation, especially among peers. Piaget's observations began with children around age three and ended at around age eleven. In my own thesis work I proposed to follow the development of moral judgment and reasoning through adolescence. Using dilemmas created by philosophers or novelists, I was struck by the fact that adolescents had distinctive patterns of thinking which were coherent and were their own, just as Piaget had seen distinctive patterns of thinking in younger children. In my dissertation I tentatively characterized these patterns as qualitative stages and added three stages to those formulated by Piaget.

When I completed my dissertation I was very well aware that by describing ninety-eight American boys, aged ten to sixteen, I had not created a universal theory. The stages I had postulated had to meet criteria which will be described shortly. The first step in determining this was to follow up my original subjects, which I have done every three years from 1955 to the present. Our empirical results have indicated step-by-step progression through a sequence, though the final stages have been found to be rare and the highest stage has yet to be definitively described. The longitudinal study has led to refinement and revision in the description and scoring of the stages. Both our philosophic assumptions as to what is more morally adequate and our psychological descriptions have been shaped by a "boot-strapping" approach in which data led to refinement of the theory which can be tested by subsequent data and research.

Coordinate with follow-up study was checking my doubts about whether the stages were really universal in non-Western cultures. This was part of my personal search for universal morality. In 1962 I chose to go to Taiwan to conduct this study because there were aboriginal Atayal villages, Taiwanese villages, and mainland Chinese children, and because a young Taiwanese anthropologist offered to help in the study. My American anthropologist friends had told me I would have to tear up my American dilemmas, like the Heinz dilemma, when I got to a different culture. I did not know if my friends would be right, and so I merely changed the Heinz dilemma from stealing a drug to one involving stealing food from a store during a famine.

My anthropologist guide and translator, who had studied the moral and religious traditions of these villages, broke out into laughter when he heard some of the responses of the village children. In the Taiwanese village some would say, "He should steal the food for his wife because if she dies he'll have to pay for her funeral, and that costs a lot." My guide was amused by these responses, but I was relieved: They were "classic" Stage 2 responses. In the Atayal village, funerals weren't such a big thing, so the Stage 2 boys would say, "He should steal the food because he needs his wife to cook for him." This means that we need to consult our anthropologists to know what content a Stage 2 child will include in his instrumental exchange calculations. But one certainly doesn't have to abandon the basic conflict posed by each dilemma. What made my guide laugh was the difference in form between the children's Stage 2 thought and his own, a difference definable independently of particular cultures.

By now, over fifty cross-cultural studies on moral stage development have been done. To summarize the findings in a sentence: the first four stages are found in almost all cultures, the fifth stage in all complex urban cultures and elaborated systems of education like Taiwan, Japan, and India.

What motivated these long years of academic research by myself and my collaborators? Essentially it was due to what seemed to me the potential importance of moral development research for educational and clinical practice. Among my thesis subjects was a group of delinquent boys. In a postdoctoral fellowship at Boston Children's Hospital, I attempted to integrate observations of the moral development of children and adolescents with their clinical diagnosis, treatment, and therapy.

At the time there were two problems with attempting to apply moral development concepts to practice. The first was the fact that there was still too much doubt about the nature and validity of the moral stages to begin confidently using them in practice. The second was the climate of the times, the suspicion of moral concepts as described in the Brown and Herrnstein quote a few pages back. That suspicion was soon to be changed by the moral clashes of the 1960s about civil rights and Vietnam. At the time of these moral controversies and student activism as a response to them I was teaching at the University of Chicago. The study of moral reasoning and its relation to conduct had become a popular subject among psychologists. Studies were done relating stage of moral judgment to behaviors from cheating to occupying administration buildings. While details of these studies caused considerable debate, the findings seemed to indicate a stage-by-stage increase in willingness to take moral responsibility for one's actions.

At the same time educators began to think once again about the role of the school and moral education. In response, my students and I began to experiment with Socratic discussion of moral dilemmas in the classroom, discussions which proved to stimulate development to the next stage. These efforts raised three controversial philosophic issues. The first we have already described, the issues of cultural relativity and moral development; the second was the claim that a later stage is a morally more adequate or better stage; the third was the role of authority and indoctrination in moral education. These concerns led me into a continuing exploration of philosophic ideas and dialogue with both critics and sympathetic philosophers.

As these educational issues became more central to my work, Harvard University's offer in 1967 to take a position focusing on moral education in the Graduate School of Education was a compelling one.

While dialogue with other scholars was important in developing a meaningful approach to moral education, I felt it was necessary to become immersed in the practice of education in dialogues with teachers and students. Work in the schools started with two assumptions of John Dewey's. The first was that one can't develop a theory of bridge building by applying pure research. It can only come out of building bridges. The second was that building a theory of education is a two- way street involving a collaboration between the teachers, students, and the educational theorist. Central to our efforts has been a faith in democracy as vehicle to creating a just and caring community.

The idea of a just community involved dealing with the hidden curriculum of the school or institution, not simply a curriculum of classroom discussion. If students were to take seriously thinking or discussion about moral issues, this discussion had to have an influence on the decisions that actually occurred in the institutional environment. To me this meant a community governed by participatory democracy—one person, one vote. Surprisingly, the institution to first embrace such an idea was a prison. A ten-year program was launched in the Connecticut Women's Prison. Then, in 1974, I started consulting with an alternative school, that was part of the Cambridge High School, committed to democratic decision making. Four years later I began consulting with a suburban New York school, the Scarsdale Alternative School.

Most recently, we have been helping to develop and research democratic programs in two very different kinds of Bronx high schools, the Bronx High School of Science which selectively enrolls intellectual, gifted students daily, and the Theodore Roosevelt High School, a school beset by the most severe problems of an innercity school. We are still learning from our experiences in this work, but I'm beginning to think I have something to say even to my old teachers who remember my behavior as an adolescent!

Chapter 2

Kohlberg's Moral Development Theory

Uwe Gielen

INTRODUCTION

The social psychological study of morality during the last sixty years has been dominated by three theoretical approaches: the psychoanalytic approach as originally formulated by Freud (1933), the social-learning view as represented by Hartshorne and May (1928-1930), and the cognitive-developmental approach as suggested by Piaget (1932) and Kohlberg (1958). The psychoanalytic view focuses on moral *feelings* such as guilt, the learning approach stresses learned *behavior*, and the cognitive-developmental position emphasizes the structure of moral *thinking*.

Freud conceived of morality as the control of sexual and aggressive instincts by the superego through feelings of guilt, shame, and inferiority. Humans are seen as possessing basic, unsocialized biological urges that have to be checked by a rigid and powerful counterforce labeled the superego. The superego consists of internalized moral and achievement values and prohibitions that the person takes over from his or her parents early in life. Later developmental changes are relatively superficial and do not touch the core of the superego. The superego contains a person's forced internalization of his or her culture as mediated by parents and other authority figures.

The social-learning view conceives of morality as a set of learned habits, attitudes, and values that are in no way distinguished from other habits. Often these are habits and values related to self-control, prosocial behavior, resistance to temptation, and underlying feelings of empathy. What a person will learn depends upon the social environment and the reinforcement contingencies that the environment sets up. Moral behavior is seen as being relative to culture.

The cognitive-developmental approach to morality focuses upon the development of universal stages of moral thinking. Such stages have been most clearly delineated by Kohlberg and are concerned with forms of thinking about interpersonal conflict situations. These forms of thinking are assumed to be identifiable in any situation where various persons may be said to have competing moral claims. Each stage of moral thinking represents a separate and coherent theory of justice that can be applied to various conflict situations. Moral thinking is said to develop from an initial concern with the physical and hedonistic consequences of one's actions, to an anticipation of, and identification with interpersonal and societal expectations, to a level where persons have worked out their own moral principles. This progression is assumed to be universal and sequential. Each person goes through the stages and levels in the same order, but the speed and endpoint of development may differ considerably from person to person and from culture to culture. The focus of Kohlberg's six stages is upon the structure or form of moral reasoning and not upon the culturally and personally variable content of moral decision making.

The theories of Freud, the behaviorists, and Kohlberg make radically different assumptions about the nature of morality. For Freud and the behaviorists, morality is ultimately irrational in nature and represents a form of social adjustment to the dictates and expectations of society. These theorists do not take the conscious moral conceptions of a person seriously enough, instead they reduce them to unconscious rationalizations (Freud), and to culturally arbitrary internalized attitudes, value systems, and behavior patterns (Learning Theories).

In contrast, Kohlberg's theory focuses upon conscious moral decision making while rejecting cultural and ethical relativism. While Freud and the behaviorists had little use for traditional philosophy, Kohlberg saw himself as the scientific and philosophical heir to the great Western philosophical tradition spanning from Socrates, Plato, Aristotle, Kant, and Mill to Dewey, Rawls, and Habermas. Kohlberg's theory is centered on the same big questions that these philosophers have asked. What is the nature of virtue? Is virtue innate; is it acquired from the environment, or must it be brought into this world through questioning and dialogue? Kohlberg asks his readers to start with Meno's psychological question to Socrates (in Plato's *Meno*):

"Can you tell me, Socrates, is virtue something that can be taught? Or does it come by practice? Or is it neither teaching nor practice but natural aptitude or instinct?" For the psychologist, it is wiser not to instantly respond with a favored theory of conditioning, instinct, or cognitive development but to recognize the prior philosophic question and to reply, like Socrates, "You must think I am singularly fortunate to know whether virtue can be taught or how it is acquired. The fact is that far from knowing whether it can be taught, I have no idea what virtue itself is.

Once the psychologist recognizes that the psychology of moral development and learning cannot be discussed without addressing the philosophical questions, What is virtue? What is justice? the only path to be taken is that by Plato and Dewey, which ends with the writing of a treatise describing moral development in a school and society that to the philosopher seems just (Kohlberg, 1984, pp. xiii-xiv).

Kohlberg's technique of assessing stages of moral reasoning is based on a structured interview containing stories posing moral dilemmas. In each of the stories the person is asked to imagine a situation where fictional characters have competing claims upon each other.

The best known dilemma is the Heinz story:

In Europe a woman was near death from a special kind of cancer. There was one drug that the doctors thought might save her. It was a form of radium that a druggist in the same town recently discovered. The drug was expensive to make, but the druggist was charging ten times what the drug cost him to make. He paid $400 for the radium and charged $4,000 for a small dose of the drug. The sick woman's husband, Heinz, went to everyone he knew to borrow the money and tried every legal means, but he could only get together about $2,000, which was half of what it cost. He told the druggist that his wife was dying, and asked him sell it cheaper or let him pay later. But the druggist said, "No, I discovered the drug and I'm going to make money from it." So having tried every means, Heinz gets desperate and considers breaking into the man's store to steal the drug for his wife. Should Heinz steal the drug? Why or why not? (Colby and Kohlberg, 1987, Vol. I, pp. 229-230).

The story is followed by a series of questions that attempt to elicit the interviewee's justifications and explanations for his or her decision.

When analyzing the answers to these stories, the rater is mostly concerned with the *structure* or *form* of the justifications rather than the specific *content* of the moral decision-making process. For instance, two children may give the following answers to the story: Child 1: "I think that Heinz should steal the drug, because his wife may be a very important person or own a lot of money." Child 2: "Heinz should not steal the drug because if he does, the police are going to lock him up." The two answers differ in their content, but not in their structure. One child proposes that Heinz should steal, the other child is against stealing. This reflects a difference in content, but the structure of the two answers is the same. Both answers are concerned with the physical aspects of the action, disregard the special moral value of the woman's life, and look at the dilemma from the point of view of a concrete, individual actor who is oblivious to shared expectations and feelings. The answers reflect a Stage 1 conception of morality, a form of reasoning found most frequently during middle childhood.

Kohlberg's approach to the study of moral reasoning is based upon a complex set of philosophical and psychological assumptions. To gain a better understanding of these assumptions, we will first discuss his understanding of the cognitive-developmental model. The model constitutes a general approach to the psychological study of the development of thought. Subsequently, we will focus on Kohlberg's delineation of the domain of justice reasoning which he sharply distinguished from domains dealing with other human values. This discussion will be followed by a description of the universal categories of moral experience, his conception of stages in the development of justice reasoning, and his approach to the problems of moral autonomy and heteronomy. The chapter will conclude by placing the development of justice reasoning within a broader framework. Much of the chapter is based upon Kohlberg (1984) and Colby and Kohlberg (1987).

THE COGNITIVE-DEVELOPMENTAL APPROACH

Kohlberg's approach to the study of moral reasoning is based upon the general assumptions and research strategies of the cognitive-developmental model as they have successively been elaborated by the philosopher-psychologist James Baldwin, the social philosopher-sociologist George Mead, and above all the Swiss epistemologist Jean Piaget. Piaget used the model to study the development of thought in children about physical objects, to study the history of science, and—to a more limited extent—to study moral development. Kohlberg (1984) extended the reach of the model to study social processes such as imitation, identification, gender identity, social attachment, and sociomoral reasoning. Close to the center of this approach lies the assumption that cognitive growth leads to qualitative transformations in worldview. Children, adolescents, and adults must be considered philosophers who are concerned about the basic categories of experience, such as time, space, and substance, causality, reality and imagination, identity, good and evil. Social experience is structured by many of the same categories as physical experience but is, in addition, characterized by the processes of role-taking and self-recognition.

The cognitive-developmental approach as elaborated by Kohlberg is based upon seven key terms and assumptions: structuralism, phenomenalism, interactionism, cognitive stages, self, role-taking, and the concept of equilibrium.

Structuralism

Cognitive structures refer to organized patterns of mental operations which often exhibit developmental regularity and cross-cultural generality. In contrast, the specific *content* of thought varies from situation to situation, person to person, and culture to culture. The function of cognition is to relate events and things to each other in an active process of information processing. The most general modes of relating are termed "categories of experience." These categories are modes of relating applicable to any experienced event and include the relations of causality, space, time, quantity, and logic" (Kohlberg, 1984, p. 10). In the moral realm, categories of experience include mental operations such as approving, blaming, assigning rights, duties, obligations, making "should" judgments, and making references to values, ideals, and norms.

Phenomenalism

Phenomenalism asserts that a person's behavior can only be understood within the framework of the person's conscious experience. In the moral realm, it is the person's interpretation of the situation that gives his or her actions a moral or nonmoral status. A person's judgments should be considered meaningful in his or her own terms and should not be reduced to unconscious motives, blindly learned habits, personality traits or external forces.

Interactionism

Cognitive structures develop through processes of interaction between the inner structures of the organism and the external structures of the environment. The structures are neither due to patterns innate in the organism nor are they due to stimulus contingencies in the environment. The structures arise out of, and are transformed by, patterned experiences which interact with organismic structures.

Cognitive Stages

The interaction between structuring tendencies intrinsic to the organism and patterned experience leads to cognitive stages which represent transformations of simpler cognitive structures into more differentiated, integrated, and complex structures. The stages are central to the cognitive-developmental model and are characterized by four general criteria:

1. Stages imply a qualitative difference in structures (modes of thinking) that still serve the same basic function (for example, intelligence) at various points in development.
2. These different structures form an invariant sequence, order, or succession in individual development. Cultural factors may speed up, slow down, or stop development, but they do not change its sequence.
3. Each of these different and sequential modes of thought forms a "structural whole." A given stage response on a task does not represent simply a specific response determined by knowledge and familiarity with that task or tasks similar to it; rather, it represents an underlying thought organization. The implication is that various aspects of stage structures should appear as a consistent cluster of responses in development.

4. Stages are hierarchical integrations. As noted, stages form an order of increasingly differentiated and integrated *structures* for fulfilling a common function. Accordingly, higher stages displace (or, rather, integrate) the structures found at lower stages (Colby and Kohlberg, 1987, Vol. I, pp. 6-7).

Self

Social development is dependent upon a sense of self and ego identity which provides continuity across time space, and role relationships. The concept of self is transformed with each new stage of development. The self and its relationships to others are reconceptualized against the background of a common social world and common social standards. The conceptions of self, others, relationships, and social standards are simultaneously transformed in a process of cognitive differentiation and integration (Kohlberg, 1984; Selman, 1980).

Role-Taking

Social cognition is based upon the process of role-taking, an "awareness that the other is in some way like the self and that the other knows or is responsive to the self in a system of complementary expectations" (Kohlberg, 1984, p. 9). Role-taking leads simultaneously to more differentiated conceptions of self and of others. Role-taking is fundamental to symbolic communication, social perspective taking, and moral development since higher stages of moral development are based upon more complex levels of role-taking. Moral reasoning involves an imaginative process of role-taking which attempts to reconcile conflicting claims of selves in a field of social expectations and standards. Social environments that provide role-taking opportunities also provide the conditions for moral growth. Role-taking is supported in groups that provide opportunities for responsibility taking, discussion of group goals, dialogue about rules and their fairness, and an atmosphere of concern for the welfare of its members.

Equilibrium

The direction of social development is also toward an equilibrium or *reciprocity* between the self's actions and those of others toward the self. In its generalized form this equilibrium is the endpoint or definer of morality, conceived as principles of justice, that is, of reciprocity or equality. In its individualized form it defines relationships of "love," that is, of mutuality and reciprocal intimacy (Kohlberg, 1984, p.9).

For Kohlberg, moral development proceeds from nonequilibrated forms of heteronomous reasoning (one-sided dependence on authoritarian claims and nonmoral considerations) to the fully equilibrated forms of principled autonomous reasoning (equal consideration for all moral claims on the basis of purely moral considerations). The fully equilibrated forms of moral reasoning are expected to uphold the demands of justice and are therefore used by Kohlberg to delineate the moral domain.

THE MORAL DOMAIN

In the social sciences, morality has been defined in a variety of ways. Often it is taken to refer to values, rules, and actions that are preferred by the members of a given society. Such a definition is very broad and relativistic in nature. It does not clearly distinguish moral values and rules from social conventions, religious values, or conceptions of the good life. In contrast, Kohlberg offers a more narrow and precise definition of the moral realm. For him, morality includes feelings, thoughts, and actions, but it is moral reasoning that gives the actions their specifically moral quality. Moral reasoning focuses on normative judgments prescribing what is obligatory or right to do. They are judgments of value, not descriptive judgments of fact. They contain universalizable prescriptions about rights, duties, and responsibilities and are not merely value judgments of preference or liking. Moral judgments tell us what we should do in situations where the claims of various persons are in conflict with each other. When people make moral decisions in situations of conflict, their reasoning frequently refers to normative rules and principles, welfare consequences for the various people in conflict with each other, the search for fair solutions, the balancing of perspectives, and the search for personal and group harmony. These moral concerns center, directly or indirectly, on issues of justice.

Moral philosophers such as Frankena (1973) have described four types of ethical judgments: 1) *deontic* judgments concerning rights and duties, 2) *aretaic* judgments evaluating the moral worth of actions and persons, 3) judgments about *ideals of the good life*, and 4) *meta-ethical* or reflective judgments about the ultimate nature of morality. *Kohlberg's theory of moral reasoning describes the ontogenesis (individual development) of deontic reasoning.* His approach centers on dilemmas of justice and assumes that universal issues of justice form the core of morality. His theory may be contrasted to aretaic theories which describe and evaluate the moral virtues of persons and societies and to theories outlining ideals of the good life (Armon, 1984).

Kohlberg makes use of the important distinction between normative ethics and meta-ethics:

> Normative ethical questions ask what is right, wrong, good, morally obligatory, and the like, and why. Normative judgments assert that a choice, action, or policy is morally right or wrong . . . meta-ethical thinking . . . addresses instead logical, epistemological, or semantic questions like the following: What is the *meaning* of the expressions *morally right* or *good*? How can ethical judgments be established or justified? What is morality? (Colby and Kohlberg, 1987, Vol. I, p. 12).

Normative thinking is focused on specific moral problems and how to solve them. Meta-ethical thinking refers to reflective reasoning one step removed from the consideration of specific moral dilemmas and actions. Kohlberg's deontic theory of justice reasoning and his coding manual deal predominantly with normative judgments, not with meta-ethics.

Kohlberg's dilemmas tend to focus on three problems of justice that go back to Aristotle. They are the problems of distributive, commutative, and corrective justice. Distributive justice concerns the way in which a society, organization, or third party distributes honor, wealth, and other tangible or intangible goods based upon equality, equity, desert, merit, and special circumstances. Commutative justice is involved in contracts, agreements, and exchange arrangements. Corrective justice applies to unfair transactions, crimes, and problems of restitution and retribution.

UNIVERSAL CATEGORIES OF MORAL REASONING

Kohlberg believed that moral judgments and justifications in a wide variety of societies are based upon similar categories. Taken together, these categories make up the universal language or deep structure of morality. Kohlberg divided the categories into three types: norms, modal elements, and value elements.

Norms

In the moral reasoning process, norms refer to the moral value or object of concern that a person deems important. Norms are used to justify moral decisions and include the following:

1. Life	6. Authority
a. Preservation	7. Law
b. Quality and Quantity	8. Contract
2. Property	9. Civil Rights
3. Truth	10. Religion
4. Affiliation	11. Conscience
5. Erotic love and sex	12. Punishment

(Colby and Kohlberg, 1987, Vol. I, p. 167)

In the Heinz dilemma, stealing the drug may be justified because "Heinz cares for his wife very much" (norm of affiliation), because "the druggist is a capitalist pig and deserves to be stolen from" (property), or because "Heinz feels strongly that saving her life is more important than following the law" (conscience).

Moral norms are of great importance because "1) they regulate human claims and conflicts, 2) define basic human rights, 3) are culturally universal, 4) are subject to sanctions, and 5) are nonreducible" (Colby and Kohlberg, 1987, Vol. I, p.49).

Norms are frequently institutionalized in systems of social roles (i.e., the legal system) which serve to reconcile conflicting claims. Norms define basic human rights such as life, freedom of conscience, and friendship. They are central to the institutions of all societies and because of this are typically protected by formal and informal sanctions.

Norms such as truth, life, friendship-affiliation, and conscience are frequently considered to be of intrinsic moral value. They constitute the issues around which many moral arguments cluster.

Modal Elements

Modal elements express the "moral mood" or modality of the moral language and include the following:

1. Obeying (consulting) persons or deity. Should obey, get consent (should consult, persuade).
2. Blaming (approving). Should be blamed for, disapproved (should be approved).
3. Retributing (exonerating). Should retribute against (should exonerate).
4. Having a right (having no right).
5. Having a duty (having no duty).

(Colby and Kohlberg, 1987, Vol. I, p. 167)

Modal elements occur in judgments such as: "Heinz has a duty to steal the drug"; "he should steal the drug to get even with the druggist"; or "he stole because he tried to be a decent husband." Modal elements imply a normative order within which duties, rights, approval, disapproval, retribution, and revenge have their place.

Value Elements

Value elements refer to the final justifications and values which go beyond norms and modal elements. Taken together, value elements constitute the "moral philosophy" of a person and include the reasons, motivations, and attitudes upon which a moral decision is based. The value elements are as follows:

Egoistic consequences:
6. Good reputation (bad reputation)
7. Seeking reward (avoiding punishment)
Utilitarian consequences:
8. Good individual consequences (bad individual consequences)
9. Good group consequences (bad group consequences)
Ideal or harmony-serving consequences:
10. Upholding character
11. Upholding self-respect

12. Serving social ideals or harmony
13. Serving human dignity and autonomy
Fairness:
14. Balancing perspectives or role-taking
15. Reciprocity or positive desert
16. Maintaining equity
17. Maintaining social contract or freely agreeing

(Colby and Kohlberg, 1987, Vol. I, p. 167)

Value elements may be seen in judgments such as: Heinz should not steal the drug because "they are going to lock him up" (7. Avoiding punishment), "he would set a bad example" (9. Bad group consequences), "the law represents the will of the people even though it may be a bad law" (12. Serving harmony), "Heinz should not do to others what he would not want done to himself" (14. Balancing perspectives/role-taking).

Norms, modal elements, and value elements provide the key terms out of which a person's moral philosophy is formed. In Kohlberg's work they play a crucial role in two respects: 1) They form the structural basis of the Standard Issue Scoring Manual. The manual translates his theory into specific coding instructions which will be described in the next chapter. 2) The norms and elements provide the "bones" for Kohlberg's six stages of moral reasoning. In the early stages, the norms and elements are only incompletely understood by a person. As the person climbs up the ladder of moral stages, norms and elements crystalize in a process of differentiation, transformation, and integration. Norms and elements are glued together by the structure inherent in the stages. At the principled level, the value elements become the principles that undergird a person's construction of a moral worldview. It is to Kohlberg's conception of moral worldviews or stages that we now turn.

Stages of Moral Reasoning

Table 2-1 describes three levels of moral reasoning, with each level being subdivided into two stages. The table characterizes each stage with reference to three questions: 1) What is the right thing to do? 2) Why is it right? and 3) Which sociomoral perspectives underlie reasoning at various stages?

We will focus first upon the sociomoral perspectives in Table 2-1, since they delineate the point of view from which a person formulates his or her moral judgment. At the preconventional level (Stages 1 and 2), societal expectations remain external to the self. The perspective is the perspective of a concrete individual actor who follows rules in order to avoid trouble, satisfy needs, and maximize his or her interests. At Stage 1, an action's physical consequences are not clearly separated from psychological consequences. Social interactions are construed from one point of view at a time, but different viewpoints are not clearly recognized or coordinated. At Stage 2, a person realizes that different indi-

Table 2.1. The Six Kohlbergian Moral Stages

Level and Stage	Content of Stage		Social Perspective of Stage
	What is Right	Reasons for Doing Right	
Level I: Preconventional Stage 1—Heteronomous Morality	To avoid breaking rules backed by punishment, obedience for its own sake and avoiding physical damage to persons and property.	Avoidance of punishment, and the superior power of authorities.	*Egocentric point of view.* Doesn't consider the interests of others or recognize that they differ from the actor's; doesn't relate two points of view. Actions are considered physically rather than in terms of psychological interests of others. Confusion of authority's perspective with one's own.
Stage 2—Individualism, Instrumental Purpose, and Exchange	Following rules only when it is to someone's immediate interest; acting to meet one's own interests and needs and letting others do the same. Right is also what's fair, what's an equal exchange, a deal, an agreement.	To serve one's own needs or interests in a world where you have to recognize that other people have their own interests, too.	*Concrete individualistic perspective.* Aware that everybody has his own interest to pursue and these conflict, so that right is relative (in the concrete individualistic sense).
Level II: Conventional Stage 3—Mutual Interpersonal Expectations, Relationships, and Interpersonal Conformity	Living up to what is expected by people close to you or what people generally expect of people in your role as son, brother, friend, etc. "Being good" is important and means having good motives, showing concern about others. It also means keeping mutual relationships, such as trust, loyalty, respect, and gratitude.	The need to be a good person in your own eyes and those of others. Your caring for others. Belief in the Golden Rule. Desire to maintain rules and authority which support stereotypical good behavior.	*Perspective of the individual in relationships with other individuals.* Aware of shared feelings, agreements, and expectations which take primacy over individual interests. Relates points of view through the concrete Golden Rule, putting yourself in the other person's shoes. Does not yet consider generalized system perspective.

Table 2.1. The Six Kohlbergian Moral Stages

Level and Stage	What is Right	Content of Stage	
		Reasons for Doing Right	Social Perspective of Stage
Stage 4—Social System and Conscience	Fulfilling the actual duties to which you have agreed. Laws are to be upheld except in extreme cases where they conflict with other fixed social duties. Right is also contributing to society, the group, or institution.	To keep the institution going as a whole, to avoid the breakdown in the system "if everyone did it," or the imperative of conscience to meet one's defined obligations. (Easily confused with Stage 3 belief in rules and authority; see text.)	*Differentiates societal point of view from interpersonal agreement or motives.* Takes the point of view of the system that defines roles and rules. Considers individual relations in terms of place in the system.
Level III: Postconventional, or Principled Stage 5—Social Contract or Utility and Individual Rights	Being aware that people hold a variety of values and opinions, that most values and rules are relative to your group. These relative rules should usually be upheld, however, in the interest of impartiality and because they are the social contract. Some nonrelative values and rights like *life* and *liberty*, however, must be upheld in any society and regardless of majority opinion.	Sense of obligation to law because of one's social contract to make and abide by laws for the welfare of all and for the protection of all people's rights. A feeling of contractual commitment, freely entered upon, to family, friendship, trust, and work obligations. Concern that laws and duties be based on rational calculation of overall utility, "the greatest good for the greatest number."	*Prior-to-society perspective.* Perspective of a rational individual aware of values and rights prior to social attachments and contracts. Integrates perspectives by formal mechanisms of agreement, contract, objective impartiality, and due process. Considers moral and legal points of view; recognizes that they sometimes conflict and finds it difficult to integrate them.
Stage 6—Universal Ethical Principles	Following self-chosen ethical principles. Particular laws or social agreements are usually valid because they rest on such principles. When laws violate these principles, one acts in accordance with the principle. Principles are universal principles of justice: the equality of human rights and respect for the dignity of human beings as individual persons.	The belief as a rational person in the validity of universal moral principles, and a sense of personal commitment to them.	*Perspective of a moral point of view* from which social arrangements derive. Perspective is that of any rational individual recognizing the nature of morality or the fact that persons are ends in themselves and must be treated as such.

Source: Lickona, T. (1976), pp. 34-35.

viduals each have their own point of view, their own needs, interests, intentions, etc. Persons are seen as relating to each other on a give-and-take basis, taking into account each other's reactions.

At the conventional level (Stages 3 and 4), conventions, rules, obligations, and expectations are experienced as being part of the self. The self identifies with and voluntarily subordinates itself to personal and impersonal (societal) mutual obligations and expectations. This does not necessarily mean that a person identifies with his or her society. The identification may instead focus on expectations prevailing in a subculture, such as a commune, religious group, or family. At Stage 3, the person sees himself or herself as being embedded in relationships. There is a perception that feelings and expectations should be shared and built upon mutual trust. Moral role-taking focuses on specific relationships and emphasizes the general characteristics of a good person, but it neglects the viewpoint of institutional or societal systems. At Stage 4, the person takes the point of view of a social or ideological system within which moral actions and expectations find their meaning and justification.

At the postconventional level (Stages 5 and 6), a person has abstracted general principles of freedom, equality, and solidarity from more specific societal or interpersonal expectations, laws, and norms. The self is differentiated from the expectations of others. It sees itself as subordinate to human or transcendent principles obligatory for all members of humanity. At Stage 5, moral reasoning reflects the prior-to-society perspective of the rational individual who is bound to society by an imagined social contract partially concretized by laws. The implicit and explicit social contract rests on principles of trust, individual liberty, and equal treatment for all, which should be the basis of societal and interpersonal arrangements and relationships. At Stage 6, a person takes "the moral point of view" that expresses an impartial attitude of respect for persons as ends in themselves. This respect should be expressed through dialogue and other forms of interaction based upon ideal role-taking. Ideal role-taking leads to the equal consideration of the claims and points of view of persons involved in a moral dilemma.

Persons at different moral levels and stages have different conceptions of what is the right thing to do in moral dilemmas, and why it might be right. At the preconventional level, moral justifications center on pragmatic considerations, satisfaction of needs and interests, avoidance of concrete harm to self and others, and obedience to rules and authority figures. At Stage 1, naive moral realism leads a person to believe that the goodness or badness of an action is self-evident, requiring little justification beyond citing rules and applying labels. At Stage 2, the moral rightness of actions is frequently judged in a relativistic manner. It is expected that people attempt to maximize their interests and that moral agreements depend upon practical considerations rather than shared moral values and expectations.

At the conventional level of moral reasoning, a person attempts to live up to shared norms, internalized conceptions of being a good person, moral or religious laws, and institutionalized rights and obligations. At Stage 3, the person orients toward shared norms that define the moral goodness of role-related behavior. A good person is one who has good motives, shows concern for others, enters into mutual relationships, lives up to the expectations of others, and respects obligations and rights customary in his or her group. At Stage 4, the individual's conscience defines and responds to obligations and rights that are embodied in the social, legal, moral, and religious institutions of society. Moral conceptions may take on a systematic, ideological character, or they may be incorporated in a more individualized conscience.

At the postconventional or principled level, a person has developed abstract moral principles which tend to focus on liberty, equality, community, benevolence, and respect for individual dignity. The principles differ from specific moral rules in several ways. Principles incorporate broadly conceived moral considerations that stand "above" more concretely conceptualized rules. Principles frequently focus on positive values (life, liberty, human dignity), while many moral rules are worded in a negative way (do not steal, kill, cheat, lie). Principles integrate specific moral rules and role conceptions and give them a broader moral meaning. At Stage 5, moral principles refer to universalizable rights and values that a rational person could agree to. Specific moral obligations, expectations, and rights must be derived from more fundamental human rights and values that form the basis of a just society. When there is a conflict, principles take priority over actual laws and cultural practices. Moral expectations refer to social welfare, social cooperation, and agreements based upon an implicit or explicit "social contract." The validity of specific laws and practices is evaluated in terms of more general moral principles. At Stage 6, moral principles refer to justice, inherent respect for human dignity, universal human care, maximum liberty compatible with the like liberty of others, and equity in the distribution of goods and respect. Social relationships must be based upon mutual respect between autonomous persons of worth and dignity.

Stage 6 constitutes the highest point on Kohlberg's developmental ladder. It embodies his conception of the "moral point of view" in its purest form. However, the fundamental nature, exact definition, and empirical status of Stage 6 have remained uncertain. None of the subjects in his longitudinal research project displayed Stage 6 reasoning, although a few subjects in other studies did (Kohlberg, 1984, ch.7). In spite of its uncertain empirical status, the nature of Stage 6 reasoning remained a crucial preoccupation of Kohlberg for theoretical and philosophical reasons. He approached developmental theory construction from a "top-down" point of view. The moral domain could only be delineated if the theoretician had at least a preliminary conception of ideal morality toward which the developmental sequence of stages pointed. Stage 6 defined for Kohlberg the "pure essence" of justice. Nevertheless, his coding guide for moral interviews describes only Stages 1 through 5.

Our discussion of the stages has so far been theoretical in nature. A more concrete feeling for the stages may be gained by inspecting the stage typed moral arguments displayed in Table 2-2. The table contains moral judgments in response to the Heinz dilemma. Judgments advising Heinz to steal the drug in order to save his dying wife and judgments advising him not to steal the drug are included in the table.

The stage structures of the judgments reflect Stages 1 through 5, including transitional stages such as 1/2, 2/3, and so on. The judgments proceed from a concern for the physical consequences of actions at Stage 1 ("if you steal you will

Table 2-2. Pro and Contra: Should Heinz Steal the Drug?

Stage	Heinz should steal the drug because . . .	Heinz should not steal the drug because . . .
Stage 1	his wife may be a very important person or own a lot of furniture . . .	if you steal you will get locked up . . . he stole without anybody knowing about it; he just stole it . . .
Stage 1/2	if you let someone die they might put you in jail . . . for stealing you won't be punished much . . .	it is not right to steal anything that doesn't belong to you . . .
Stage 2	if your wife is dying, you'd steal too. . . the druggist was ripping him off . . . it's up to Heinz to decide how badly he wants to save his wife . . .	then he might end up in jail, and then he would not be able to raise the money . . .
Stage 2/3	if he were desperate enough he'd have to do it . . .	the druggist worked hard and earned the money, and you shouldn't steal from him . . .
Stage 3	whether he likes her or not, she's still a living human being . . . the druggist is mean and deserves to be robbed . . . the children will be desolate and the family will fall apart . . .	if he explains the situation to the druggist he will understand . . . it is better to die with honor than live as a thief . . .

Stage	Heinz should steal the drug because . . .	Heinz should not steal the drug because . . .
Stage 3/4	only God has the right to take a human life . . . the husband would feel a responsibility to care for her . . .	if you trust God you will leave life and death in his hands . . . it will set a bad example . . .
Stage 4	life is more important than maintaining society . . . there is something special in a human being, perhaps some spark of the divine . . .	he would violate the rights of the druggist . . . taking the law into one's own hands breeds disrespect for the law . . .
Stage 4/5	stealing the drug may be a good way of bringing this injustice to the attention of the public . . . the laws of humanity are more important than the law against stealing . . .	
Stage 5	there is an obligation to respect human life which transcends the rights of the druggist . . . the right to life is universal and has universal applicability . . .	

Note: The table has been contructed based upon criterion judgments contained in Colby and Kohlberg (1987; Vol. 2).

get locked up"), to a pragmatic concern for fulfilling one's desires and interests at Stage 2 ("it's up to Heinz to decide how badly he wants to save his wife"), to a concern for role-related virtues and feelings at Stage 3 ("it is better to die with honor than live as a thief"), to a concern for socially defined rights and duties at Stage 4 ("he would violate the rights of the druggist"), to moral principles based upon a hierarchy of values at Stage 5 ("there is an obligation to respect human life which transcends the rights of the druggist").

MORAL AUTONOMY AND HETERONOMY

Starting with his dissertation research in 1958, Kohlberg's work was much influenced by the ideas of the German philosopher Immanuel Kant, the American philosopher-psychologist James Baldwin, and the Swiss epistemologist Jean

Piaget. These three thinkers emphasized that the development of moral judgment proceeds from moral heteronomy to autonomy. A morally autonomous person may be defined as a person who takes an independent and self-legislative stance toward moral decision making. Autonomous decision making does not rely on the authority of tradition, law, or holy books but freely appeals to universalizable moral considerations that should apply equally to all moral actors. In contrast, heteronomous moral judgments exhibit unilateral respect for tradition, law, power, and other forms of authority. Autonomous moral decision making stresses the autonomy of the moral domain over nonmoral domains and incorporates ideals of human freedom. Moral autonomy should not be confused with rugged individualism stressing self-assertion and the expression of personal desires and interests. The morally autonomous person gives priority to universalizable moral ideals which supersede self-interest and self-expression in situations of moral conflict. In contrast, heteronomous judgments tend to appeal to pragmatic, instrumental, and nonmoral considerations.

Kohlberg and his co-workers developed a typology that describes autonomous and heteronomous moral decision making (Kohlberg, 1984; Colby and Kohlberg, 1987). The typology is partially independent of his stage theory although there is a gradual shift from heteronomous to autonomous moral decision making along the sequence of stages. Autonomous judgments can be distinguished from heteronomous judgments within each stage.

When formulating the concepts of heteronomy and autonomy, Kohlberg followed the ideal type method of the German sociologist Max Weber. The method constructs "ideal types" based upon clusters of characteristics and themes that seem to "hang together" on the basis of an underlying, invisible structure. The ideal types of moral autonomy (sometimes referred to as Type B or Substage B) and moral heteronomy (Type A) are each based upon nine characteristics that appear to form an inner unity. The criteria for moral autonomy include intrinsic respect for persons, mutual respect in cooperative situations, reciprocal role-taking, precedence of moral values over other values, autonomous choices in moral dilemmas, and others. Specific scoring rules for these characteristics are discussed in chapter 4. However, it should be noted that the moral decision making of specific persons only very rarely approaches the inner unity of Type B or A. Kohlberg's moral types do not exhibit the same logical tightness and inner consistency that his moral stages do since the types intermingle structure and content to a considerable degree.

Following Piaget, Kohlberg and his co-workers have proposed three hypotheses regarding the heteronomy-autonomy typology. The first hypothesis states that moral growth throughout the stages of moral reasoning should be accompanied by a gradual shift toward moral autonomy. This has been shown to hold true in varying degrees in several countries. The second hypothesis proposes that moral autonomy develops most consistently in institutions and societies emphasizing democracy, equality, cooperation, and mutual relationships. In contrast, social environments emphasizing authority, social hierarchy, obedience, generational respect, and the immutability of tradition are expected to interfere with the development of moral autonomy. Tentative support for this hypothesis has been found in a number of cross-cultural studies (Colby and Kohlberg, 1987). Finally, it has been hypothesized that moral autonomy leads to moral behavior, because moral autonomy is based upon an intrinsic respect for moral principles and a sense of inner obligation. Empirical research lending support to this hypothesis is discussed in chapter 3.

For Kohlberg, the concept of moral autonomy expressed an aspect of mature moral reasoning not fully captured by his stage theory. His philosophical ideals which had been shaped by his readings of Plato (Socrates), Kant, Dewey, Baldwin, Hare, Rawls, and Habermas pointed toward principled forms of moral autonomy as the ideal endpoint of moral development. At the same time, his conception of moral autonomy was influenced by his experience of moral life in an Israeli kibbutz. The kibbutz ideology favored a socialist emphasis on democracy, cooperation, and egalitarian relationships. His students Bar-Yam, Reimer, and Snarey have also studied the moral conceptions and the moral atmosphere prevailing in collectivist kibbutzim. Based upon these experiences, Kohlberg has suggested that moral autonomy develops most easily in egalitarian societies and groups including "just communities." In this way, the concept of moral autonomy has served as a bridging concept linking together differences in sociocultural environments, ideal forms of moral decision making, morally inspired action, and ideals of the just community.

THE PLACE OF MORAL REASONING IN COGNITIVE AND SOCIAL DEVELOPMENT

Kohlberg's Piagetian model of moral development led him to place a heavy emphasis on the importance of cognitive skills. In his view, intellectual development sets the stage for sociomoral development but does not guarantee it. He has postulated that theories of cognitive development (Piaget), social reasoning development (Selman), moral development (Kohlberg), and ego development (Loevinger) define increasingly narrow domains of structural development. Developmental changes occurring in the broadly defined domains create the necessary but not sufficient conditions for development in the more narrowly defined domains. The more narrowly defined domains stand in a relationship of partial dependence to the more broadly defined domains:

Cognitive Development ⟶ Social Reasoning ⟶
Moral Reasoning ⟶ Ego Development

According to this sequence, Piagetian cognitive development is a necessary but not sufficient condition for the development of Selman's social perspective taking levels. These levels in turn provide the necessary but not sufficient conditions for the development of moral reasoning. Finally, the development of moral reasoning sets the stage for possible ego development.

The relationships between the four forms of development may be clarified by an example. At Piaget's stage of concrete operations (found around ages six to nine), a child becomes able to separate objective characteristics of an object from actions relating to it, learns to classify objects systematically, develops the ability to order objects along physical dimensions, and understands that objects may keep their underlying identity in spite of apparent perceptual changes. These abilities may then be transferred into the social realm where they are applied to social role-taking and the interpretation of social actions. The child begins to understand that another person can view the self as a subject just as the self can view the other as a subject. This understanding forms the basis of Selman's stage of self-reflection. The stage of self-reflection, in turn, may lead the child to construct cooperative (moral) interactions in terms of hedonistic exchange where self and other are perceived as having diverse desires, needs, and interests (Kohlberg's Stage 2). Finally, moral reasoning in terms of exchange between need-oriented persons will influence a person's character type or stage of ego development. In Loevinger's (1969) theory, persons at the Delta Stage are described as being wary, pragmatic, manipulative, and oriented toward the satisfaction of concrete needs and impulses—a stage that has clear parallels to Kohlberg's hedonistic stage.

Walker (1988) has reviewed a considerable amount of empirical research that lends support to Kohlberg's hypotheses about the relationships between different cognitive and social domains. In the studies, moral reasoning skills appear to depend upon social reasoning skills which in turn appear to presuppose general intellectual abilities. Intellectual abilities, however, are no guarantee for advanced levels of moral reasoning. While intellectual and social reasoning skills make sophisticated forms of moral reasoning possible, prolonged exposure to social relationships based upon mutual respect and concern equally contributes to moral and ego development.

CONCLUSIONS

Kohlberg's cognitive-developmental approach to the study of justice reasoning has been based upon a set of philosophical (meta-ethical) assumptions dramatically different from the positivistic assumptions underlying the behaviorist study of morality. His liberal optimism also diverges sharply from the deep distrust of human nature that forms the basis of Freud's irrational conception of moral inhibitions and identifications. Kohlberg placed "moral meaning making" and a conscious concern for principles of justice at the center of his theory. He rejected the cultural and ethical relativism that has pervaded modern social science in favor of a philosophically conceived, and empirically tested, concept of moral autonomy. In his view, moral psychology must contribute to the solution of educational and societal problems in order to justify itself. Such a contribution can only be worthwhile if it succeeds in delineating a conception of ideal justice. This conception serves as the underlying telos of his psychological theory and informed his educational efforts to create just communities.

Behind his theory there stands a Socratic and Platonic conception of the nature of virtue. He summarized this Platonic conception as follows:

> *First*, virtue is ultimately one, not many, and it is always the same ideal form regardless of climate or culture.
>
> *Second*, the name of this ideal form is justice.
>
> *Third*, not only is the good one, but virtue is knowledge of the good. He who knows the good chooses the good.
>
> *Fourth*, the kind of knowledge of the good that is virtue is philosophical knowledge or intuition of the ideal form of the good, not correct opinion or acceptance of conventional beliefs.
>
> *Fifth*, the good can then be taught, but its teachers must in a certain sense be philosopher-kings.
>
> *Sixth*, the reason the good can be taught is because we know it all along dimly or at a low level and its teaching is more a calling out than an instruction.
>
> *Seventh*, the reason we think the good cannot be taught is because the same good is known differently at different levels and direct instruction cannot take place across levels.
>
> *Eighth*, then the teaching of virtue is the asking of questions and the pointing of the way, not the giving of answers. Moral education is the leading of people upward, not the putting into the mind of knowledge that was not there before.
>
> (Kohlberg, 1981, p. 30)

This Platonic view stands in direct contradiction to the empiricist and Freudian viewpoints that predominate in modern American psychology. Surprisingly, Kohlberg was able to translate his Platonic philosophical assumptions into a rigorous methodology and research program. His universal moral categories—the norms, modal elements, and value elements described above—map with great precision the coding instructions contained in his elaborate Standard Issue Scoring Manual. One of his greatest strengths has been his ability to interweave meta-ethical assumptions with the psychological description of normative reasoning, and the systematic assessement of the moral ideas of his subjects. It took him more than thirty years to fully develop his theory, methodology, and longitudinal research projects. This development was based upon his "bootstrapping" approach which led to constant revisions based upon feedback between philosophical assumptions, psychological theories, methodological issues, and research results.

Kohlberg restricted his Piagetian "hard stage model" to the development of justice reasoning. The "hard state model" is based upon Piagetian assumptions regarding structured wholeness, invariant sequence, and hierarchical integration. Kohlberg believed that the domain of justice reasoning lent itself to explanation in terms of a Piagetian stage model but that other forms of ethical reasoning were best explained by looser "soft stage models." Kohlberg preferred to focus on "morality as justice [since it] best renders our view of morality as universal. It restricts morality to a central minimal core, striving for universal agreement in the face of more relativistic conceptions of the good" (Kohlberg, 1984, p. 306).

Other theorists such as Erikson, Fowler, Gilligan, Kegan, and Perry have explored alternative visions of ethicality that do not fully satisfy the rigorous Piagetian criteria of stage development. Toward the end of his life, Kohlberg began to work with his colleague, Thomas Lickona, on a book describing a variety of broad trajectories toward ethical development. His theory of justice reasoning provides us only with a very incomplete account of ethical development. Nevertheless, this incomplete account constitutes the most sophisticated and rigorous conception of moral development now available.

Chapter 3

Research on Moral Reasoning

Uwe Gielen

INTRODUCTION

In 1983, Colby et al. reported the results of Kohlberg's twenty-year longitudinal study of American males. The study had been conducted with two goals in
mind: to develop a reliable and valid scoring system and to use this scoring system to demonstrate the existence of an invariant sequence of internally consistent stages of moral reasoning. The study was successful in achieving the two
goals, but it left a number of questions unanswered. Among the questions, three
have been asked most persistently: 1) Is the sequence of stages universal in
nature, or does it apply merely to persons growing up in American or Western
societies? 2) Does Kohlberg's focus on justice reasoning among males lead to a
truncated vision of morality that distorts and invalidates the moral development
of women? 3) What relationships, if any, exist between moral reasoning and
moral action?

Many critics of Kohlberg's approach have been highly skeptical about his
answers to these questions. They have argued that his theory and methodology
is ethnocentric in nature (Dien, 1982), that his approach misconstrues the moral
experience of women (Gilligan, 1982), and that moral reasoning and moral
action may be unrelated to each other in most real-life situations. In response to
these criticisms, Kohlberg tightened up his scoring system, provided more precise and focused theoretical discussions, worked out in considerable detail the
philosophical assumptions underlying his theories, and conducted, together with
his students and colleagues, an enormous amount of empirical research. Prior to
his death in 1987, he had planned to edit a comprehensive volume of empirical

studies using the Moral Judgment Interview (MJI). This was not to be, and so we will limit ourselves here to a very selective survey of relevant research projects.

While Kohlberg's critics have raised many important theoretical and empirical issues, the critics have also frequently been misled. The research evidence suggests that Kohlberg's theories and methods can be meaningfully applied in a wide variety of cultural contexts. The MJI appears to be a reliable and valid measure of moral reasoning. Gender differences on structural measures of moral reasoning are minimal, or they reflect educational and occupational differences. Social experience appears to be associated in theoretically understandable ways with moral reasoning, while measures of moral reasoning are frequently related in a meaningful way to moral actions.

Typically, methodological issues and research results led Kohlberg to raise important theoretical and philosophical issues. In line with his "bootstrapping" approach, philosophical assumptions, psychological theories, methodological issues, research results, and educational efforts stood in a relationship of constant mutual feedback. Therefore, our discussion of research results will include a number of theoretical considerations. Since for Kohlberg the concept of morality was basically a philosophical concept, psychological research on morality had to serve philosophical ends. To him, the main purpose of psychological research on morality was to empirically investigate and jeopardize the meta-ethical and normative assumptions underlying his theory and the normative conceptions of justice embodied in his stages and types. This grandiose, philosophically inspired conception of empirical research separated Kohlberg from most of his psychological colleagues who have attempted to be scientifically objective and philosophically neutral. Kohlberg did not believe that such neutrality was possible or desirable. For him, all psychological research on morality was based upon philosophical assumptions, and he used his psychological research to simultaneously test his philosophical assumptions. The empirical success of his psychological approach to the study of morality appeared to him to vindicate his deontic conception of the nature of justice.

A LONGITUDINAL STUDY OF AMERICAN MALES

Kohlberg tested his stage model most rigorously in his twenty-year longitudinal study of moral development. He started with an original sample of ninety-eight boys aged ten to sixteen, many of whom were reinterviewed a number of times. Since some of the boys could not be reinterviewed, and since the interviews of seven subjects were used to construct the Standard Issue Scoring Manual, Kohlberg and his team reported longitudinal data for fifty-one subjects only (Colby and Kohlberg, 1987). At the end of the study, the subjects ranged in age from thirty to thirty-six. The study included information about parental social class, level of intelligence, and sociometric status. All subjects were given oral interviews on Forms A, B, and C of the MJI. The interviews were scored by highly experienced raters.

The results of the study give strong support to the stage model. Individually and as a group, the subjects moved slowly but steadily upward on the moral stage ladder. When the results for Forms A, B, and C were integrated, 67 percent of all reasoning occurred at the individual's modal stage, and 99 percent of all reasoning fell into two adjacent stages. Although certain scoring rules may have inflated these estimates of stage consistency somewhat, the results nevertheless point to highly consistent reasoning across the nine dilemmas and six issues. None of the subjects skipped a stage. On a nine-point stage scale, only 3 percent of the reinterviews were rated lower than the immediately preceding interviews.

At age ten, 59 percent of the subjects' moral reasoning was rated at Stage 2, 26 percent was rated at Stage 1, and 14 percent at Stage 3. At age eighteen, Stage 1 reasoning had completely disappeared. About 20 percent of the reasoning was now rated at Stage 2, 58 percent at Stage 3, and 20 percent at Stage 4. At age thirty-six, Stage 1 and 2 reasoning was absent, Stage 3 reasoning had declined to 31 percent, Stage 4 reasoning had increased to 62 percent, and Stage 5 reasoning was used in 7 percent of the arguments. After age twenty-six, every subject was scored at Stage 3 or above. Moral development occurred throughout the whole age range represented in the research project.

Age accounted for 60 percent of the variability in the subjects' moral judgment scores. Parental social class and the subjects' level of intelligence correlated moderately with the moral reasoning scores, but the subjects' sociometric status during the school years appeared to have little relevance to their later moral development. However, their educational experience had an important influence on their moral reasoning skills. Subjects did not attain a consistent Stage 4 rating unless they had attended college for some time, and all the subjects rated at Stage 4/5 had completed college.

For Kohlberg, the success of the longitudinal research project validated his "bootstrapping" approach to psychological research. The project led to the development of a highly reliable scoring methodology. The methodology, in turn, was applied to the moral reasoning interviews of the remaining fifty-one subjects. The subjects reasoned consistently across the nine dilemmas, suggesting the presence of a coherent moral domain united by a single underlying organizational structure. Development followed an upward path toward more abstract, differentiated, and inherently moral forms of reasoning. Movement on this path was supported by intellectual skills, longterm exposure to educational experiences, and an upper-middle-class environment.

CROSS-CULTURAL RESEARCH ON MORAL REASONING

A Theoretical Perspective on Cross-Cultural Research

One of Kohlberg's most stimulating and controversial claims concerns his contention that moral reasoning develops according to a universal sequence of stages that transcends or cuts across culturally specific ethical value systems, religions, political ideologies, and conceptions of the cosmic order. The cross-cultural empirical validation of his approach and related approaches has made considerable progress in recent years (Edwards, 1981, 1986; Gielen, 1990; Moon, 1986; Snarey, 1985; Vine, 1986). More than fifty studies employing the MJI in a wide variety of cultures are available, while more than thirty studies using the Defining Issues Test (DIT) outside the USA have been reported (Gielen, Miao, and Avellani, 1990; Moon, 1986).

Kohlberg's proposition is based on the following assumptions:

1. In all societies there exists a common set of moral problems, issues, and conflicts. These common issues ensue because they are based upon the very nature of social living and social role-taking.

2. Social role-taking is based upon the recognition that self and others share universal human features regardless of more specific personal differences. This is true in all societies.

3. Moral conflicts can be conceptualized in a limited number of ways that reflect underlying sociomoral perspectives based upon role-taking.

4. A developmental hierarchy of increasingly differentiated, integrated, and universal conceptions will be found in all societies, unless powerful social pressures and fundamentalist ideologies prevail over this "natural hierarchy."

5. These hierarchies of increasingly differentiated conceptions will be empirically and universally found, regardless of more specific, culturally variable social roles, moral prescriptions, and choices. Philosophical, religious, and political value systems may have a powerful influence upon the content of moral reasoning, but they influence structural development only indirectly.

6. The MJI can be easily adapted to specific situational and cultural circumstances and can be successfully employed with persons from widely differing educational backgrounds. The DIT, however, as a demanding written test, can be used only with selected literate groups, depending upon their educational background and test-taking experience.

As can be seen, these six assumptions reflect the very nature of Kohlberg's theory. To test them cross-culturally means to jeopardize his theoretical claims in a profound manner. Kohlberg early on reported a number of studies which were conducted in Mexico, Taiwan, and Turkey (Kohlberg, 1969). Although age trends in moral reasoning based upon these studies were widely reprinted in developmental and introductory psychology textbooks, Kohlberg's report omitted crucial details regarding sample size, translation and adaptation of interview procedures, and means and range of scores. This information did not become available until Snarey published his authoritative overview of cross-cultural research in 1985. Kohlberg's early studies were based upon his Aspect-Scoring system and are best considered pilot studies. Their results should be compared only with great caution to the later, more thorough investigations by Edwards, Lei, Nisan and Kohlberg, Snarey, Vasudev, and others.

Many critics of Kohlberg have asserted that his theory incorporates a fundamental ethnocentric bias because it takes "the rationalistic, individualistic, 'lib-
eral-democratic' values of the white, male, American intellectual as distinctively mature" (Vine, 1986, p. 432). In a similar and more specific vein, Dien
(1982) has argued that Kohlberg's conception of moral autonomy is incompat-
ible with the traditional Chinese vision of moral maturity. This vision sees
humanity as being embedded in an orderly universe and governed by an innate
sense to maintain moral harmony. Kohlberg's emphasis on autonomous, free, and
rational decision making is said to misconstrue the Chinese moral experience.

Most of Kohlberg's critics have argued from a position of cultural relativism.
They claim that moral development cannot be captured by any cross-culturally
valid, one-dimensional scale which reduces the rich variety of culturally structured moral experience to an arbitrary, inherently ethnocentric focus on the
development of moral autonomy. Kohlberg's theory is said to lead to scientifically unsound and morally invidious conclusions that fail to respect the uniqueness and moral dignity of non-Western cultures. (See Kohlberg, 1984, pp. 320-
338 for a summary of some of these criticisms and his response to them.)

Besides criticizing Kohlberg for his allegedly ethnocentric theory, critics
have also doubted whether Kohlbergian moral dilemmas and interview procedures
are realistic or appropriate for many non-Western cultures. We may call this
general "suspicion" (it really is no more than that) potential for *methodological
and theoretical imperialism* in developmental approaches.

Cross-Cultural Research Findings

Following Edwards (1981; 1986), we will now consider three broad questions
about the significance of cross-cultural research on moral reasoning: 1) Can the
interview method and the DIT be successfully adapted to a wide variety of cultural situations? 2) Does moral reasoning develop according to a universal
sequence of stages? 3) Can cross-cultural research contribute to our understanding of sociomoral experiences that support or hinder the development of
moral reasoning? These experiences may include differences in education, presence or absence of literacy, fundamentally different cultural value systems, societal complexity, immigration and cross-cultural contact, and gender roles in
different societies.

Kohlberg's MJI is readily adaptable to a wide variety of cultural situations.
As an example, we may refer to my use of the famous Heinz (= Jules) dilemma
in a small Haitian village. For the mostly illiterate, desperately poor respondents (both women and men), this dilemma was far more realistic and "ecolog-
ically valid" than it has been for my German or American middle-class respondents. The large majority of Haitian villagers firmly rejected stealing as a valid
alternative in the (adapted) Heinz dilemma, though in a comparable, real-life situation it would have been in their (or their wives') "naked self-interest" to steal.
Most Haitian villagers reasoned at Stages 2 and 3 (see also White, 1984). In

real life, stealing in the villages occurred fairly infrequently, especially given the extreme poverty of the villagers. Other researchers working in rural, non-Western areas such as Kenya have also reported that the MJI elicits a rich variety of understandable moral arguments (Harkness, Edwards, and Super, 1981). Moral dilemmas indigenous to a culture can be readily developed although this has only been reported for a few research projects (Lee, 1973). Many adults in isolated villages in traditional cultures have been reported to reason predominantly at Stages 3 and 2. Among the Kipsigis of Kenya, moral judgment scores were systematically correlated with people's ratings of each other's moral integrity (Harkness, Edwards, and Super, 1981).

The research evidence for the cross-cultural usefulness of the DIT presents a mixed picture, as may be expected from a written, complex test. While East Asian students from Hong Kong, Japan, South Korea, and Taiwan readily respond to and understand the DIT (Gielen, Miao, and Avellani, 1990), many students from the Sudan (Ahmed, Gielen, and Avellani, 1987) and Kuwait do not readily understand the test. The testing format and the nature of the moral arguments provided by the DIT present major difficulties for many of these Arabic students.

The strongest research evidence supporting the cross-cultural validity of Kohlberg's moral stage theory derives from longitudinal studies conducted in Israel, Taiwan, and Turkey (Snarey, Reimer, and Kohlberg, 1984; Lei, 1990; Nisan and Kohlberg, 1982). These studies, employing the Standard Issue Scoring Manual, followed children and adolescents over a number of years. In Israel and Taiwan, both females and males were included in the samples. The Israeli sample came from a kibbutz, an intentionally created, highly integrated community embracing a socialist-collectivist ideology. The Turkish study included males from rural and city areas.

The results of these studies strongly support the existence, coherence, and sequentiality of moral stages in three widely differing societies. In the studies, stage scores could be reliably assigned to the large majority of interview protocols although some of the principled moral arguments by the Israeli and Chinese respondents displayed thinking not found in the coding manual (see below). Subjects typically increased their stage scores over time but never skipped a stage. The answers of the respondents tended to be internally consistent, that is, moral judgment scores across issues and dilemmas were systematically correlated with each other. No systematic gender differences were found either in the Israeli or in the Taiwanese study.

Figure 3-1 depicts average moral stage scores for five samples: American males, Israeli females and males from a kibbutz, Chinese females and males from Taiwan, Turkish males from a village, and Turkish males from two large cities. When comparing the five samples, it should be kept in mind that these samples do not constitute national random samples, nor are the samples fully equated for educational background. Nevertheless, some conclusions can be drawn

FIG. 3-1. Development of Moral Reasoning in Four Countries

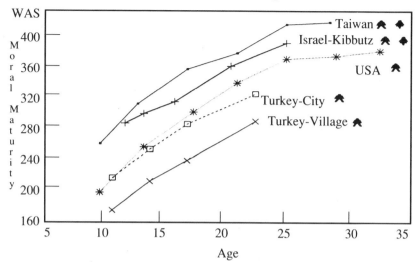

Source of Data: Colby and Kohlberg (1987);
Kohlberg and Nisan (1984); Kohlberg, Snarey,
and Relmer (1984); Lei (1990)

from the data: In all five groups there is a steady increase of moral maturity scores with increasing age and education. There is no evidence that the MJI favors American male interviewees over non-American or female interviewees. For instance, the Chinese male-female sample received higher scores than the male American sample. Rural background among the Turkish interviewees tends to be associated with low moral judgment scores, a finding that matches other studies conducted in rural areas. Principled moral thinking occurs somewhat more frequently in the Chinese and Israeli samples than in the American sample.

It is important to note in this context that East Asian students from Taiwan, Japan, Hong Kong, and South Korea have also consistently received high P%-scores (principled morality) on the DIT (Gielen, Miao, and Avellani, 1990), while respondents from villages in Third World countries only rarely endorse Stage 5 and 6 reasoning on the DIT, nor do they display much Stage 4 and 5 thinking on the MJI. This suggests that the commonly drawn distinction between Western and non-Western cultures is misleading for moral judgment research. Moral judgment scores are much more strongly influenced by the complexity and institutional integration of societies, by educational levels, and by the influence of rigorous ethical systems such as Confucianism than by degrees of Westernization. Traditional, face-to-face village societies can reach a satisfactory moral equilibrium based upon role-oriented, interpersonal expectations which are reflected in Stage 3 reasoning (Edwards, 1986). Stage 4 conceptions, however, are based upon a system-perspective. A system-perspective develops when persons, through secondary and tertiary education, migration, exposure to the mass media, national and religious ideologies, and diverse value systems become fully aware of a widening sociomoral world. It does not seem to matter much whether the widening world is a Western or Eastern world. This is so because Stage 4 reasoning responds to prevalent societal structures and does not merely reflect dominant cultural ideologies. The moral integration of large societies depends on the development of Stage 4 reasoning among its members, but in turn it also contributes to this development.

Postconventional thinking is reported only in studies conducted among well-educated, predominantly urban females and males from a variety of Eastern and Western countries. The research evidence suggests the following conditions for the emergence of postconventional thinking: 1) Postconventional thinking emerges among individuals living in structurally complex societies. 2) The individuals have been exposed to formal schooling at least through late adolescence. The schooling does not have to be Western in nature. 3) The individuals have been exposed to competing, complex value systems and display ideological awareness. 4) The value systems include abstract considerations such as may be found in Hindu metaphysics, Confucian ethics, or socialist ideals of an egalitarian society. 5) Postconventional thinking presupposes a high level of formal or postformal operations (Commons et al., 1984). 6) Individuals have been exposed to highly generalized and abstract role-taking opportunities through education, opportunities for reflective thinking, and responsible decision making in secondary institutions. These six empirically found conditions for the emergence of postconventional thinking agree well with the tenets of cognitive-developmental theory. In addition, individuals from a variety of cultural backgrounds may evaluate postconventional thinking positively although they themselves are unable to produce principled moral arguments (Moon, 1986).

The Nature of Principled Moral Thinking in Cross-Cultural Perspective

One of the most important tasks of cross-cultural research on moral reasoning concerns the investigation of culturally varied forms of postconventional moral thinking. Such investigations can determine the degree to which Kohlberg's conceptions of a highest level of moral thinking may be culture-bound. In recent years, several investigators in India, Israel, Japan, and Taiwan have identified postconventional forms of moral reasoning which are poorly represented in the Standard Issue Scoring Manual. For instance, Snarey (1982) conducted interviews in an Israeli kibbutz which appeared to reveal a postconventional principle emphasizing communal equality and collective happiness. Cheng (1989) reports that several of her Chinese university students interpreted father-son conflicts from a Confucian point of view stressing principled notions of filial piety. In an earlier study, Lee (1973) had also provided postconventional examples of the Chinese norm of filial piety.

Among research projects investigating alternative versions of postconventional thinking, the study by Vasudev and Hummel (1987) is especially provocative. Vasudev interviewed Indian females and males from privileged economic and educational backgrounds. The moral reasoning of about 11 percent of her adults was judged to be postconventional in nature. These postconventional interviewees frequently used both Indian and Western forms of moral thinking. The Hindu conceptions included principles of justice, *Ahimsa* (nonviolence), human dignity, freedom, and the fundamental value of all forms of life. The respect for all forms of life included an emphasis on connectedness and harmony within the human world, and between the human world and other life forms. *Ahimsa* does not simply mean an absence of violence but also includes universalizable values of love, compassion, sympathy, and impartiality. "*Ahimsa* may be as important to Indian thought as justice is to Kohlberg's theory" (Vasudev and Hummel, 1987, pp. 113-116).

The cross-cultural research by Cheng, Lee, Lei, Snarey, and Vasudev suggests an interesting interpretation of Kohlberg's writings. According to this interpretation, his writings present "both a global and a relatively more restricted view of morality. In the global view, morality represents ideals of human life, dignity, personality, and autonomy. In the restricted view, stages of moral reasoning represent 'a rational reconstruction of the ontogenesis of the justice principle'" (Vasudev and Hummel, 1987, p. 116). The global view emphasizes that "principled moral thinking appeared first in human history in the period 600-400 B.C., when human ideals and rational criticism of customary morality developed in Greece, Palestine, India, and China" (Kohlberg, 1981, pp. 378, 383). Kohlberg identifies here principled moral thinking with the postconventional moral perspectives found in the sayings of historical figures such as Socrates, various Jewish prophets, Siddharta Gautama (Buddha), and Confucius. In classical Chinese philosophy, the postconventional perspective is exemplified by the virtue of *ren* (*jen*). *Ren* emphasizes a principled point of view supporting benevolence, humanitarian considerations, the Golden Rule, and the responsible weighing of conflicting claims (Roetz, 1990).

The global interpretation of Kohlberg's postconventional perspective suggests that it is compatible with a rich variety of worldviews and does not necessarily reflect the details of Stage 5 thinking, as currently identified in the Standard Issue Scoring Manual. Principled moral thinking may be conceptualized in broader terms than allowed for in the Standard Issues Scoring Manual. The developmental sequence of preconventional, conventional, and postconventional levels of moral thinking may indeed be universal, but Stage 5 thinking in its presently recognized form may not be. The present conception of Stage 5 does not give sufficient expression to collectively oriented moral conceptions of human dignity and interpersonal harmony which may be found in societies less individualistically oriented than present-day American society.

GENDER DIFFERENCES

Carol Gilligan's Theory of Gender Differences

When Carol Gilligan's book *In a Different Voice* appeared in 1982 it had a powerful impact upon the psychological study of moral development. By now, close to half a million copies of her feminist critique of Kohlbergian research have been sold. The book advances three claims: 1) That the distinctively feminine voice of care, connection, and responsibility in human relationships has been suppressed in Kohlberg's male-oriented account of justice reasoning; 2) that Kohlberg's methods and theories misrepresent women's moral development which leads to artificially depressed scores by females on his justice reasoning scale; and 3) that the early development of girls favors the fusion of social attachment and empathy with identity development, while the early development of boys favors the fusion of separation, individuation, and strivings for autonomy. In the following, we will focus on Gilligan's first and second claims. These have in recent years dominated the study of gender differences in moral reasoning and elicited detailed responses from Kohlberg and his followers.

Gilligan (1982) and Gilligan, Ward, and Taylor (1988) have proposed that two distinct orientations or voices may be traced in the development of moral thinking. These orientations may be found at different developmental stages and in different age groups. One voice emphasizes themes of responsibility in human relationships, care for others, interpersonal sensitivity, empathy, avoidance of hurting others, conflicts between opposing responsibilities, and "a mode of thinking that is contextual and narrative rather than formal and abstract" in nature (Gilligan, 1982, p. 19). Much of Gilligan's research focuses on how girls and women define moral problems for themselves, including their reconstruction of the moral dilemmas they previously experienced. Much of the moral experience of women is said to revolve around the nature of relationships between the self and others. The moral self with its unique history, psychological characteristics, states of mind, hopes, and fears is perceived in-responsive-and-responsible-relationship-to-others. Sensitivity to others may be experienced as being in conflict with one's own "selfish" needs.

According to Gilligan, women often speak in a moral voice quite different from the abstract, formal, impersonal, rights-oriented voice of men that she sees reflected in Kohlberg's theory of justice reasoning. Justice reasoning focuses on the clash of rights, fairness in adjudicating conflicting moral claims, rules and principles, resistance to illegitimate authority, and the logic of equality and reciprocity. In contrast, an ethic of care leads us to respond to the human needs of those for whom we feel responsible. It remains unclear in Gilligan's writings whether she favors the voice of care over the voice of justice and rights, or whether she believes that the two voices should express themselves in a coordinated fashion. While a mixture of the two voices is commonly found in interviews, Gilligan remains wedded to the idea that the two voices are quite distinct in nature. One may therefore ask whether a true integration of these voices is desirable or even possible.

In Gilligan's theory the nature of the moral self is quite broadly conceived, including conceptions of "the good life," aretaic judgments of approval or disapproval, moral traits such as selfishness, preoccupations with fears and hopes evoked in social relationships, and opposing themes of connection and disconnection in one's social life. While Gilligan's theory focuses on a broadly defined "moral self," Kohlberg's deontic conception of moral reasoning is restricted to moral decision making in situations involving the clash of competing moral claims (Puka, 1988). Much of Gilligan's theorizing focuses on personality differences, while Kohlberg's deontic theory specifically does not center on personality differences. In Gilligan's theory there exists a distinct danger that processes of moral judgment are assimilated to, and confused with, personality organization (Rest, 1986b).

In contrast to Gilligan, Kohlberg (1984) believes that his own principled stages of moral reasoning integrate themes of justice and benevolence-caring. A person, especially at the higher stages of moral reasoning, cares about others by persistently taking the role of others and giving equal weight to their claims. Thus, a concern for the needs of others and the avoidance of arbitrary harm-doing is built into the very nature of "justice reasoning." For Kohlberg, the theoretical opposition between the voices of care and rights/justice is misleading and overlooks the structural integration of these two voices in much of his theory. Following Nunner-Winkler (1984), he has also suggested that many aspects of Gilligan's theory refer to possible gender differences concerning "moral content" or "moral style" rather than to structual differences. Such stylistic differences may be expected to vary by dilemma, life situation, gender, and cultural background. For instance, moral dilemmas involving personal relationships are likely to evoke a care orientation while moral dilemmas occurring in secondary institutions may elicit a rights or justice orientation.

Are There Two Distinct and Gender Related Voices?
The Empirical Evidence

The empirical study of Gilligan's two voices has made only slow progress in recent years. The research on gender differences is thoroughly and skeptically reviewed by Walker (in press) whose own studies have provided little support for Gilligan's contentions. While the two studies by Lyons (1983) and Gilligan and Attanucci (1988) suggest a disproportionate emphasis on "response considerations" in the self-constructed, real-life moral dilemmas of females, other studies have not found significant gender differences in moral orientation. Furthermore, the alternative use of a response versus a rights orientation in moral decision making seems to be quite unstable over time and to vary widely across real-life and hypothetical dilemmas. In Walker's (in press) study, only 50 percent of his subjects used the same basic moral orientation in a real-life dilemma over a time span of two years. Pratt et al. (1988) asked their sample to recall and discuss two real-life dilemmas. They found little consistency in moral orientation across the two dilemmas. In general, a response orientation is more likely to predominate in personal relationship dilemmas than in impersonal relationship dilemmas.

Gilligan's contention that two distinct, relatively stable moral orientations exist is not supported by much of the research currently available. While females are sometimes more likely to employ a response orientation than males, the link between gender and moral orientation appears to be quite variable in nature. So far, little sustained cross-cultural research on the question of two distinct moral orientations is available.

Does Kohlberg's Theory Favor Males? The Empirical Evidence

We now turn to Gilligan's second contention: that the theoretical focus and research methods of Kohlberg and his followers systematically and unfairly favor men over women. To be sure, Gilligan made her strongly worded claims without providing a systematic review of the relevant literature. Equally surprising, Gilligan et al. (1982) in their own Kohlbergian study found no systematic gender differences in eight different age groups. Nevertheless, her claim has been widely reported and endorsed.

Two surveys by Walker (1985; in press) and one survey by Thoma (1986; see also Rest, 1986, pp. 111-118) fail to give any support to Gilligan's claim. Walker (in press) surveyed 80 studies employing 152 samples and 10,637 subjects. The studies include many North American samples and a sprinkling of samples from other societies. All studies included females and males, reported statistical tests for gender differences, were based upon the MJI, and employed a variety of coding guides for the MJI. For 85.5 percent (n=130) of the samples, no significant gender differences were reported. For 5.9 percent (n=9) of the samples, females received significantly higher scores than males, while for 8.6 percent (n=13) of the samples, males received higher scores than females. The latter group included several studies that did not match females and males with respect to educational and/or occupational background. When researchers controlled for educational and occupational differences, gender differences in moral reasoning disappeared. Walker also performed a meta-analysis with respect to gender differences. The meta-analytic procedure allowed him to statistically integrate the results of the various studies. Across the studies, gender explained a mere one-twentieth of one percent of the variance of moral reasoning development. In other words, the gender of the 10,637 subjects could not be used to predict their moral reasoning development.

Thoma (1986) has provided us with a similar review of 56 DIT studies employing over 6000 subjects. In his review, he divided the 56 samples into five age groups. In all five groups, females received slightly higher P%-scores (principled thinking) than the males! Again, gender differences were negligible in size. Based upon Thoma's meta-analytic analysis, gender accounted for one-half of one percent of the variance in DIT moral reasoning scores. Age/education taken together accounted for over 250 times the variance in DIT scores than was accounted for by gender.

The question of gender differences in moral reasoning competence was also investigated by Lind, Grocholewska, and Langer (1986). They tested large samples of female and male students from Austria, West Germany, and Poland. Lind et al. employed the "MUT" in their study and found no consistent gender differences with respect to moral judgment competence. Their conclusion agrees with the findings by Gibbs, Arnold, and Burkhart (1984). These authors employed the SRM to investigate structural gender differences in moral reasoning among American subjects. They found no structural differences, although females displayed a greater orientation toward empathy and conscience.

Gilligan's work has been enormously successful in directing the attention of psychologists and the educated public toward the study of gender differences in moral reasoning. Perhaps her greatest contribution has been the expansion of the moral domain to include an emphasis on caring, responsibility, and responsiveness to the needs of others. Her richly textured theoretical work includes many fruitful new ideas, but it also includes a rather diffuse conceptual framework and premature claims. Empirical support for her conception of two distinct, stable moral orientations remains contradictory and weak, while her claims regarding structural Kohlbergian research are consistently contradicted by the empirical evidence available. This is not to deny that the cognitive-developmental approach to the study of gender difference in moral thinking and behavior has so far failed to elucidate gender difference in moral behavior. For instance, males in a wide variety of societies engage much more frequently in antisocial activities than do females. These differences cannot be due to differences in moral reasoning development (as defined by Kohlberg) since moral reasoning development differs little by gender.

THE RELATIONSHIP OF MORAL JUDGMENT TO MORAL ACTION

Kohlberg's Theory of Moral Action

In 1963 and 1964, Kohlberg reviewed empirical studies that attempted to relate measures of superego strength or emotive measures of conscience strength to behavioral measures of honesty and resistance to temptation. Many of these studies were psychoanalytically inspired and used projective tests to measure guilt feelings and fantasy punishment reactions. In general, these studies did not succeed in showing clear relationships between emotive measures of conscience strength and behavioral measures of honesty. Similarly, Hartshorne and May's (1928-1930) studies of moral traits such as self-control, service (prosocial behavior), and honesty found little consistency between or within these behavioral traits, nor were these traits clearly related to tests of moral knowledge and opinions. These disappointing findings contributed much to Kohlberg's insistence that the cognitive-developmental approach provides us with a clearer understanding of moral development than the psychoanalytic and behavioristic approaches do (Kohlberg 1963, 1964).

For Kohlberg, a theory of moral action by its very nature must be both a psychological theory and a philosophical theory. His theory emphasizes two criteria that must be fulfilled before a person's conduct can be considered moral in nature. First, the individual's own judgment must be considered. Moral conduct refers here to conduct consistent with the individual's own moral conceptions and ideals. Yet there are cases where a person's judgment of moral rightness is wrong. Throughout history, moral judgments have supported slavery, aggressive actions against out-group members, racial inequalities, etc. In such cases, actions must be analyzed from the point of moral principles, such as equal respect for the dignity of persons. Behavior is most clearly moral in character when the individual's point of view coincides with the consensus of principled persons. However, adequate moral reasoning is only a necessary, but not a sufficient condition for moral actions to take place. Moral actions also depend on a person's understanding of the factual, non-moral aspects of a situation, the person's sense of responsibility for an action, and certain non-moral "executive skills" that a person must possess in order to complete an action sequence successfully.

Figure 3-2 depicts a model of the relationship between moral judgment and moral action which is based upon Kohlberg's extended discussion of the problem (Kohlberg, 1984, ch. 7). Moral action and moral thought are linked together in a four-step sequence which leads from the person's interpretation of the sociomoral situation (What is going on here? What moral claims do the persons involved have?), to a deontic moral decision (What is the right thing to do in this situation?), to a follow-up judgment of responsibility (Am I the person who is obligated to perform this action?), to a consideration of non-moral executive skills and ego controls. These controls include stable attention, an internal sense of efficacy, self-esteem, the ability to control impulses, delay gratification and avoid procrastination, a longterm perspective, physical and mental energy, and intelligence.

The model suggests that a number of cognitive-affective operations have to come together before a person engages in moral actions. The initial operations display a specifically moral or "should character," and depend on the person's moral stage, moral orientation, and on specific values. These come together to lead to the deontic moral choice which prescribes morally obligatory or desirable actions. Deontic reasoning, however, is not necessarily addressed to anyone in

Fig. 3-2. The Relationship Between Moral Reasoning And Moral Action

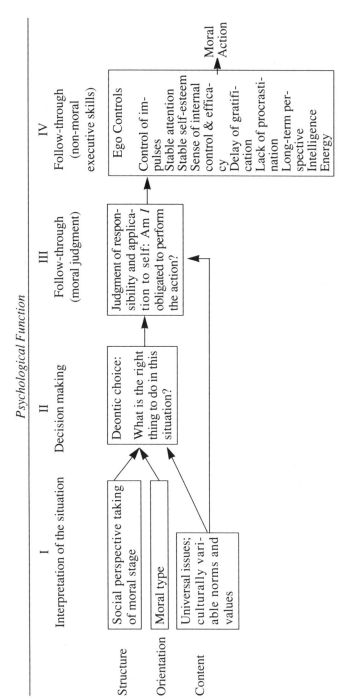

Psychological Function

Note: This figure constitutes an expanded and modified version of Figure 7.2 in Kohlberg (1984)

particular. Therefore, it must be followed by a further judgment which ascribes responsibility for the action to the self. Finally, a moral action typically requires executive skills which taken together may be termed ego-strength or willpower. They facilitate moral action in the face of distractions and temptations, and may overcome practical problems, cognitive drifting, social disapproval, feelings of embarrassment and inadequacy, and fatigue.

Judgments of Responsibility

Kohlberg makes a clear distinction between deontic judgments and judgments of responsibility. Judgments of responsibility go beyond deontic judgments in one of four ways:

1. Judgments that consider the needs and welfare of the other as an individual where the other's welfare seems to be a matter of a right or claim the other has or where it is a matter of not harming the other's welfare [reflect] a deontic concern. Judgments that consider filling the other's need when it is not based on a right or claim or where it is a matter of enhancing his or her welfare, not just preventing harm, [reflect] a responsibility concern.

2. Judgments of responsibility consciously consider the involvement and implication of the self in the action or in the welfare consequences to the other.

3. Judgments of personal moral worth (aretaic) of the kind of self the actor wants to be (perfecting character) or would be if he or she failed to perform the action (judgments of blame, guilt, loss of integrity) are judgments of responsibility when explicitly used as a basis for action rather than rights or obligations.

4. Judgments that use an intrinsic valuing of social relationships such as friendship or relationships of community as justification for performing a moral action are judgments of responsibility (Higgins, Power, and Kohlberg, 1984, p. 80 quoted from Kurtines and Gervirtz, *Morality, Moral Behavior, and Moral Development*, Wiley, 1984).

Responsibility judgments play an important mediating role between deontic conceptions of what is morally right and corresponding moral actions. Responsibility judgments develop according to a sequence of stages which parallel stages of deontic reasoning.

Predicting Moral Behavior

Kohlberg's four-step model makes numerous predictions about relationships between moral reasoning, judgments of responsibility, and moral action. Only some of these predictions have so far been tested in a systematic manner. Predictions based upon the four-step model include the following:

1. Persons at the higher moral stages are more likely to feel responsible for engaging in moral actions than are persons at lower moral stages. For instance,

persons reasoning at the preconventional level feel much less true responsibility for performing prosocial actions than do persons reasoning at the principled level. Moral reasoning at higher stages is more prescriptive and more likely to focus a person on his or her responsibilities.

2. Persons are likely to reason at similar moral stages in hypothetical and real-life moral dilemmas. They tend to bring similar structures of reasoning into the two types of situations. This does not imply, however, that the *content* of their reasoning will necessarily carry over from hypothetical to real-life dilemmas.

3. In some practical situations, a person's moral judgment *performance* may fall below his or her level of *competence*. Self-interest, utilitarian considerations, and social pressures may at times depress the level of practical moral decision making. Non-moral goals may win out over moral goals. In total institutions such as prisons and military organizations, the moral decision making of individual members may undergo a process of "segmentation." In such cases, the structure of individual moral reasoning is assimilated to the perceived structure of institutional decision making (Hickey and Scharf, 1980).

4. Persons reasoning at higher moral stages are more likely to engage in moral actions (as defined previously) than persons reasoning at lower stages. More consistency exists between moral reasoning and action at the higher stages.

5. Persons judged to be autonomous in type are more likely to engage in moral actions than persons judged to be heteronomous in type.

6. When cultural values and institutional prescriptions coincide with moral choices supported by structural moral considerations, corresponding moral actions are especially likely to ensue.

7. Relationships between moral reasoning and moral behavior are strongest when persons reasoning at widely differing stages are compared to each other.

8. Persons high in ego-strength (stable attention, a sense of internal control, high intelligence) are more likely to perform actions consistent with their moral, or not so moral, convictions than persons low in ego-strength. In some cases, a person may reason at Stage 2 and, in addition, may endorse anti-social or sociopathic beliefs. In such a case, ego-strength makes it more likely that a person will perform antisocial actions. Ego-strength pushes a person toward moral or immoral actions, depending upon the content and structure of the person's reasoning.

9. A considerable discrepancy between sociomoral judgment competence and sociomoral judgment performance may exist when a person is low in ego-strength. Very low ego-strength may be related to attention deficit problems, emotional instability, and a high level of cognitive inconsistency. Low ego-strength is partly based upon décalage, that is, the stage structure of cog-

nitive operations changes rapidly between and within situations. Moral reasoning becomes inconsistent and loses some of its guiding force. (See chapter 12 for a pertinent discussion of Selman's clinical work.)

10. When a moral action requires defiance of malevolent authority figures, persons reasoning at the principled level and in an autonomous manner, and possessing ego-strength, will be the most likely to resist morally dubious orders by the authorities.

11. Individual moral action is importantly influenced by the "moral atmosphere" of a group. The "moral atmosphere" is not merely a reflection of individual structures of reasoning, but reflects group norms of caring, loyalty, and responsibility that influence the content of the individuals' moral thinking. (Relationships between structures of individual moral thinking, the moral atmosphere of "just communities," and moral actions are discussed in chapters 7 and 9.)

12. Over time, moral reasoning and moral action develop in a reciprocal relationship to each other. Moral reasoning leads to moral action, but reflection upon important moral actions will in turn lead to advances in moral reasoning competence.

Research on Moral Reasoning-Moral Action Relationships

While many of the predictions concerning relationships between moral reasoning and moral action have not yet been systematically investigated, a considerable number of interesting empirical studies have already been completed. Blasi (1980) has provided us with a broad review which includes forty-seven studies using various versions of the MJI. The studies focused on moral behaviors such as delinquent actions, sociopathy, everyday behaviors measured by teacher ratings, peer nominations, observer reports or self reports, cheating, honesty, altruistic behavior, and resistance to social pressure or malevolent authority. Most of the studies reported statistically significant relationships between Kohlbergian measures of moral reasoning and relevant moral behavior. In studies of delinquents and sociopaths, 70-80 percent were rated as preconventional in their reasoning. Very little Stage 4 and 5 reasoning was reported for seriously delinquent adolescents, unless the studies employed the earlier, more unreliable and lenient moral judgment coding guides (see also Jennings, Kilkenny, and Kohlberg, 1983). In many of the studies reported by Blasi, individuals receiving high moral judgment scores were especially likely to engage in prosocial or altruistic behavior. Subjects receiving high stage scores tended to resist social pressures in conformity situations, while lower-scoring subjects were more likely to cheat or display dishonesty.

An additional review of moral reasoning-moral action studies has been provided by Thoma and Rest (1986) who sum up twenty-eight research reports connecting DIT-scores to a wide variety of behavioral measures. Again, the majority of studies found the expected relationships between moral reasoning and moral behavior. Delinquents and cheaters received relatively low DIT scores while attendees at social justice meetings, conscientious objectors, and leaders in juries and small groups received relatively high scores. All in all, the reviews of Blasi (1980), Jennings, Kilkenny, and Kohlberg (1983), and Thoma and Rest (1986) provide consistent support for the supposition that moral reasoning and moral action are interrelated. In the studies reviewed, correlations between stage scores and moral behavior were usually modest to moderate in size, but they covered a considerable variety of situations.

While many studies have shown significant correlations between moral reasoning and moral action, the studies often suffer from methodological and theoretical shortcomings. Because many of the research projects had been conducted before the new Standard Issue Scoring System had become available, scoring procedures now considered outdated were frequently used. Very few of the studies report scores for moral heteronomy and autonomy. Theoretical predictions in the studies are at times only loosely related to cognitive-developmental theory. Given this unsatisfactory situation, Kohlberg and his co-workers decided to rescore moral judgment interviews for some of the studies and to introduce questions about moral responsibility into some of their research designs. We will briefly review a few of these "new look studies," since their results have a close bearing on Kohlberg's conception of the origins of moral action.

The Finnish psychologist Helkama asked his subjects whether "Heinz is responsible if his wife should die?" While only 17 percent of the Stage 3 and 3(4) subjects held Heinz responsible, 53 percent of the Stage 4/5 and 5 subjects did so (Kohlberg, 1984, p. 520). In McNamee's (1978) study, subjects had an opportunity to help a fellow student who was feeling ill because he had taken drugs. Only 36 percent of the subjects reasoning at Stage 2 thought they should help the victim, and only 9 percent did indeed help. In contrast, 83 percent of the subjects reasoning at Stage 5 thought that they should help, and 88 percent of those acted in accordance with their convictions. Dramatic differences were also found in an early version of Milgram's famous electrical shock experiment. In this experimental situation, naive subjects are asked to administer electrical shocks of up to 450 volts to an innocent victim who is supposed to complete a verbal learning task. Many subjects in this experiment give in to the pressures of the experimenter and "shock" the victim (who, however, does not really receive the electrical shocks). Kohlberg found that all of the subjects rated as "heteronomous" obeyed the orders of the malevolent experimenter, while 86 percent of the subjects rated as "autonomous" disobeyed the experimenter at some time (Kohlberg, 1984, pp. 546-548).

Next we come to a well-known study of participants in the Free Speech Movement at the University of California in Berkeley. The study had originally been conducted by Haan, Smith, and Block (1968) during the 1960s and included the administration of the MJI to students who had been arrested for a sit-in. Candee and Kohlberg rescored the interviews based upon the Standard Issue Scoring System and compared them to interviews by students not involved in the sit-in. The results show a clear relationship between stage of moral reasoning, moral type, and participation in the sit-in. While 0 percent of the subjects rated as Stage 3 and being "heteronomous" sat in, 83 percent of the subjects rated as Stage 4/5 and "autonomous" in their judgment participated in the sit-in (Kohlberg, 1984, pp. 541-546). These results may be compared to an earlier study conducted by Gielen (1986) at the University of Cologne. Based upon an earlier coding system, the German students were classified as displaying conventional, transitional, or principled moral reasoning. Principled and transitional students were much more likely to have participated in a variety of political protest activities than the conventional students.

Relationships between moral reasoning, moral type, judgments of responsibility, and moral action are undoubtedly complex in nature. The available empirical studies suggest that Kohlberg's model of judgment-action relationships is a fruitful one. In a considerable variety of situations, persons reasoning in a principled and autonomous manner are especially likely to engage in responsible, morally desirable behavior, such as helping people in need, avoidance of harm doing, involvement in activities related to civil rights, resistance to immoral orders given by dubious authority figures, and keeping explicit or implicit social contracts. But much empirical work needs to be done before moral reasoning-action relationships can be properly understood. Studies on the role of ego-strength in moral decision-making situations are very much needed and should be of special interest to the clinician (Kohlberg, 1984, pp. 556-560). For the educator, however, Kohlberg's most important work on judgment-action relationships is related to his efforts to create a moral atmosphere of caring, loyalty, and responsibility in "just communities." Such a moral group atmosphere forms a bridge between individual moral thinking about justice issues, loyalty to collective norms, and responsible action.

CONCLUSIONS

Our brief survey of a number of Kohlbergian research projects has provided impressive evidence that many of Kohlberg's ideas have withstood the challenge of empirical research. A rich variety of variables appears to be related in an understandable way to role-taking experiences which in turn are connected to moral stage and type. When moral stage, moral type, attribution of responsibility for actions to the self, and ego-strength act in concert, they lead to moral actions consistent with moral reasoning. On the other hand, efforts to show that Kohlbergian measures of moral reasoning are based upon male-oriented, Western ideologies have not met with much success. Cross-cultural research has suggested the existence of some moral visions not fully accounted for in the Standard Issue Scoring system, but researchers have generally been able to recognize a postconventional moral perspective in their subjects' reasoning even in the absence of specific scoring criteria. Cross-cultural research suggests that well-educated adults in non-Western countries such as India and Taiwan are exposed to competing traditional and modern value systems. This situation may actually support the development of principled moral thinking since it provides a challenge to develop broad, integrative vistas.

In Kohlberg's work, deontic philosophical assumptions were for the first time translated into a vigorous research methodology that reached a new level of precision and complexity. Kohlberg succeeded in combining a philosophical focus on the deep structure of moral reasoning with a seemingly contradictory focus on precise measurement that can be admired even by hard-boiled, positivistic researchers. This combination of theoretical and methodological sophistication served as a model for a whole generation of developmental psychologists. They took his theoretical and methodological approach and extended it to the study of social reasoning (Selman), ego-ideal development (van den Daele), prosocial reasoning (Eisenberg), notions of forgiveness (Enright), faith development (Fowler), religious reasoning (Oser), moral reasoning among young children (Damon), evolving structures of the self (Kegan), conceptions of social conventions (Turiel), aesthetic experience (Parsons), the development of categories of natural philosophy (Broughton), conceptions of the good (Armon, 1984), and to alternative methods designed to study moral reasoning (Damon, Eckensberger, Gibbs, Lind, and Rest). Some of these contributions should be of special interest to clinicians and are discussed in Part III of the book.

Kohlberg's earlier tendency to equate the moral domain with justice reasoning may have induced tunnel vision in some of his followers, but it kept his early theoretical and methodological efforts sharply focused on a fundamental dimension of morality. In his later years, he expanded his vision to include concerns for benevolence, beneficence, caring, and responsibility, although his drive toward a broader conception of the ethical self was cut short by his death. The expansion of his moral vision is most salient in his educational efforts which also added a sociological dimension to his work. But his conception of the stages of moral reasoning remained in many ways at the center of his philosophical, psychological, and educational vision. Without justice, there could be no true morality for him. Caring and beneficence were important considerations in his own personal life, and they remained important for his interpersonal theory of morality. But he insisted that while care cannot be expanded to include everybody—a commitment to justice can. The ultimate aim of education in a democratic society was to develop free, morally autonomous persons who would feel respect for the human dignity of all. This aim could only be achieved if social psychologists developed a practical and realistic theory of the development of moral reasoning and moral action. Such a theory could then be applied to education. Part II of the book will discuss Kohlberg's efforts to integrate this "old" conception of individual moral development with emerging sociological conceptions of group-based moral development in just communities.

While Kohlberg readily admitted that there are many strands in the fabric of human development, the "moral reasoning strand" remained at the center of his vision from the beginning to the end of his scientific career. When he started his work, moral psychology and moral education had almost ceased to exist as viable fields of scientific and practical endeavor. The traditional concerns of moral philosophy appeared to have no relevance to the goals of scientific psychology and practical education. Kohlberg declared this to be an illusion. More than any other philosopher-psychologist-educator during the last fifty years, he succeeded in returning moral reasoning to the agenda of educators and psychologists. While the details of his stage model must surely remain subject to revision, expansion, and change, his general approach to the problems of human ethicality remains exemplary. Those of us who have been impressed by his contributions can only hope that his legacy will not disappear among the constantly changing fashions and trends of American psychology and education.

Yet whether his legacy will endure is difficult to judge at this time. When Kohlberg began to publish his early work during the late 1950s and early 1960s, he thought of himself as an outsider to American psychology. Psychology was then dominated by behaviorists, psychoanalysts, and a sprinkling of humanistic psychologists. The influence of Chomsky, Piaget, and Kohlberg helped to usher in the "cognitive revolution" which has since changed the face of psychology. But both the substance and the style of Kohlberg's philosophically informed approach continue to place him outside the mainstream of American psychology. After his death in 1987, Harvard University dissolved his Center for Moral Education in an astonishingly brief period of time. His idealist, rational, Socratic vision of morality may have been too discrepant for the more empiricist and irrational notions of social adjustment that continue to dominate much of American psychology and education.

Chapter 4

The Measurement of Moral Reasoning

Uwe Gielen with Ting Lei

INTRODUCTION

In chapter 2 we considered in some detail Kohlberg's theory concerning the development of stages of moral reasoning. The basic outlines of that theory were already visible in his dissertation (Kohlberg, 1958), but in the subsequent twenty-nine years many theoretical and methodological improvements and revisions were added to that early outline. Two of the most dramatic areas of progress concern his radical revisions of the scoring procedures and the large corpus of empirical studies which trace moral development among persons widely differing in socio-moral experience. Moral reasoning was shown to be related to moral action, and some of Kohlberg's students have developed alternative methods to measure moral reasoning skills.

In this chapter we introduce Kohlberg's approach to measuring moral judgment development which culminated in the Standard Issue Moral Judgment Interview and Scoring System. This detailed scoring system is one of Kohlberg's greatest achievements and has not been surpassed by any other methodical approach to the study of sociomoral development. Subsequently, we will discuss two alternative methods to the measurement of moral reasoning skills: Gibbs' Social Reflection Method and Rest's Defining Issues Test. The Social Reflection Method is a group-administered, written test that hews closely to Kohlberg's Moral Judgment Interview. The Defining Issues Test is a multiple choice test measuring a person's preferences for prefabricated, stage-typed moral arguments. The tests by Kohlberg and Rest have been used in numerous research projects which taken together constitute much of our present scientific knowledge about the nature and development of moral thought.

A SHORT HISTORY OF KOHLBERG'S SCORING SYSTEMS

Kohlberg began his twenty-year longitudinal study of American males in 1956. Seventy-two boys aged ten to sixteen were periodically reinterviewed using nine hypothetical dilemmas. At first, their moral reasoning was assessed by the "Aspect Scoring" method which included two procedures, the "Global Story Rating" procedure and the "Sentence Scoring" procedure. The "Aspect Scoring" method assessed twenty-five aspects of moral judgment while focusing on the content concerns that each boy brought to the moral dilemmas. The content concerns included a focus on punishment (said to be typical of Stage 1 reasoning), utilitarian exchanges with another person (Stage 2), empathic concern for another person (Stage 3), respect for law and societal order (Stage 4), an orientation toward social contract (Stage 5), and an orientation toward universal principles (Stage 6). Moral stages were identified with the content-oriented concerns. Kohlberg constructed a manual that listed prototypical sentences for each of the twenty-five aspects and for each dilemma ("Sentence Scoring"). In addition, a person's overall response to a moral dilemma was assigned a stage based upon the "Global Story Rating" procedure (Kohlberg, 1958, 1969).

As the boys grew older, many of them were reinterviewed every three or four years. Based upon the longitudinal changes in their moral judgment, the "Aspect Scoring" method was abandoned. The data showed too much stage mixture, and sometimes a subject's moral judgment level would develop in an inconsistent manner from one testing period to the next. Rather than giving up his developmental theory, Kohlberg decided that his scoring methodology was deficient and had to be thoroughly revised. A number of more rigorous new coding systems were developed. These included the Structural Issue Scoring system (Kohlberg, 1971) and the final version of the Standard Issue Scoring system (Colby et al., 1987). As Kohlberg's scoring systems evolved, two issues remained central to the process of methodological refinement. These concerned "the differentiation of content and structure and the definition of the unit of analysis. . . . Each major scoring change has involved an important redefinition of the content-structure distinction, and each definition has led to (or been accompanied by) a redefinition of the unit of analysis" (Colby, 1978).

In the 1958 scoring systems, content and structure remained largely undifferentiated. The concerns for punishment, affiliation, law, contract, etc., were treated as structural in kind, while in the later scoring systems they became content issues. At first it was not realized that persons at any stage could reason about issues such as affiliation or the law but that their reasoning about the same issues would differ qualitatively from stage to stage. These qualitative differences became the focus of the later scoring systems.

The Structural Issue Scoring of 1971 constituted a significant theoretical and methodological advance over the earlier system. It introduced new stage definitions centering on the broadly conceived socio-moral levels of perspective and on role-taking. The Structural Issue Scoring system required much interpretation on the part of the rater who had to derive the levels of perspective from overall interpretations of the subject's view. A considerable amount of subjectivity crept into the scoring process and made it too unreliable, since the unit of analysis had become too large. Nevertheless, experienced raters using the 1971 system could gain a much better grasp of moral stages than raters using the 1958 system.

Several versions of the Standard Issue Scoring Manual became available in the late 1970s and early 1980s, but it was not until 1987 that the definitive version of the manual was published (Colby et al., 1987). The Standard Issue Scoring method achieved greater objectivity and specificity in the scoring process when compared to the previous Structural Issue Scoring guides. The new scoring method introduced specific "criterion judgments" defining the stage structure for a large number of moral ideas. Based upon the criterion judgments, well-trained scorers can now reliably assign stage scores to specific interview responses.

The long history of introducing steady changes into the scoring system has led to many problems in the interpretation of the research literature. Correlations between earlier coding systems and the final coding system may run as low as the thirties, indicating poor comparability between earlier and later stage definitions and research results. It is a good practice to indicate in research reviews what scoring guide has been used in each study. Snarey (1985) provides a good example in his review of the cross-cultural literature.

In general, redefinitions of the preconventional stages have been much less extreme than the redefinitions of higher stages. Stage 6 was completely removed from the new scoring manual, and Stage 5 scores are much less frequently reported in the research literature based upon the new scoring system than in the earlier literature. As a dramatic example, we cite Kohlberg and Candee's (1984) reanalysis of the Haan, Smith, and Block (1968) study conducted at the University of California, Berkeley, during the mid-1960s. Kohlberg and Candee rescored some of their protocols by using the new Standard Issue Scoring procedure. While Haan, Smith, and Block report that, based upon the Aspect Scoring system, 23 percent of their protocols were rated at Stages 5 or 6, not a single protocol was unequivocally scored as principled in the reanalysis, and only 11 percent of the protocols were rated at Stage 4/5.

The new Standard Issue Scoring procedure uses much more stringent stage definitions than the older, more lenient scoring systems. Protocols formerly rated at Stages 5 or 6 now tend to be scored at Stage 4B or Stage 4/5, while some protocols formerly rated at Stage 4 may now be scored at Stages 3/4 or 3. The new stage definitions, however, appear to capture structural aspects of moral reasoning in a much more convincing way than the older stage definitions. The new Standard Issue Scoring procedure appears to cleanly separate content from structure. However, the new manual is not a definitive guide for understanding the most advanced forms of moral reasoning, nor can it be used to assess the moral reasoning of young children.

THE STANDARD ISSUE SCORING MANUAL

The Moral Judgment Interview

The Moral Judgment Interview (MJI) is a semi-openended interview consisting of three parallel forms: Forms A, B, and C. Each form contains three moral dilemmas in which a conflict between two moral issues is described. With one exception, the three forms focus on the same six universal issues, namely life, law, morality and conscience, punishment, contract, and authority (left out in Form C). The moral dilemmas are followed by 9-12 standardized probing questions which attempt to elicit the interviewee's justifications or reasons for a course of action. The interviewee is asked to accept the factual aspects of the hypothetical dilemmas as stated.

Forms A, B, and C contain the following nine moral dilemmas:

FORM A   Dilemma III: Should Heinz, a poor husband, steal an exorbitantly priced drug in order to save his dying wife?

III': Should Heinz be punished after he steals the drug?

I: A father promises his son that he can keep his self-earned money in order to go to camp. Subsequently, the father changes his mind. Should the son refuse to give the money to his father?

FORM B   IV: A terminally ill patient in severe pain requests euthanasia. Should a doctor go along with the patient's request?

IV': Should the doctor be punished for mercy killing?

II: A girl lies to her mother after the mother broke a promise to her. Should the girl's sister tell on her?

FORM C   V: Should an army captain order a soldier to his almost certain death if this helps the soldier's company to escape?

VIII: A convict escapes from prison and subsequently leads a model life. Should a man who recognizes him twenty years later report him to the police?

VII: What is worse, stealing from a store or cheating an old man out of his money?

It takes around forty-five minutes to administer one form of the MJI. Details of the dilemmas can be easily adjusted to fit most cultural circumstances. The test is best administered as an oral, tape-recorded interview which is later transcribed. In some research projects, the subject's responses are hand-recorded, or a written version of the questionnaire is used. Written interviews are only practicable with older, literate, well-motivated subjects. Children less than ten years old may experience considerable difficulties in understanding the stories.

The interviewer must have a good grasp of moral development theory and be able to elicit the moral philosophy of the respondent. Above all, this means that the interviewer poses the right follow-up questions when the respondent's answers contain insufficient information. The respondent is repeatedly asked to provide reasons or justifications why a chosen course of action should be followed and why chosen values and norms should be upheld. The respondent is not asked what he or she would do in the dilemmas but what the *right* solution to the dilemmas is. Respondents reasoning at the preconventional level may find it difficult to distinguish clearly between what they would do and what one ideally should do.

Scoring Procedures

When constructing the Standard Issue Scoring Manual, Kohlberg and his group followed the theoretical approach of *hermeneutic objectivism*. Hermeneuticism concerns itself with the interpretation of texts and meaning systems, an approach that tends to prevail in the humanities. It is the goal of hermeneuticism to discover hidden structures of meaning. When using the Standard Issue Scoring Manual, the interviewer and the rater become hermeneuticists who confront the task of understanding the subject's point of view. Interviewer and rater must be able to see the moral world through the eyes of the interviewee.

The rater's interpretations, however, can easily become subjective and arbitrary in nature. The interpretations may read nonexistent ideas into the subject's responses. Therefore, the new coding guide establishes strict interpretive guidelines which must be followed in the scoring process. The coding guide successfully establishes a balance between the philosophical-psychological need for deep interpretation and the scientific need for objectivity and reliability. It is this balance that makes the coding guide such a striking example of objective hermeneutics. The tender-minded approach of the humanities and the tough-minded approach of the natural sciences are reconciled in Kohlberg's psychological work.

The Standard Issue Scoring Manual describes an elaborate, time-consuming, precise procedure to establish the stage structure(s) and moral type of an individual's interview. To establish the stage structure, an interview is successively broken down into smaller and smaller units, in order to isolate specific *interview judgments*. Interview judgments represent a basic moral idea or judgment by the respondent. The interview judgments are then matched against the stage-typed *criterion judgments* which are outlined and analyzed in the manual. Based on the stage scores assigned to the combined interview judgments, a *Weighted Average Score* (WAS) and the overall *Global Stage Score* of the subject are computed.

Breaking down the interview into interview judgments: Breaking down the

interview into manageable units constitutes a crucial part of the scoring procedure since it demands of the trained rater that he or she understand the basic
syntax of the subject's moral language. The breakdown process follows a three-
step sequence. The rater divides up the answers for each dilemma into two standard *issue* categories, isolates the moral *norms* that a subject supports, and finally identifies the *elements* or reasons that make the norm valuable to the subject.
The elements are crucial for the definition of interview judgments. They lead the
rater to an understanding of the subject's moral philosophy. The reader may
recall from chapter 2 the discussion about universal norms, modal elements,
and value elements that together make up the universal deep structure of moral
discourse. The Standard Issue Scoring Manual operationalizes the categories
and applies them to the interpretation of moral judgment interviews.

In the scoring process, responses for each dilemma must be divided into two
predetermined issue categories. For the Heinz dilemma, the two issues are life
and law. All the responses supporting the stealing of the drug are classified as supporting the *life issue*, while arguments against the stealing are said to support the
law issue. Let us take as an example the following response which was given to
the Heinz dilemma: "Heinz should steal the drug because he has been living
with his wife for all these years. Wouldn't he feel close to her and think that
he has to help her?" The response would be assigned to the *issue of life*.
Subsequently, the moral argument is listed under the *norm of affiliation* since it
appeals to the value of mutual sharing. Finally, the argument is classified under
the *element of reciprocity or positive desert* since in the response, affiliation is
construed from the point of reciprocity: Heinz is said to appreciate his wife and
feel an inner obligation to help her.

The rater has now classified the interview judgment by issue, norm, and element and is ready to compare the interview judgment against a variety of *criterion judgments* contained in the manual. Criterion judgment #15 which is
described in Table 4-1 fits best. The criterion judgment describes Stage 3 thinking in which a person appeals to relationships of mutual sharing ("Wouldn't he
feel close to her . . .?) and to natural obligations felt by "Mr. Everybody"
("Wouldn't he . . . think that he has to help her . . .?").

The Standard Issue Scoring Manual contains approximately 900 pages of
criterion judgments, since they occupy center stage in the coding process. As can
be seen in Table 3-1, a criterion judgment explicates the stage structure, provides
critical indicators, describes match examples, and points to characteristics distinguishing a given criterion judgment from similar sounding yet different judgments. For many criterion judgments, guess examples and potentially misleading nonmatch examples are also provided. The use of guess examples may
become necessary when an interview is poorly probed, or when it contains culturally unusual forms of moral reasoning.

After the rater has matched the interview judgments against the stage-typed
criterion judgments, the *Global Stage Score* and the *Weighted Average Score*

Table 4-1. Criterion Judgment #15

DILEMMA:	III
ISSUE:	Life
NORM:	Affiliation
ELEMENT:	Reciprocity or positive desert (15)
STAGE:	3

Criterion judgment [Heinz should steal the drug even if he doesn't love his wife] out of gratitude or appreciation; *OR* because she has shared her life with him, and the least he can do is to save her.

Stage structure In this judgment obligation is based on a relationship of mutual sharing. The sharedness of experience creates not only feelings of affection but a generalized obligation.

Critical indicators Required for a match is an appeal to either: a) the prior sharing; or b) the gratitude Heinz should express.

Distinctions *Between Other Stages*
Do not confuse the idea of mutual sharing with the Stage 2 conception of the relationship in terms of Heinz's probable needs and useful exchanges (CJ#7), or with the Stage 4/5 conception of relationships in terms of mutual commitment (CJ#32).

Match examples 1. *If the husband doesn't love his wife, is he obligated to steal the drug for her? Why or why not?*

Yes, he should still steal the drug—he did love her once and no doubt she loved him (possibly she still does)—that is, she shared a great part of herself with him. The least he can do is help her when she needs help.

2. *What if Heinz doesn't love his wife?*

Well, both have shared at least a time together, so that he should feel the necessity to help her.

Source: Colby and Kohlberg, Vol. 2, p. 28.

(WAS) can be calculated. Stage scores are initially established for each of the six issues in the MJI and then combined. Interview judgments supporting the subject's moral decision are weighted most heavily while tentative guess scores are weighted less heavily. Global Stage Scores may be pure stage scores (1, 2, 3, 4, 5) or mixed stage scores (stages 1/2, 2/3, 3/4, 4/5). Mixed Global Stage Scores indicate that the second stage in the score is represented by at least 25 percent of the reasoning in the interview. Mixed stage scores are quite commonly found in research studies. In samples of college students, a stage score of 3/4 may be more frequently represented than any other stage score. Theoretically, a mixed score could be made up of more than two stages, but in practice this rarely occurs. The Weighted Average Score (WAS) provides a continuous, numerical assessment of the subject's reasoning. It can range from 100 (pure Stage 1 reasoning) to 500 (pure Stage 5 reasoning). Because the Manual contains an insufficient number of criterion judgments at Stages 1 and 5, extreme scores close to 100 and to 500 occur infrequently.

Establishing Moral Types A and B: Besides establishing Weighted Average Scores and Global Stage Scores, the coding manual can also be used to assign Type A and Type B ratings to an interview. The type ratings are based on nine criteria which point to the presence of autonomous moral reasoning or Type B. When a given interview does not meet the nine criteria, it is assigned a Type A rating indicating the presence of heteronomous reasoning. Moral type ratings are based upon a guided clinical evaluation procedure which focuses on the dilemma as a whole. The procedure is less detailed in character than the procedures used to establish stage scores.

The coding manual assumes that moral types are "ideal typical" constructions which intermingle content and structure. Moral type ratings are not designed to replace stage ratings but to provide additional information about a subject's moral reasoning. Moral type ratings are important when a researcher wishes to predict moral behavior. For the educator, the concept of moral type may serve as a guide to design and evaluate educational interventions which attempt to support the development of autonomous moral reasoning.

The moral type rating procedure uses the following nine criteria to establish the autonomous nature of an interview:

1) The subject supports and justifies *autonomous choices* that appear to be just and fair from a postconventional point of view. Heinz, for instance, should steal the drug and not be punished for it, while Joe has a moral right to refuse his father the money.
2) The judgments of the interviewee reflect a clear *hierarchy* of moral values. Moral values are placed above pragmatic or consequential considerations.
3) Autonomous judgments express respect for persons and value persons *intrinsically.*
4) Autonomous reasoning *prescribes* moral obligations which supersede

desires and pragmatic considerations.

5) Autonomous moral judgments are felt to be *universal* or binding for everybody in comparable positions.

6) Justifications for autonomous judgments appeal to inner *freedom* rather than to tradition, authority, or law.

7) Autonomous judgments refer to *mutual respect* in cooperative situations.

8) Autonomous judgments reflect *reversibility* or reciprocal role-taking.

9) Autonomous moral judgments treat rules and laws as humanly created, flexible guidelines for decision making (*constructivism*) (Colby and Kohlberg, 1987, Vol. 2, pp. 913-914).

Given ideal conditions, the Standard Issue Scoring Manual provides very reliable assessments of stage structure and moral type. Threats to the validity and reliability of the scoring procedure derive from three main sources. The interview may not contain appropriate probing questions, either because it was given in a written form or because the interviewer is inexperienced. The interview may contain culturally unusual forms of moral reasoning that cannot be easily matched against criterion judgments. This may occur when an interviewee uses elaborate religious-metaphysical arguments and parables to support his or her choice in the dilemmas. Finally, the rater may experience general difficulties in matching interview judgments with criterion judgments. This may reflect insufficient training by the rater and a lack of understanding of the numerous subtle distinctions contained in the scoring manual. Raters learning the scoring procedure need to establish satisfactory interrater reliability against expert scorers. While it is possible to learn the procedures based upon an extensive study of the manual, additional attendance at scoring workshops is to be preferred.

THE SOCIAL REFLECTION MEASURE

Given the lengthy and complex nature of the Standard Issue method of assessment, a number of efforts have been underway to construct alternative and simpler tests of moral reasoning development. John Gibbs had been a member of the original research team that constructed the Standard Issue Scoring Guide. His Social Reflection Measure (SRM) retains several of Kohlberg's moral dilemmas, his emphasis on subject-produced reasoning, and his general approach to coding moral justifications. The questionnaire contains two of Kohlberg's dilemmas (an alternative form of the SRM is available), and focuses the subject's thinking on sociomoral norms associated with the dilemmas. The SRM facilitates the data collection process since the test can be group-administered and does not rely on individualized follow-up questions. Filling in the test takes about thirty-five to sixty minutes. The SRM also uses a simplified scoring procedure. The procedure can be learned in about thirty to forty hours based upon Gibbs and Widaman's (1982) test manual. The scoring manual provides copies of the questionnaire, general stage descriptions, and criterion judgments for the eight norms of affiliation, life, law and property, legal justice, conscience, family affiliation, contract, and property. Practice protocols and statements are also included in the manual. In many ways, the SRM "unabashedly rides piggyback on the Standard Issue manual" (Gibbs and Widaman, 1982, p. XIII).

Gibbs introduces one theoretical innovation in his test. Gibbs does not believe that Kohlberg's Stage 5 is truly a Piagetian "hard" stage based upon new thought operations representing internalized schemata of action. Rather, he introduces two types of "theory-defining discourse": theoretical relativism and theoretical principles. The two types of theory-defining discourse represent explicit, reflective, philosophical, or intellectual positions about issues such as the relation between individual and societal rights. "Theoretical relativism" emphasizes that the claims of individuals cannot be reconciled with the claims of society because the very nature of individual and societal claims makes them incommensurable with another. This position seems to be comparable to Stage 4 1/2 in Kohlberg's system. The "theoretical principles" orientation represents the systematic prioritizing of rights in relationship to other rights. For instance, the right to life may be logically analyzed as taking priority over other rights or claims. Kohlberg would interpret such statements as reflecting Stage 5 thinking, but Gibbs believes that such statements merely represent a certain meta-ethical or theory-defining position. Markoulis (1989) has recently studied the cognitive and sociomoral operations of educationally advantaged Greek adults. His data suggest both the usefulness of the SRM but also the possibility that Gibbs' "theory-defining discourse" does, in fact, represent postconventional thinking.

Gibbs' test represents a valid, more practical alternative to the Standard Issue Scoring approach. Correlations between Kohlberg's and Gibbs' measures range from r = .50- .85, suggesting that in many research projects the SRM could be fruitfully used in place of the Standard Issue Scoring method. At present, not enough research using the SRM is available for many comparative purposes, yet the use of the SRM often appears to be preferable to the use of Rest's DIT when Kohlbergian hypotheses are under investigation. Gibbs has also developed a recognition test, the Sociomoral Reflection Objective Measure (SROM), (Gibbs et al., 1984). Gibbs, Basingper, and Fuller (in press) have developed a shorter version of the SRM which appears promising.

THE DEFINING ISSUES TEST

The Defining Issues Test (DIT) was developed by James Rest, formerly a research associate of Kohlberg and now a leading authority in the field of moral development research. Rest realized early on that the administration and scoring of the MJI is very cumbersome. Therefore, he developed an objective multiple choice test that indexes moral development based upon the recognition of, and preference for, seventy-two moral arguments. The DIT is based upon a stage model somewhat different from the final version of Kohlberg's moral reasoning theory. Therefore, the test cannot be used to rigorously test assumptions and predictions derived from Kohlberg's strict stage model (Rest, 1979, 1986a, 1986b).

The DIT contains three political and three moral dilemmas some of which are taken from the MJI. For each dilemma, twelve arguments are provided that can be used to solve the conflict. The arguments reflect different moral stages. Respondents are asked to rate the importance of each argument. In addition, subjects are asked to select and rank the four most important arguments. Examples of arguments pertaining to the first dilemma (the Heinz story) are as follows: Stage 2: Is Heinz willing to risk getting shot as a burglar or going to jail for the chance that stealing the drug might help? Stage 3: Isn't it only natural for a loving husband to care so much for his wife that he would steal? Stage 4: Do the druggist's rights to his invention have to be respected? Stage 5A: Does the law in this case get in the way of the most basic claim of any member of society? Stage 6: What values are going to be the basis for governing how people act toward each other?

The DIT is objectively scored and provides moral stage scores for Stages 2, 3, 4, 4 1/2 (A), 5A, 5B, and 6. No items for Stage 1 are included in the DIT. Preferences for principled thinking (Stages 5A, 5B, and 6, combined) are expressed by the P%-Score. The P%-Score indicates the percentage of a person's rankings that fall in the principled range. The P%-Score is by far the most frequently used indicator of moral judgment maturity in the DIT literature. A further, less frequently used overall indicator of moral judgment maturity is provided by the D-Score. The D-Score is based upon a complex mathematical formula that takes into account and weighs a subject's ratings of the seventy-two moral arguments provided by the DIT.

The DIT also contains three validity and "consistency" checks to establish whether the person taking the test understands it and is reasonably careful in filling it out. Among the seventy-two items, there are a few "meaningless" items (M-items) based upon lofty-sounding, but senseless statements. Subjects endorsing a number of the pretentious sounding but meaningless moral arguments should be removed from the research sample. A second checking procedure looks for consistency between items *rated* high and items *ranked* high. A third checking procedure determines whether a protocol reflects response sets on the rating task. It is good research practice to analyze inconsistent DIT protocols separately. Delinquents, younger teenagers, and persons not used to multiple choice tests frequently fail the validity checks.

The DIT is based upon a theoretical model which differs from Kohlberg's mature stage model in five respects: 1) Rest uses stage definitions that go back to Kohlberg's earlier stage conceptions in use during the 1960s; 2) Rest uses a quantitative model which assumes that people liberally intermingle stages in their evaluative thinking; 3) the DIT locates a person in terms of a number on a developmental continuum rather than assigning persons to one or two stages (this is similar to the Weighted Average Score on the MJI); 4) the DIT is not a production test but rather measures a person's preferences for prefabricated moral arguments; and 5) the DIT intermingles structure and content to a much larger extent than does the Standard Issue Scoring System.

Table 4-2 describes Rest's conception of six moral stages as they are partially reflected in the DIT. The six stages focus on the coordination of rules and expectations, the balancing of competing interests and moral claims, and on basic conceptions of rights and duties. Each stage represents an internally consistent integration of these aspects. But the attentive reader will soon notice that these stages do not fully differentiate structure from content. For instance, at Stage 3 the central consideration for a morality of interpersonal concordance is said to be: "Be considerate, nice, and kind, and you'll get along with people." While such considerations are compatible with Kohlberg's mature interpretation of Stage 3, they are not necessary considerations in his structural conception of Stage 3. For instance, Stage 3 thinking in some persons, cultures, and historical periods may instead emphasize rigid role conceptions and a focus on "tougher" virtues such as honor, courage, and loyalty.

One important difference between Kohlberg and Rest concerns the degree to which people's moral reasoning is said to reflect a variety of stages. Kohlberg believes that the active conceptualization of moral arguments is based on one stage, or two adjacent stages. The MJI is said to measure "hard" Piagetian stages and to provide evidence for consistency in reasoning across dilemmas. However, when a person evaluates prefabricated moral arguments on the DIT, he or she may well prefer arguments reflecting a variety of stages. This is so because the evaluation process is influenced both by the content and the structure of the moral arguments. Consequently Kohlberg applies his strict Piagetian stage model only to production processes and not to evaluation processes. Rest sees it differently and believes that stage mixture predominates throughout the domain of moral reasoning.

Rest (1979, 1986a, 1986b) has provided extensive evidence which documents the reliability and validity of the DIT. There exist now around 600 studies employing the DIT, making it the most frequently used moral judgment test in the scientific literature. Since such an extensive research basis is available, the results of any new study can be fruitfully compared against a massive set of data. The test appears to pick up more or less latent patterns of moral reasoning that precede structures of reasoning identified by Kohlberg's interview method. Because it is easier to judge moral arguments than to produce them, persons are usually 1 - 1 1/2 stages "ahead" on the DIT when compared to the MJI. The gap between DIT scores and MJI scores tends to be larger during adolescence than during the later years. Adolescents and adults frequently endorse principled moral arguments on the DIT though they may be quite unable to produce these arguments in interviews.

Correlations between Rest's and Kohlberg's test tend to be moderate, indi

Table 4-2. Stages of Moral Development According to Rest

Stage	Coordination of Expectations About Actions (How Rules Are Known and Shared)	Schemes of Balancing Interests (How Equilibrium Is Achieved	Central Concept for Determining Moral Rights and Responsibilities
Stage 1	The caretaker makes known certain demands on the child's behavior.	The child does not share in making rules but understands that obedience will bring freedom from punishment.	The morality of obedience: "Do what you're told."
Stage 2	Although each person is understood to have his own interests, an exchange of favors might be mutually decided.	If each party sees something to gain in an exchange, then both want to reciprocate.	The morality of instrumental egoism and simple exchange: "Let's make a deal."
Stage 3	Through reciprocal role-taking, individuals attain a mutual understanding about each other and the ongoing pattern of their interactions.	Friendship relationships establish a stabilized and enduring scheme of cooperation. Each party anticipates the feelings, needs, and wants of the other and acts in the other's welfare.	The morality of interpersonal concordance: "Be considerate, nice, and kind, and you'll get along with people."
Stage 4	All members of society know what is expected of them through public institutionalized law.	Unless a societywide system of cooperation is established and stabilized, no individual can really make plans. Each person should follow the law and do his particular job, anticipating that other people will also fulfill their responsibilities.	The morality of law and duty to the social order: "Everyone in society is obligated and protected by the law."
Stage 5	Formal procedures are institutionalized for making laws, which one anticipates rational people would accept.	Law-making procedures are devised so that they reflect the general will of the people, at the same time insuring certain basic rights to all. With each person having a say in the decision process, each will see that his interests are maximized while at the same time having a basis for making claims on other people.	The morality of societal consensus: "You are obligated by whatever arrangements are agreed to by due process procedures."
Stage 6	The logical requirements of nonarbitrary cooperation among rational, equal, and inpartial people are taken as ideal criteria for social organization which one anticipates rational people would accept.	A scheme of cooperation that negates or neutralizes all arbitrary distribution of rights and responsibilities is the most equilibrated, for such system is maximizing the simultaneous benefit to each member so that any deviation from these rules would advantage some members at the expense of others.	The morality of nonarbitrary social cooperation: "How rational and impartial people would organize cooperation is moral."

Source: Rest (1983, p. 588) (From Mussen (Ed.), *Handbook of Child Psychology*, Vol. IV, Wiley, 1983).

cating that the two tests measure overlapping yet distinct cognitive skills. Correlations between age/education and DIT scores in a variety of national and cross-national samples are often substantial and support the notion that the DIT provides, indeed, a developmental measure. As with the MJI, measures of intelligence show modest to moderate correlations with moral judgment ability. Parental social class contributes only slightly to the DIT scores of adolescents, and gender differences tend to be minimal. A preference for principled moral arguments on the DIT tends to go together with adherence to liberal political and religious viewpoints (Rest, 1979, 1986a, 1986b).

COMPARISONS BETWEEN MJI, SRM, AND DIT

The student of moral reasoning contemplating a research project or ploughing through the research literature may ask the following questions: Which moral reasoning test is most useful for my project? What are the limitations of the various tests? What theoretical and empirical conclusions can be drawn from data based upon these moral reasoning tests?

Table 4-3 compares three moral judgments tests and attempts to give preliminary guidance for answering some of these questions. The MJI is without a doubt the most precise and comprehensive test for the strict investigation of Kohlberg's theoretical claims. The test can easily be adapted to various social and cultural circumstances, provides reliable structural estimates of a person's moral reasoning, gives the researcher the opportunity to establish heteronomous and moral types, does not rely on the subject's reading abilities, and as a production test gives the subject the opportunity to express his or her own idiosyncratic moral convictions and considerations. Learning to code provides a thorough introduction to Kohlberg's conception of moral stages and types. The MJI is an especially useful test when relationships between moral reasoning and moral actions are explored. The test can also be combined with other approaches to moral reasoning when the researcher wishes to explore new aspects of the moral domain. In such cases, the data derived from the MJI can serve as a baseline against which the new conceptions and findings can be compared.

The disadvantages of the MJI are above all practical in nature. When the test is given in the preferred, oral form, tapes of the interviews must be transcribed. The interviewer must be trained to ask the right follow-up questions. Learning to score it is a time-consuming, difficult process, and the researcher may not have access to a scoring workshop. If the researcher's first language is not English, the coding manual is indeed difficult to grasp.

The SRM can serve as a useful alternative test to the MJI in many research situations. Although the SRM lacks some of the precision and adaptability of the MJI, it frequently gives results reasonably close to the results that would be obtained with the MJI. When the researcher wishes to compare the level of moral reasoning prevalent in a variety of groups, or if the purpose of the study is to establish correlations between moral reasoning and other variables, the SRM may well be the test of choice. The test assumes a reasonable level of literacy and a reasonable degree of motivation on the part of the subjects. Careless

Table 4-3. Comparison of Three Moral Judgment Tests

Test	NATURE OF TASK	REASONING OF SUBJECTS EXPLORED?	READING KNOWLEDGE	MORAL TYPES/SUB-STAGES	FOCUS OF TEST	TEST-RETEST RELIABILITY	PRACTICAL CONSIDERATIONS AND LIMITATIONS
MJI (Kohlberg)	Production (3 stories—3 alternate versions available)	Yes	Not necessary, if given verbally (preferable)	Yes Heteronomous vs. Autonomous	Choices: Orientations: Stages 1-5; Some metaethical questions	High	Individual test administration (written group administration tests sometimes used). Considerable flexibility in administration —can be modified for cross-cultural purposes; Transcription of interviews is cumbersome; trained interviewers and scorers are needed; scoring difficult to learn and time consuming; large body of studies
SRM (Gibbs)	Production (2 stories— 2 alternate versions available) Shorter version available	Yes	At least 4th—6th grade Oral administration possible	None	Choices, Stages 1-4 Theoretical Relativism & Theoretical Principles orientations.	Rather high	Written group administration; motivation of Ss important; can be adapted for cross-cultural purposes; trained scorers needed (30+ hours training); cannot be used for nonliterate or semiliterate Ss or cultures; few studies available; moderate-high correlation with MJI
DIT (Rest)	Recognition— Preference (6 stories; 3 story version available)	No. Test explores evaluative, not justificatory thought	At least 8th—10th grade	Some (4^1/2, 5A, 5B)	Choices: Stages 2, 3, 4, 4^1/2. 5A, 5B, 6	Moderately high; variable	Group administration; objective standard scoring procedures; motivation of Ss important; systematic adaptation to different cultures difficult; cannot be used for nonliterate or semiliterate Ss or cultures; very large body of studies; moderate correlation with MJI

subjects may produce unscorable protocols. The scoring procedures for the SRM are of moderate complexity and can be mastered by most researchers in three to eight weeks. The SRM does not allow for the scoring of moral types, and it may not be the test of choice when the nature of postconventional moral thinking is being explored.

The DIT is the most practical of the three tests in many research situations. It can be administered to groups, can easily be scored by hand or by computer, provides a variety of stage scores, does not demand special training for interviewers or scorers, and can be easily integrated into the research process. Given Rest's (1979, 1986a, 1986b) useful summaries of the enormous DIT research literature, test results can usually be interpreted in a straightforward manner. The test is probably most useful when the focus of the research is on broad comparisons between group means. The DIT may also be used to study the effectiveness of educational interventions which focus on the improvement of sociomoral reasoning skills. The test is also useful in order to establish to what extent principled moral thinking is valued by a society or group of people when most of the group members are unable to formulate moral principles for themselves.

Among the three tests, the DIT makes the greatest demands on the cognitive and reading skills of the subjects. The test requires formal operations (Piaget) which must be applied to moral-political situations. Younger subjects may lack these cognitive skills, or they may lack the motivation to confront the difficult task established by the DIT. Researchers should guard themselves against a tendency to use the DIT merely for the sake of convenience. The DIT is neither theoretically nor empirically a replacement for the MJI, although the DIT has often been treated in this manner in the research literature.

Besides the MJI, SRM, and the DIT, there exist a number of alternative moral reasoning tests and scoring procedures. Two tests may be mentioned in this context. Gibbs' Sociomoral Reflection Objective Measure (SROM) has already been mentioned, and should be considered as a possible alternative to the DIT. The SROM appears to have a somewhat closer relationship to the MJI than does the DIT, but until now it has not been used very much in research projects. For further information, J. Gibbs at the Ohio State University should be contacted.

In German-speaking countries, Lind's *Moralisches-Urteil-Test* (MUT) has been frequently used. It is a preference test based upon two moral dilemmas and is available in an English translation. The test measures both the intensity of stage-typed preferences and the consistency with which stage-typed preferences are upheld across different choices, arguments, and dilemmas. The test has been applied in a number of European capitalist and socialist countries and has led to novel interpretations of the Kohlbergian research enterprise. Interested readers should consult the book by Lind, Hartman, and Wakenhut (1985) which was translated from the German. We may add in this context that the German philosophical, methodological, and empirical literature on moral reasoning is quite extensive in scope. It is characterized by its theoretical sophistication and by an awareness of Kohlberg's contributions to philosophy, psychology, and education.

CONCLUSIONS

We have described or touched upon a variety of research methods that can be used to study the structural development of moral judgment competence in relationship to social experience and moral action. The methods include Kohlberg's Moral Judgment Interview, Gibbs' Social Reflection Measure, Rest's Defining Issues Test, Lind's *Moralisches-Urteil-Test*, and Gibbs' Sociomoral Objective Reflection Measure.

The tests appear to be satisfactory tests by the conventional criteria of psychological test construction. In Kohlberg's longitudinal research project, the new Standard Issue Scoring approach proved to be a highly reliable method (Colby et al., 1983). Using different raters, test-retest correlations of .96, .99, and .97 were found in three different data sets. Interrater reliability was also excellent for the three Forms A, B, and C. Gibbs' Social Reflection Measure also appears to be a reliable measure of moral judgment competence for adolescents and adults. Reliability coefficients for the Defining Issues Test are less consistent from one study to the next, depending on socio-cultural factors, age, and subjects' motivation (Moon, 1986).

It is important to realize that the tests were developed with a very specific purpose in mind. The tests attempt to measure sociomoral role-taking skills, and the concepts, strategies, and value hierarchies that are used by people to solve predetermined moral dilemmas. These structural tests do not attempt to establish a person's moral character, mental health, or personality organization. They should not be used to determine the moral worth of a person or group of persons, since adequate judgments of moral worth must take into account moral actions, self-conceptions, personality organization, and the normative content of moral decision making. Since the tests employ predetermined dilemmas, they may fail to measure a person's ability to spontaneously notice subtle moral implications in real-life situations. Finally, the tests may not measure moral motivation very well. A person may use sophisticated moral decision-making strategies, yet value non-moral goals over moral goals in some situations (Rest, 1986c).

Kohlberg's methodological and theoretical approach to the nature of justice reasoning is both very narrow and very broad in scope. It is a narrow approach because it only focuses on moral decision-making situations that raise questions of justice. It is a very broadly conceived approach because it perceives problems of justice in a wide variety of situations and because it claims that it has identified universal structures of moral reasoning. The moral reasoning tests described above should be seen in this light. By now, far more than a thousand research projects based upon these tests have been completed. The projects have been conducted in a wide variety of societies and social situations. The research evidence suggests that in many situations, tests of moral reasoning give valid estimates of a person's approach to moral decision making. In conjunction with other measures, the moral reasoning tests can also be employed to predict moral action and to study the effectiveness of educational interventions.

SUGGESTED READINGS FOR CHAPTERS 2-4

Lawrence Kohlberg (1987) *Child psychology and childhood education: A cognitive-developmental view,* New York: Longman, is written in a nontechnical fashion and integrates many findings in the areas of child development and child education as seen from Kohlberg's perspective. Chapters 2 and 7 describe his theoretical assumptions and his view of moral development. Lawrence Kohlberg (1984) *The psychology of moral development,* New York: Harper & Row chapters 1-4, covers similar ground in a more detailed and technical fashion. Chapter 2, "Stage and sequence: The cognitive-developmental approach to socialization," represents the most important psychological essay on social development written during the last fifty years. Chapter 4 includes Kohlberg's assessment of the many criticisms that have been directed at his theory. The most comprehensive assessments of his philosophical, psychological, and educational theories and research projects can be found in Sohan Modgil and Celia Modgil (Eds.) (1986) *Lawrence Kohlberg: Consensus and controversy,* Philadelphia, The Falmer Press. The book includes essays both supportive and critical of his approach, as well as Kohlberg's extensive reply to his critics. The book, unfortunately, does not cover some of Kohlberg's later writings. Many essays in it assume that the reader is thoroughly grounded in moral philosophy, psychology, and education as well as Kohlberg's work. The philosopher Dwight Boyd (1988) edited a special issue of *The Journal of Moral Education,* Vol. 17, 3, October 1988, entitled: *In honour of Lawrence Kohlberg: Some directions of current work.* Kohlberg provided inspiration for numerous empirical and theoretical projects, but he always left his students and colleagues with enough "breathing space" so they could follow their own path. Personal reminiscences of Kohlberg by some of his students may be found in: James R. Rest (Guest Editor) (1988) *Special issue: The legacy of Lawrence Kohlberg, Counseling and Values,* Vol. 32, 3, April, 1988.

Broad overviews of moral psychology are presented in James R. Rest (1983) "Morality," in *Manual of child psychology* (Ed. P. Mussen); Vol. 3: *Cognitive Development* (Eds.: J. Flavell and E. Markham) New York: Wiley, pp. 556-629.; and in Thomas Lickona (Ed.) (1976) *Moral Development and Behavior: Theory, Research and Social Issues.* New York: Holt, Rinehart, and Winston. Rest is sympathetic to Kohlberg's position but reviews other theories as well. Lickona's book contains essays written from a wide variety of viewpoints. A more recent set of essays by an international group of authors is contained in: William M.

Kurtines, and Jacob L. Gewirtz (Eds.) (1984) *Morality, Moral Behavior and Moral Development. Basic Issues in Theory and Research.* New York: Wiley. Ann Colby and Lawrence Kohlberg (1987) *The Measurement of Moral Judgment,* Vols. 1-2. Cambridge, Mass.: Cambridge University Press, constitutes the final version of his coding guide. Volume 1 provides a concise summary of Kohlberg's theoretical assumptions, reliability and validity data, results from three longitudinal studies in the USA, Turkey, and Israel, instructions for scoring, and practice cases. Volume 2 contains Forms A, B, and C of the Moral Judgment Interview as well as scoring criteria. John C. Gibbs and Keith I. Widaman (1982) *Social Intelligence: Measuring the Development of Sociomoral Reflection.* Englewood Cliffs, N.J.: Prentice Hall, describes Gibbs' SRM (Social Reflection Questionnaire) and coding system.

James R. Rest's (1986) *Manual for the Defining Issues Test,* 3rd edition, may be obtained from the Center for the Study of Ethical Development, University of Minnesota, 141 Burton Hall, Minneapolis, MN 55455 which will also provide information concerning DIT computer scoring services and programs. DIT research is surveyed in James R. Rest (1979) *Development in Judging Moral Issues.* Minneapolis, Minn.: University of Minnesota Press. More recent DIT research and its implications are described in: James R. Rest (1986) *Moral Development: Advances in Research and Theory.*

Standard surveys of the cross-cultural literature include: John Snarey (1985) Cross-cultural universality of social-moral development: A critical review of Kohlbergian research. *Psychological Bulletin, 97,* 202-32; Carolyn Pope Edwards "Cross-cultural research on Kohlberg's stages: The basis for consensus", and Ian Vine: "Moral maturity in socio-cultural perspective: Are Kohlberg's stages universal?" both in Sohan Modgil and Celia Modgil (1986) *Lawrence Kohlberg: Consensus and Controversy:* London: The Falmer Press, pp. 419-453. A useful earlier survey may be found in Carolyn Pope Edwards: "The comparative study of the development of moral judgment and reasoning," in: Ruth H. Munroe, Robert L. Munroe, and Beatrice B. Whiting (Eds.) (1981) *Handbook of Cross-Cultural Development.* New York: Garland Publishing, pp. 501-527. A special issue of *Behavior Science Research,* 1986, *20,* (1-4) reports eight cross-cultural papers dealing with moral reasoning, including a useful survey of DIT studies by Y.L. Moon. Lutz H. Eckensberger (1983) reviews a highly active research scene in: "Research on moral development in Germany," in *The German Journal of Psychology, 7,* 195-244. Uwe P. Gielen (1990) critically evaluates "Some recent work on moral values, reasoning, and education in Chinese societies," in *Moral Education Forum,* Vol. 15, *1,* 3-22. The review discusses both Kohlbergian and non-Kohlbergian studies.

Lawrence J. Walker surveys "Sex differences in moral reasoning," in W.W. Kurtines and J.L. Gewirtz (Eds.) (in press) *Moral Behavior and Development: Advances in Theory, Research, and Application* (Vol. 2). Hillsdale, N.J.: Erlbaum. While Walker focuses on MJI studies, Stephen J. Thoma (1986) reviews and integrates DIT studies in: Estimating gender differences in the comprehension and preference of moral issues. *Developmental Review*, 6: 156-180. Gilligan's feminist conception of moral development may be found in: Carol Gilligan (1982) *In a Different Voice. Psychological Theory and Women's Development*. Cambridge, Mass.: Harvard University Press. The Center for the Study of Gender, Education and Human Development, Harvard Graduate School of Education, has begun to issue a series of monographs, including: Carol Gilligan, Janie Victoria Ward, and Jill McLean Taylor (Eds.) (1988) *Mapping the Moral Domain*. The book expands her earlier theoretical framework and applies it to a variety of life situations. Bill Puka's (1988) *Caring concern and just regard: Different voices or separate realities?* MOSAIC Monograph No. 4. University of Bath, provides a concise comparison between Kohlberg's and Gilligan's approaches to the study of morality. Kohlberg's own response to Gilligan's claims is outlined in Kohlberg (1984: 224-235; 338-370).

The relationship between moral reasoning and moral action is discussed by Lawrence Kohlberg and Daniel Candee, in Kohlberg (1984, see above), chapter 7. Augusto Blasi's (1980) earlier survey: Bridging moral cognition and moral action: A critical review of the literature. *Psychological Bulletin*, 88: 1-45, remains the best empirical survey of moral reasoning - moral action studies. The relationship between moral reasoning and unlawful activities is discussed by William S. Jennings, Robert Kilkenny, and Lawrence Kohlberg: "Moral-development theory and practice for youthful and adult offenders," in William S. Laufer and James M. Day (1983) *Personality Theory, Moral Development, and Criminal Behavior*. Lexington, Mass.: Lexington Books, pp. 281-355. Relationships between DIT scores and behavior/attitudes are reviewed by Stephen J. Thoma and James R. Rest (with Robert Burnett). "Moral Judgment, Behavior, Decision Making, and Attitudes," in James R. Rest (1986) *Moral Development: Advances in Research and Theory*. New York: Praeger, pp. 133-175. Helen Weinreich-Haste discusses "Kohlberg's contribution to political psychology" in: Sohan Modgil and Celia Modgil (1986, see above), chapter 22.

Relationships between the social environment and moral development have been investigated by: Betsy Speicher-Dubin (1982) *Relationships between parent moral judgment, child moral judgment and family interaction: A correlational study*. Unpublished dissertation, Harvard University; and by Georg Lind, Hans Hartman, and Roland Wakenhut (Eds.). (1985). *Moral Development and the Social Environment: Studies in the Psychology and the Philosophy of Moral Judgment and Education*. Chicago: Precedent Publishing. The latter volume contains research using Lind's MUT (*Moralisches-Urteil-Test*).

Kohlberg consistently emphasized that all psychological and educational work on morality must ultimately rest on a sound philosophical basis. He discusses his own basis in: Lawrence Kohlberg (1981) *The Philosophy of Moral Development. Moral Stages and the Idea of Justice*. New York: Harper & Row. Chapter 4 in this volume (*From Is To Ought*) is especially pertinent. Certain later modifications in his philosophical position are outlined in Lawrence Kohlberg's "A current statement of some theoretical issues," in: Sohan Modgil and Celia Modgil (1986; see above), chapter 30. Chapters 2-4 in the volume summarize discussions by other authors of his philosophical views. For a short introduction to moral philosophy, see: William K. Frankena (1973) *Ethics*. Englewood Cliffs, N.J.: Prentice Hall.

The spring issue of every volume of *The Moral Education Forum* features a complete listing of new books, monographs, and articles on moral development research and education. The fall or winter issue of each volume carries an annotated description of all doctoral dissertations in the field. In addition to articles and book reviews, the Forum also has a Shop Talk section that is open to news and inquiries from readers. *The Journal of Moral Education*, and *The Exchange for Philosophy and Moral Psychology,* and *Mosaic* all carry relevant articles and news items. Information on addresses and contact persons can be procured from the *Association for Moral Education*, at the University of Minnesota, 141 Burton Hall, 178 Pillsbury Drive, S.E., Minneapolis, Minn. 55455.

POSTSCRIPT

John C. Gibbs, K. S. Basinger, and R. L. Fuller (in press) *Moral Maturity: Measuring the Development of Sociomoral Reflection,* Hillsdale, N.J.: L. Erlbaum, contains a discussion of an abbreviated version of the Social Reflection Questionnaire.

William M. Kurtines and Jacob L. Gewirtz (Eds.) (in press) *Handbook of Moral Behavior and Development.* Vol. I: Theory, Vol. II: Research, Vol. III: Application, Hillsdale, N.J.: L. Erlbaum, promises to become a standard reference for the 1990s.

PART II

KOHLBERG FOR THE EDUCATIONAL PRACTITIONER

Chapter 5

An Overview of Kohlberg's Contributions to Education

Lisa Kuhmerker

During Lawrence Kohlberg's lifetime the transition of his moral development theory into practice was basically of three kinds: 1) the use of hypothetical dilemmas in the form of a series of classroom discussions, generally spaced at weekly intervals; 2) the application of teaching strategies to curriculum content in traditional courses; and 3) the creation of "just community schools" whose goal was nothing less than the transformation of the governance structure of the school.

DILEMMA DISCUSSIONS

A generation of teachers who has had no personal contact with the moral development movement sparked by Kohlberg, *can test the power* of dilemma discussions by introducing occasional hypothetical moral dilemmas into the traditional curriculum or by planning a series of such discussions as a unit. The teacher is likely to be impressed by the capacity of the hypothetical dilemmas, and the suggested probe questions, to engage student interest and to create the dissonance that calls forth the students' best thinking. The teacher is likely to find that his or her awareness and increasingly skillful use of instructional strategies for creating dissonance, and focusing student attention on issues of fairness, "spills over" into other curriculum areas and into issues of classroom management.

Incorporating occasional hypothetical dilemmas into the curriculum, or using those strategies to spur discussion, can be accomplished in the individual classroom and need not involve educational change on a school-wide level. Commercially available audio-visual materials can assist and augment the effort. The section on dilemma discussions on pages 91-102 provides the theory, rationale, and suggestions for teaching needed to initiate such activities.

FOSTERING MORAL DEVELOPMENT THROUGH TRADITIONAL CURRICULUM

The teaching strategies Kohlberg's colleagues developed in the course of using hypothetical dilemmas in the classroom are well-suited to being applied to courses that are part of the traditional curriculum. There are many instances in which developmental theory and Kohlbergian-type probe questions became integrated into course content. On pages 115-122 three examples of such influence on secondary school courses are described. The first is a literature course created specifically to foster cognitive dissonance and perspective taking, as well as the traditional skills of literary analysis. The second example provides an overview of a social studies program where historical incidents are framed in terms of the dilemmas they created for their protagonists. The third example describes a unit on the Holocaust and human behavior, designed to help students to face both history and themselves.

TRANSFORMING THE SCHOOL INTO A JUST COMMUNITY

There comes a time when the introduction of yet another hypothetical dilemma is counter-productive. The solution at this point is not to invent a more "realistic" dilemma—a task that is far more difficult than one might imagine—but to move to real-life issues of fairness in the school or other educational setting. On pages 103-115 are descriptions of programs that Kohlberg labeled "just community schools" and that reflect not merely the limits of moral development through dilemma discussions but Kohlberg's conviction that the capacity for moral reasoning must be wedded to the creation of community norms within the school setting.

When Kohlberg first attempted to involve students in moral discussions it became quickly apparent that the students wanted to question all kinds of adult authority. The result was that Kohlberg was "un-invited" by these schools and carried out some of his substantive early research with groups in prison populations. When he returned to the schools, it was with the knowledge that commitment on the part of the administration was essential. It should be noted that each of the just community interventions was carried out in an alternative school setting where both students and staff elected to participate. This does not mean that regular public schools cannot become just community schools, but it emphasizes that the leadership in the school must be firmly committed to the goal.

During the last ten years of his life Kohlberg acted upon his conviction that the creation of just community schools was the most logical outgrowth of his theories and the strategy most consistent with the education of citizens of democratic nations. The goal of just community schools is radical; it is no less than the transformation of the school governance structure from the traditional mode, where adults set and enforce standards of behavior as well as curriculum content, to one where the major proportion of decisions are made jointly by students, faculty, and administrators. With the making of rules comes the responsibility of abiding by them and enforcing them within the school community. It is this link between decision making and sense of responsibility that can change the moral atmosphere of the school, reduce violence and discipline problems, and create conditions for moral development. It is a process involving soul-searching, stress, conflict, patience, and lots and lots of time. Turning a traditional school into a democratic just community is not a decision to be made lightly. The experience of the just communities in which Kohlberg was involved showed that it also took an extended period of staff preparation, staff support, and the funding to make this preparation and support possible.

There are only two reasons why a school would wish to move from a traditional governance structure to a just and democratic one. One reason is that a lot of things are not going well! The atmosphere of the school is confrontive and violent, substance abuse is prevalent, absenteeism and drop-outs are commonplace, student achievement is low, disrespect for authority is blatant, and teacher burnout is a major issue. In such a situation educators are understandably reluctant to share what little authority and power they feel they have, but they can see the need for drastic change. On a deeper level, they also long for the possibility of community and communication; ideals that probably drew them to the teaching field and then inexplicably eluded them.

The second reason why a school would be willing to turn from a traditional governance structure to a just and democratic one with full student participation, is that *it is the best way we know — perhaps the only reliable way — to prepare young people to become active and responsible members of a democratic society*. This would be the primary motive for the transformation of public schools in stable communities and for private schools who already pride themselves on their academic excellence.

No school in the second half of the twentieth century is so troublefree that it shares none of the problems that plague our innercity schools; the staff of no innercity school is so totally burned out that it has discarded the goal of preparing young people to be well-adjusted adults and good citizens of a democracy. Thus it may be that educators and parents of children in "good" schools may yet feel that students are apathetic, self-centered, and vulnerable to the influence of drugs and corruption in the wider society. Such concerns are more than reason enough to transform the governance structure of the school.

The process of creating a just community school is time consuming, and the teacher education and development phase can be complex and extensive. The smaller and more cohesive the faculty group, the greater its chances of success.

Thus, a small private school might transform itself with little or no trauma, a school-within-a-school may be a viable option within a large high-school setting, or an alternative school could exist parallel to the traditional high school. Still another option is to incorporate some features of the just community school into a large school setting. One such example is described on pages 114-115.

Documentation on programs that put them into the category of democratic or just community schools is uneven, but this book includes enough examples, from schools inspired by Kohlbergian ideas and Kohlberg's participation, to give readers a sense of whether or not they would like to propose the creation of a just community and what steps might lead them in that direction (Chesbrough, 1981; Codding and Aranella, 1981; Mosher, 1980; Power, 1979a, 1979b, 1985; Power, Higgins, and Kohlberg, 1989; Wasserman, 1975, 1977, 1979). Two words of caution:

1) To date, no school has instituted a substantive program of this kind without having been "seeded" by an administrator who had prior knowledge and experience with such a program or which benefited from a consultant team that had such experience.

2) A school with multiple problems might well need a year of teacher preparation—and the funding this requires—before implementing its program.

MORAL DEVELOPMENT PROGRAMS
FOR THE ELEMENTARY SCHOOL YEARS

Kohlberg did not formally measure the moral development of preadolescent children and took no direct role in school programs for the elementary school years. With his colleagues Selman, Fenton, and Lickona he was a consultant to Guidance Associates (1972, 1976) in the development of film strips and discussion guides. Thomas Lickona, a colleague of Ralph Mosher as well as Kohlberg, has interpreted the implications of moral development theory during the early years for a general audience in "Raising Good Children" (Lickona, 1983) as well as in academic publications (Lickona, 1980; Lickona and Paradise, 1980). In Mosher's edited volume, "Moral Education: A First Generation of Research and Development" (Mosher, 1980) there are several chapters focused on the elementary years. A focus on the moral education of young children through a democratic school governance structure and the fostering of friendship is central to the publications of Kuhmerker and Shaheen (Shaheen and Kuhmerker, in press).

MORAL EDUCATION PROGRAMS IN
PART-TIME EDUCATIONAL SETTINGS

Realistically, it is unlikely that the majority of students across the nation will have the opportunity to attend a just community school in the next few years. Yet perhaps there is an opportunity for large numbers of students to have such an experience for significant periods of time, albeit they do not have such an opportunity on a year-round basis. Similarly, the teaching strategies developed through research into the effect of dilemma discussions on moral development can benefit part-time and after-school programs.

Sunday School and CCD Programs: Sunday schools provide excellent opportunities for fostering moral reasoning through the use of hypothetical dilemma discussions. Research on the effects of the use of dilemma discussions has shown consistent and reliable growth in the structure of students' thinking about moral issues. There is no doubt whatsoever that the incorporation of dilemma discussions can enrich the curriculum of programs of any denomination. Indeed, in summer workshops at Harvard's Center for Moral Education in the 1970s, extensive adaptations of Kohlberg's theory were made by religious educators as diverse as the Ethical Culture Society, the Seventh-Day Adventists, and the Roman Catholic Archdiocese of Ontario. They perceived, correctly, that Kohlberg's theory of moral development was "content-free," i.e., it could accommodate diverse religious beliefs and content.

The workshop kits that have been developed for training leaders of dilemma discussions (Guidance Associates, 1972, 1976) are suitable for Sunday school teachers who may not have a formal background in education, and their cost puts them within the reach of the average church or synagogue budget.

After-School and Weekend Programs: Often limited to custodial care, sports, and arts and crafts activities, such programs can be enriched by dilemma discussions. In some communities, demand for group experiences on Saturdays and during holiday periods has led to numerous small private entrepreneurs who offer "enrichment" of various sorts. Moral dilemma discussions could be a welcome addition to their range of activities. While after-school programs also have great potential for involving participants in self-governance and fairness issues that can overshadow the relevance of hypothetical dilemmas, the fact that dilemma discussion can be satisfactorily begun and completed in a single session may be a major advantage.

Summer Camps: Summer camps are an ideal setting for the creation of just communities. No full-scale attempt to institute or assess summer programs materialized during Kohlberg's lifetime. However, it may well be that ten years from now Kohlbergian theory and strategies may yet be a major aspect of the Kohlberg legacy.

There are multiple reasons why summer camps are "naturals" for the creation of just communities. The function of summer camps is to bring a group of young people together for a community experience and the away-from-home-and-school setting of camp is ideal for creating a social structure. The fact that academic requirements do not have to be primary provides the leisure for exploration of ideas. Everyone is "new" on the first day of camp, and the concrete need for establishing rules that are fair is "up-front agenda." Yet most camp administrators do not have a rationale for moral development in such a setting. This is why camp experience is so liberating for some youngsters and so painful for others.

The camp experience needs a structure for discussing the fairness of rules and the feelings of others. Within the month or two-month scope of togetherness, campers can create a world and not just try to fit into a structure that has been created for them. While most parents cannot shop around for an ideal school, parents do select the summer camp of their choice. An explicit focus on fairness issues and a democratic governance structure might be seen as a greater "plus" in the eyes of thoughtful parents than many of the other features through which camp administrators try to attract their clients.

Publicly funded summer programs for remediation and recreation for innercity youngsters may likewise adopt the just community model as an optimally effective way to reach disaffected youngsters. Whether they are day programs or sleep-away programs, they may be the most cost-effective way to reach the students who are at social risk, and the effect of such programs may well "spill over" to benefit the regular school setting.

The transformation of the mainstream of education is a daunting task and may well be beyond the realm of possibility within the professional setting of most educators. The potential for creating summer programs that are just communities, both in the private and public sector, is waiting to be explored. It may well be that ten years from now this will be the arena in which the Kohlbergian legacy is most vital and alive.

Chapter 6

Fostering Moral Development through Dilemma Discussions

Lisa Kuhmerker

Dilemma discussions are not a panacea to cure the ills of American education. I think about them as a modest contribution to curriculum improvement and pedagogical techniques firmly grounded in research about cognitive moral development and resting on sound philosophical assumptions. They can make a significant contribution to American education only if educators see them as one aspect of a developmental approach to curriculum which . . . implies fundamental rethinking of the nature and purpose of education in a democracy (Edwin Fenton, in Gomberg et al., 1980, p. 161).

Lawrence Kohlberg did not set out to create hypothetical dilemmas designed to promote moral reasoning in classroom settings. He created them in order to assess the reasoning about justice issues of the sample of adolescent boys he set out to study for his doctoral dissertation (Kohlberg, 1958). As he used to tell us, he stationed himself in front of a local candy store, and as teenagers drifted in and out he buttonholed them to pose hypothetical dilemmas. The famous "Heinz dilemma" and the other eight dilemmas which became the content of Forms A, B, and C of the Moral Judgment Interview (MJI) were all created to tap the moral reasoning of the subjects for his dissertation on "The Development of Modes of Thinking and Choices in Years 10 to 16."

A doctoral student, Moshe Blatt, used Kohlberg's dilemmas in a Sunday school setting (Blatt, 1969). He tested the students for their stage of moral judgment, met with them as a group once a week for twelve weeks, and then retested them. To his surprise, he found that 64 percent of them had developed one full stage in their moral reasoning.

Blatt them set out to replicate these findings in two sixth and two tenth grade public school classrooms. Students were divided into three groups; one group met with Blatt for eighteen sessions, another met for the same length of time in a peer-led discussion group, and a control group received no educational intervention. The Blatt group showed an average gain of one-third of a stage; the other groups showed almost no change. In a follow-up test one year later, the Blatt group maintained its lead over the others (Blatt and Kohlberg, 1975).

The work of Blatt demonstrated that the development of moral judgment could be affected by an educational intervention and that such an effect was not a temporary phenomenon when the intervention provided opportunities for cognitive conflict, role-taking, and an exposure to moral reasoning above one's own stage of reasoning. Kohlberg rescored the Blatt data after he had developed his final scoring system, but the basic finding, that a relatively short intervention can effect stage change, remained unchanged.

"Since Blatt's pioneering research on moral discussion, there have been a large number of studies which have replicated his findings. These have been reviewed by Lockwood (1978), Higgins (1980), Leming (1981), Enright, Lapsley, and Levy (1983), Schafli, Rest, and Thoma (1985), and Lapsley, Enright, Harris, and Serlin (in press). Unfortunately there has been little research conducted to clarify what are the critical conditions in these discussion programs that promote development (Schafli, Rest, and Thoma, 1985)." (Power, Higgins, and Kohlberg, 1989, p. 13).

The integration of the research on the use of hypothetical dilemmas into educational practice took three forms:

1) The development of audio-visual kits and teacher discussion guides for the elementary school level (Guidance Associates, 1972, 1974) and the intermediate or secondary school level (Guidance Associates, 1976),

2) The development of curricula in social studies for the secondary school level which focus both on hypothetical and real-life dilemmas faced by historical figures and which use probe questions and other teaching strategies typical of hypothetical dilemma discussions, and

3) The development of teacher education workshops and curriculum guides for leaders of dilemma discussions in mainstream educational settings (Fenton, 1977; Fenton, 1980; Gomberg et al., 1980).

LEADING DILEMMA DISCUSSIONS

Dilemma discussions help students to progress toward generally accepted educational goals. It is good for teachers to remember that the skills needed to lead dilemma discussions successfully are the same kinds of skills teachers need to function effectively as discussion leaders in other aspects of the curriculum.

The process of leading dilemma discussions is the same whether these be hypothetical or historically based.

Edwin Fenton of Carnegie Mellon University was one of the two prominent educators who bridged the gap between Kohlbergian research and the classroom teacher. Fenton translated moral education theory into language with which teachers were familiar, clarified the parallels between moral education and education in general for teacher audiences, and developed workshop programs suitable for in-service education. (The other prominent educator has been Ralph Mosher (Mosher, 1978; Mosher, 1979; Mosher, 1980; Mosher and Sullivan, 1976) whose work will be discussed in connection and juxtaposition with the "just community school" concept.) The workshop guide for leading dilemma discussions, conceptualized by Fenton and developed by a team of educators at Carnegie Mellon (Gomberg et al., 1980), was widely used in the 1970s and 1980s but remained in mimeographed form. It is no longer available through Carnegie Mellon University, so highlights of its contents will be summarized or quoted liberally in this volume.

GENERAL EDUCATIONAL GOALS AND THE GOALS OF DILEMMA DISCUSSIONS

Dilemma discussions can help students progress toward at least five general educational goals:

1) The development of basic *participatory skills*, such as speaking . . . and working in small groups.

2) Acquisition of *knowledge* about subject areas such as literature or history or about contemporary affairs or the life of the school.

3) *Personal development*, particularly growth in self-knowledge and self-esteem.

4) The development of *reasoning abilities*; in other words, movement from pre-operational to concrete and from concrete to formal operation on the Piagentian scale.

5) The development of the ability to understand democratic values, or movement to higher stages of moral reasoning on the Kohlberg scale (Gomberg et al., 1980, p. 1).

Fenton cautions teachers to remember that students may understand vocabulary and basic concepts in terms of their own stage development, rather than from the societal or principled level that the teacher assumes. For example, a teacher might say, "The Supreme Court declared the law unconstitutional because it violated fundamental principles of justice protected by the Constitution." By justice, the teacher might mean principles such as the equal worth and dignity of all individuals, while students at Stage 2 might think justice means paying people back for something done or not done, and students at Stage 3 might think that justice means what the majority of ninth graders think about an issue (Gomberg et al., 1980, p. 113).

The awareness of how differently children and adolescents may make mean-ing of vocabulary and concepts whose common meaning is assumed by adults first struck Fenton when a Harvard team of Kohlberg's joined with a Carnegie Mellon University group in a joint project sponsored by the W. Clement and Jessie V. Stone Foundation. Even as the testing and incorporation of some dilem-mas led to some success in helping teachers to lead discussions (Galbraith and Jones, 1976), Fenton felt that he did not grasp the implications of dilemma dis-cussions clearly enough to make them an integral part of a school curriculum. So, after having successfully authored and/or edited some thirty social studies texts, Fenton spent a sabbatical year at Harvard studying and learning.

> I began to focus on two major questions: How can teachers and curriculum workers facilitate the development of formal thought so that students can employ the inquiry processes which lie at the heart of the social studies dis-ciplines? And how can teachers facilitate the development of principled thought on the Kohlberg scale, thought which students must use in order to understand fully humanistic disciplines such as history, religion, literature, and philosophy? Out of this reflection and learning grew a project in civic edu-cation based on developmental psychology, multiple curricular goals, a sequential and integrated curriculum, and a participating government struc-ture. . . . But we called it civic education rather than moral education (Gomberg et al., 1980, p. 154).

Fenton is quoted here at length to highlight the fact that the reasons for using dilemma discussions go far beyond the desire to "create a lively discussion" or even beyond the goal of stimulating moral reasoning and stage change. Dilemma dis-cussions are a primary vehicle for fostering the overarching goals of the school.

TEACHING SKILLS AND STRATEGIES NEEDED IN GENERAL EDUCATION AND IN THE LEADING OF DILEMMA DISCUSSIONS

Teachers require four essential skills to lead dilemma discussions with max-imum effectiveness. They must be able to 1) establish a nonthreatening classroom atmosphere, 2) organize time effectively, 3) encourage student-to-student inter-action, and 4) develop skills in using probe questions (Gomberg et al., 1980, pp. 114-115).

The establishment of a nonthreatening classroom atmosphere is critical, for students will hesitate to speak freely if they feel that they may be ridiculed by other students or the adult. It requires skill and tact on the teacher's part to challenge the reasoning of students with probe questions or have one student confront another with reasoning of another stage but at the same time keep the student from feeling threatened or put down (Gomberg et al., 1980, p. 114).

Organizing time effectively may require some relearning on the part of the teacher. For example, a successful dilemma discussion may require that the class break up into small discussion groups but reassemble into the class-as-a-whole before every subgroup is finished with its discussion. "Straw votes" may be another strategy with which teachers are unfamiliar but one that is helpful in deciding what issues might be discussed by small groups in the class or what probe questions might best stimulate a divergence of opinion.

Moral reasoning is most successfully encouraged when there is a diversity of opinion in the class. Brief small group discussions can be used to elicit the two or three "best reasons" for a position. It is perfectly acceptable for some students not to be sure how or on what basis to resolve a dilemma; such a situation adds to the vigor of the discussion when the class-as-a-whole reconvenes. If there is no controversy, or if students propose problem-solving strategies that circumvent the need to make a moral decision, the teacher can use additional probe questions to increase the dissonance.

Because a typical class contains students who reason at two or more stages of the Kohlberg scale, discussion of reasons at contiguous stages will often occur spontaneously. The teacher should try to keep the discussion concentrated on the argument at the stage most students use and at one stage higher in order to give students an opportunity to examine more adequate reasoning than they ordinarily employ (Gomberg et al., 1980, p. 118). It is not necessary for the teacher to accurately identify the stage of student remarks; it suffices that the teacher has a general "feel" for which statements are more comprehensive and adequate solutions to the dilemma. It is not only unnecessary, but undesirable, to bring the issue of stages into the discussion of the class.

Relying on any one method to present dilemmas, or one way to discuss them, will soon lead to boredom among students. Fenton and his co-authors suggest a variety of strategies. A teacher might present five statements about an issue and ask students to respond in writing about whether they agree, disagree, or can't decide, and what their reasons are. Discussion would follow. Students might be asked to pick the "best" reason from a list of reasons and justify their decision. The list of reasons could include one or more sentences typical of Stage 2, 3 or 4 (Gomberg et al., 1980, pp. 118-120).

ISSUES OF NOMENCLATURE

A variety of names have been attached to the process of fostering moral reasoning through discussion of dilemmas. "Hypothetical dilemma discussions," "sociomoral dilemmas discussions," "moral dilemma discussions," "civic dilemma discussions" all reflect the process with some accuracy. On the basis of many years of experience in the mainstream of American education, Fenton suggested that the term "dilemma discussions" was not only accurate and comprehensive but likely to avoid the confusion and controversy that the term "moral dilemma discussion" might evoke. In workshops he often demonstrated ways in which dilemma discussions contribute to knowledge of subject matter in a deliberate attempt to tie discussions to the attainment of knowledge—still the major goal of most teachers.

> Teachers must be convinced that dilemma discussions can contribute to general educational goals and become an integral part of their courses if these discussions are to reach their full potential in the schools. Stage change occurs slowly; students reason at one stage for several years as they develop through childhood and adolescence. They should encounter more sophisticated thought constantly in order to facilitate cognitive moral growth. This conclusion implies that dilemma discussions ought to take place in required courses year after year so that all students will have an opportunity to develop to the limit of their cognitive capacities. For this reason, teachers must be convinced that dilemma discussions mesh smoothly with their general educational goals if we are to persuade a majority of teachers in a school to utilize them. A single course in ethics or moral education for a semester will not do the job, although it may offer a superb capstone to a carefully devised developmental curriculum extending over many years. To put the issue in a deliberately provocative way, cognitive moral development is far too important a matter to be left exclusively in the hands of moral educators (Gomberg et al., 1980, pp. 156-157).

AUDIO-VISUAL CURRICULUM MATERIALS DESIGNED TO STIMULATE DILEMMA DISCUSSION

Kohlberg, Harvard colleagues like Robert Selman, Fenton, and some of his associates at Carnegie Mellon all had input into a series of filmstrips, audiotapes, and teacher guides published by Guidance Associates in the early and mid-1970s. (First Things: Values, 1972; First Things: Social Reasoning, 1975; Values in a Democracy, 1975; Universal Values in American History, 1976; Relationships and Values, 1976; Guidance Associates, a subsidiary of New York: Harcourt Brace Jovanovich). Four to ten moral dilemmas are in each curriculum packet. Each of the four full-color film strips takes about five minutes to present, leaving ample time for discussion. The script of the film strip is part of each comprehensive discussion guide. This material is the most fool-proof entry point to the application of Kohlbergian theory for the novice teacher.

SOCIAL STUDIES CURRICULA FROM A KOHLBERGIAN PERSPECTIVE

A wide range of materials, of which the curricula listed below are a sample but which are not currently in print, looked at social education from a cognitive developmental perspective (Gomberg et al., 1980, pp. 15-16):

Fenton, E. (Ed.), (1973-1975). *The Carnegie Mellon Social Studies Curriculum*. New York: Holt, Rinehart and Winston. The second edition of this series of social studies and audio-visual materials includes dilemmas as an integral part of each individual course. The course titles are: *Comparative Political Systems, Comparative Economic Systems, The Shaping of Western Society, Tradition and Change in Four Societies,* and *A New History of the United States.*

Wyeth, T. J. and E. Fenton (Eds.), (1980). *Reasoning About Literature and Social Studies: Dilemmas for Junior and Senior High School*. Pittsburgh: Carnegie Mellon Education Center.

Fenton, E. and L. Kohlberg (1976). *Universal Values in American History*. New York: Guidance Associates.

Fenton, E. and L. Kohlberg (1976). *Values in a Democracy*. New York: Guidance Associates.

Ladenburg, T. and M. and P. Scharf (1978). *Moral Education: A Classroom Workbook*. Davis, Calif.: Responsible Action Press.

Galbraith, R. E. and T. M. Jones (1976). *Moral Reasoning: A Teaching Handbook for Adapting Kohlberg to the Classroom*. Anoka, Minn.: Greenhaven Press.

Perhaps the most popular and widely used dilemma has been "Holly's Dilemma." (First Things: Values, 1972, Guidance Associates) It was made into a film-strip and was also widely used by teachers who merely presented the dilemma verbally.

HOLLY'S DILEMMA: A HYPOTHETICAL DILEMMA FOR ELEMENTARY SCHOOL AGED CHILDREN

Holly's Dilemma has been cited in a variety of contexts. The wording used below comes from the mimeographed materials of the Carnegie Mellon workshops for leading dilemma discussions (Gomberg, 1980).

Holly is an eight-year-old girl who likes to climb trees. She is the best tree-climber in the neighborhood. One day, while climbing down from a tall tree, she falls off the bottom branch but does not hurt herself. Her father sees her fall. He is upset and asks her to promise not to climb trees anymore. Holly promises.

Later that day, Holly and her friends meet Shawn. Shawn's kitten is caught up in a tree and can't get down. Something has to be done right away or the kitten might fall. Holly is the only one who climbs trees well enough to reach the kitten and get it down, and she remembers her promise to her father.

Should Holly help Shawn by climbing the tree to get the kitten down? Why or why not?

Probe questions:

1) Suppose there is a good chance Holly's father will never find out what happened? Would that make a difference in your decision?

2) What's more important to you, helping a friend or keeping a promise to your father?

3) Would it make any difference in your decision if there were a good chance that Holly would get caught and punished?

4) If Holly doesn't save the kitten, Shawn will be mad at her. Should that make any difference in what she does? Why?

Holly's dilemma is meant to be a dilemma that both reveals the moral reasoning of the participants and stimulates them to reach for more comprehensive ways of resolving dilemmas. The teacher does not encourage the children to find a solution to the problem. He or she does not ask: "What would you do in Holly's place?" Although the teacher does not "pull" toward a problem-solving solution, children may still lock in to problem-solving solutions. Calling the fire department is such a solution, but it evades the dilemma. In the early 1970s when these dilemmas were developed, Kohlberg was much more focused on ascertaining stage level than he was in later years. Thus, the teacher guide for these dilemma discussions emphasizes strategies that refocus children's attention on the dilemma and sharpen the conflict and does not encourage general problem-solving strategies.

Are there pitfalls in using dilemmas in this way with very young children? Perhaps. The dilemmas force children to prioritize, therefore to break one rule in favor of another. This could be confusing to children who have not yet learned to value a rule, such as promise keeping. Before you are asked to produce reasons why a promise might be broken, you need to understand that promise keeping is important.

At what grade levels and how frequently should hypothetical dilemmas be introduced into the elementary school curriculum? Kohlberg and his associates did not direct themselves to answering this question. Common sense suggests that children's responses serve as a guide and that any good activity can become boring with over-use.

SHARON'S DILEMMA: A HYPOTHETICAL DILEMMA FOR ADOLESCENTS

"Sharon's Dilemma" engages the imagination of adolescents without fail. This summary is taken from the mimeographed material for the workshop on dilemma discussions (Gomberg, 1980).

Sharon and her best friend Jill walked into a department store to shop. As they browsed, Jill saw a blouse she really liked and told Sharon she wanted to try the blouse on. Sharon continued to shop.

Soon Jill came out of the dressing room wearing her coat. She caught Sharon's attention with her eyes and glanced down at the blouse under her coat. Without a word, Jill turned and walked out of the store.

Moments later the store security officer, a sales clerk, and the store manager approached Sharon . . .

Sharon gives the store personnel permission to inspect her bag, they correctly assume that Jill has the blouse and press Sharon to give them the name of the girl she was with. The store manager asserts: "I can't let the shoplifters off the hook and expect to run a successful business. . . . If you don't tell us, you can be charged with the crime of aiding the person who committed the crime."

Question: Should Sharon tell Jill's name to the security officer? Why or why not?

Contrary to the Heinz dilemma, which many teachers consider unrealistic, Sharon's dilemma is immediately identified as a perfect dilemma for use with adolescents. What may not be immediately apparent is how skillfully Sharon's dilemma is constructed.

1) The question is what *should* Sharon do, not what would you do in Sharon's place. Focus on what ought to be done forces subjects to produce reasons that have validity for everyone.

2) The dilemma leaves the personalities and history of the two friends undefined enough so that the students can project assumptions and a scenario of their choice on the information given. They are not tempted to compare how similar or different the characters in the story are from their best friend and themselves. If the depth and history of the friendship might affect the solution in the eyes of some students, such information can be accommodated, but the "givens" are succinct enough to make it equally possible that the discussion takes a different focus.

3) The dilemma does not offer extraneous or extenuating circumstances; if we don't wish to do so, we don't need to take into consideration whether or not Jill is poor or whether or not she has ever done this before.

4) The forced choice of the dilemma is structured so that the conflict must be faced. Sharon cannot solve the problem by talking Jill out of the shoplifting plan; she has no foreknowledge of Jill's plan; Jill disappears before Sharon might take action.

Some students will go to great lengths to turn a dilemma discussion into a problem-solving discussion. In real life it is appropriate for us to avoid dilemmas and to seek solutions where we do not have to choose one good over another, but if the goal of the discussion is moral development the pressure of a forced decision necessitates producing *reasons* for prioritizing.

5) The dilemma centers on the primary agenda of one stage, the friendship orientation of Stage 3, it accommodates a lower Stage 1 and Stage 2 orientation that

is focused on the self as "Number One," and it gives voice to the rationale of the next stage without being "preachy" about it. Loyalty to a friend is clearly a "good," but the societal perspective of the proprietor and the law-enforcing officer are also verbalized. Students who may be deeply rooted in Stage 3, where loyalty to friends is paramount, can understand the societal perspective, not only because they have heard over and over again that stealing is wrong, but also because of the "plus-1 effect." Moral development research has documented that persons can understand one stage beyond the predominant stage in which they are embedded and for which they can produce a rationale.

A study of the probe questions reveals how effectively they tap issues that might be glossed over if the teacher merely presented the dilemma and "winged" the discussion. A wide range of answers is acceptable; the important thing is that students give *reasons* for their positions. Instead of asking students to produce the "right" answer, the questions encourage them to look at the dilemma from as many perspectives as possible and to find a solution that is comprehensive enough to take these multiple perspectives into account.

REFLECTING ON CLASSROOM
DISCUSSION OF DILEMMAS

Recording a classroom session and analyzing student interaction and his or her teaching strategies is always an illuminating experience for the teacher. Taping a dilemma discussion can be especially illuminating because a good dilemma highlights the subtleties of classroom interaction. Whose voice emerges as most influential? Did the highest stage of reasoning "carry the day" or are students drawn to rationales or personalities on the basis of other criteria? Who takes a position and sticks to it? Who changes position, perhaps more than once? Is it the reasoning, or the peer pressure, that seems to account for a change of mind? Is the thinking of many students tapped, or did a few students monopolize the discussion? Does repeated listening to the session suddenly reveal a totally unexpected insight?

For illustrative purposes, excerpts of one teacher's reflection on a discussion of the Sharon dilemma is presented (Saltzman, 1981). Working with a bright group of tenth graders, Saltzman found that when students were asked what one should do in Sharon's place, they asked all kinds of specific questions designed to elaborate and clarify the situation. They discussed every legal aspect of Sharon's behavior, the security guard's behavior, and even the store owner's behavior. For some students this may have been a strategy for putting distance between the dilemma and themselves. The more faults they could find with the situation, the less seriously they would have to take it. (The experienced dilemma discussion leader recognizes when the digression fosters perspective taking and when it might better be refocused on the main issue.)

Yet the dilemma was powerful in eliciting dissonance within individual students' thinking as well as between students. Replaying the tape, Saltzman noticed that one student changed or modified her position three times. At the start she stated emphatically that under no circumstances should Sharon tell on her friend, that friends owed each other loyalty. A bit later, she said that the crime was not *big* enough to warrant telling on a friend. Then she further modified her position by saying that she would not tell the police but perhaps should tell Jill's parents. When the discussion turned to Sharon's possible arrest, the student felt that when Sharon was actually charged, she should reveal Jill's name. (Only in retrospect did Saltzman realize that she had missed the opportunity of asking "Why?" which would have placed the focus on reasoning rather than on action.)

The tape confirmed a clear example of the peer pressure so prevalent among young adolescents: Adam raised his hand and volunteered: "If they are good friends, maybe she should tell, maybe this is what the girl (Jill) needs—a shock—so she won't go through life thinking she can get away with it." All around him his friends said, "Oh no!" "Not a good idea." "Are you serious?" In the very next breath Adam recovered by saying, "I guess that's a bad way to handle it." He didn't pull back on his concern for Jill's future, only on the method he had proposed to handle it.

From the point of view of trying to understand adolescent development, Saltzman's most provocative finding was the qualitatively different ways in which students projected themselves into the dilemma of Sharon and teenagers like themselves, versus the positions they took when asked to take the role of various adults. When asked to take Sharon's role, the students argued and deliberated at length. When asked to role-switch to the parental perspective, they did not hesitate at all. It was as if they did not perceive that the adults might be having a dilemma as well. In this particular discussion, the teenagers assigned Stage 1 responses to the adults, as if the latter were not capable of higher levels of thought. "What would Sharon's parents want her to do?" Most students decided that Sharon's parents would want her to tell on Jill because they did not want their daughter to get into trouble. Not that Sharon should tell because stealing is wrong, or because telling is the lawful thing to do—or even, as Adam had suggested, because telling might be for Jill's own good—but rather because of the fear of punishment.

Do teenagers often assign Stage 1 reasoning to their parents or adults in general? To ask such a question would have been impossible without Kohlberg's groundbreaking research. Utilizing a "lesson" based on a hypothetical dilemma that grew out of psychological research into the sequential structures of thinking about moral issues, suddenly the teacher recognizes not only the reality of such structures in her students' responses but finds herself asking a totally new question.

Now the teacher can hardly wait to use a new dilemma and to think of probe questions that might corroborate or negate the tentative hypothesis. If it were true that teenagers in her class assume that adults act upon preconventional moral reasoning, what might be the reasons for this? What might be the educational opportunities for expanding their social perspective? Would dilemma discussions at different grade levels, with students from differing socio-economic backgrounds reveal the same patterns? Suddenly the teacher does not feel "burned out," but curious, engaged! Stage-level responses and the discussions that tap them are "real," and so is the Kohlberg legacy for the classroom teacher!

Chapter 7

From Theory to Practice: Kohlberg's Participation in Secondary School Programs

Lisa Kuhmerker

The just community approach in practice involves an effort to develop more responsible moral action as well as improving moral reasoning. It holds that responsible moral behavior is a function not only of individual psychological disposition . . . but also of shared group norms and a sense of community, the moral component of school climate or group characters (Lawrence Kohlberg, in Kohlberg and Higgins, 1987, p. 105).

THE CLUSTER SCHOOL

In the spring of 1974 Kohlberg received grants from the Danforth and Kennedy foundations to undertake the training of high-school teachers in developmental education and the just community approach. Part of the grant went to Carnegie Mellon University, where Ted Fenton and collaborators developed social-studies and English high-school curricula. The grant application also called for two programs in the Cambridge schools: one to train teachers in a variety of moral discussion-based curricula, and one to create a small just community school-within-a-school.

It so happened that just at this time an existing alternative school within Cambridge Rindge and Latin High School was in the process of expanding and rethinking its educational goals. At the suggestion of the superintendent of the Cambridge schools, Kohlberg was invited as a consultant to the planning group.

The planning group, with Kohlberg's participation, came up with four primary principles for governing the new school:

1. The school would be governed by direct democracy. All major issues would be discussed and decided at a weekly community meeting at which all members (students and teachers) would have one vote.
2. There would be additionally a number of standing committees to be filled by students, teachers, and parents.
3. A social contract would be drawn between members which would define everyone's responsibilities and rights.
4. Students and teachers would have the same basic rights, including freedom of expression, respect from others, and freedom from physical and verbal harm (Power and Higgins and Kohlberg, 1989, p. 64).

The summer of 1974 was spent in planning, and school opened in September with eight teachers from the Cambridge high school serving half-time, offering a cluster of English and social-studies courses—hence the name, Cluster School—which permitted a flexible use of time for moral discussion and the creation of a democratic school structure. The students, likewise, spent half their school day in this cluster and took the rest of their courses in the regular high-school program.

Two excellent narratives describing the beginning of the Cluster School and its gradual development are in print, and the reader with more than a casual interest in the typical and unique aspects of getting an ambitious alternative school to function owes it to himself or herself to become acquainted with them (Wasserman, 1980; Power, Higgins, and Kohlberg, 1989). Both narratives agree that the Cluster School began in chaos, because of the usual logistical foul-ups and because the students actively tested every conceivable limit of this novel school experience. The process of establishing a relative degree of order on the chaos of the Cluster School, *in a just and democratic way,* demonstrates how theory can serve practice. It is this Kohlbergian contribution that makes the history of the Cluster School and the other just community schools worthy of study when many alternative school programs have come and gone with little notice.

In small and large group meetings the effort to stimulate moral growth involved the exposure of students to cognitive moral conflict, to opportunities for role-taking, to considerations of fairness, to exposure to "plus-1" moral reasoning, and to active participation in group decision making.

When Kohlberg and his associates used dilemma discussions to stimulate moral thinking the group that discussed such moral dilemmas was not conceptualized as having a normative role. The participants were simply fellow-classmates. There is nothing wrong with this level of interaction. In a departmentalized high-school program, for example, teachers in any of the subject areas could use these principles for fostering thinking about sociomoral issues. When a student body is to be united in such a way as to become a just community, a new approach is required.

"The just community approach represented Kohlberg's effort to balance "justice" and "community"; to introduce the powerful appeal of the collective while both protecting the rights of individual students and promoting their moral growth" (Power, Higgins, and Kohlberg, 1989, p. 53). This involved reconsideration of some fundamental issues in moral education.

As a result of Kohlberg's involvement in the Cluster School, his view of conventional moral judgment changed and deepened. When confronted with the widespread preconventional morality in the high-school setting, Kohlberg gained a new appreciation of conventional morality as a goal for this age group. "While in the 1960s Kohlberg could take for granted the claims of conventional morality and argue for the merits of principled morality, after Vietnam and Watergate that commonly held belief in social conventions could no longer be taken for granted. The just community approach was fashioned in the 1970s to initiate adolescents into creating a conventional moral system which they could believe in because it embodied on a conventional level the values of fairness, equality, and community" (Power, Higgins, and Kohlberg, 1989, p. 54).

Kohlberg gained an increased appreciation for "content" as well as "structure." *What* is decided is important, as well as *why* the decision is reached. The reality of Cluster School Community Meetings also brought home the affective components of moral motivation. "Kohlberg (1980) at this point introduces the power of the collective—the moral authority of the group—to provide a support system for adolescents to act on their higher-stage modes of reasoning. If students who operate at a Stage 2 or 3 level lack the consistent internal motivation to act on what they judge to be right, then the group or community can provide the external motivation for such action. That motivation comes in the form of what Durkheim calls 'attachment to the group'—an affective bond between the individual and his peers which leads the individual to want to live up to the normative expectations of the group" (Power, Higgins, and Kohlberg, 1989, p. 57).

The Cluster School narratives of Wasserman (1980) and Power, Higgins, and Kohlberg (1989) illustrate Kohlberg's insistence that school rules be upheld. One example from the latter text describes an incident when Cluster School students were invited to view a film at Harvard University. An agreement had been democratically reached that there would be no smoking in the viewing room. As soon as the lights went out, some students began to smoke. The teachers said nothing, but Kohlberg ordered the film stopped and took the teachers into the hallway for consultation. They agreed that to permit students to violate the rules without reacting was to undercut the democratic process. "This incident also illustrates the relation between advocacy and the role of the consultant. Kohlberg, as consultant, advocated to the faculty a position based on the just community approach. They, agreeing with his point, in turn advocated a position to the students about the importance of upholding social agreements. The consultant in this model of intervention does not wait to be consulted; he or she takes an active, interventionist stance in relation to the staff" (Power, Higgins, and Kohlberg, 1989, p. 69).

The most severe test of whether the Cluster community could learn to make and stand by its own rules centered around the issue of drug use. It was not difficult for students to vote democratically to establish rules, as long as they expected that the teachers would enforce them. Standing most directly in the way of achieving this goal was a well-established norm among students against "ratting":

> If someone breaks a rule that does not personally harm or affect you, leave its detection to the authorities. Do not rat on anyone lest that person rat on you. Seen in this light, almost any student enforcement of a rule is ratting. The only way the perception could be undone was for the majority of students to reinterpret student enforcement as involving a group of people protecting the community by collectively upholding their agreements and helping the person breaking the rule to become a better community member. Community meeting participation was meant to be an education in reinterpretation by learning to see behavioral problems from the perspective of their effect on the community and not simply as an act of one individual which may or may not affect a second individual (Power, Higgins, and Kohlberg, 1989, p. 72).

THE LEGACY OF CLUSTER SCHOOL

The Cluster School was dissolved at the end of five years and reorganized with program changes and staff changes as the K-100 School. During the time of its existence, however, the primary features that were to characterize the other just community schools were established. Each of these schools was committed to democratic decision making, to emphasis on justice and fairness, and to a structural organization designed to support students' moral development and capacity for democratic self-government. The Cluster School, and subsequent just community schools in Scarsdale, the Bronx, and Manhattan, each had advisory groups, discipline or fairness committees, and core groups that offered the emotional support and skill practice needed to function in the weekly community meeting.

BROOKLINE'S SCHOOL-WITHIN-A-SCHOOL: AN ALTERNATIVE SCHOOL INFLUENCED BY KOHLBERG

> The aim of education is development of individuals to the utmost of their potentialities. But this statement in isolation leaves unanswered the question as to what is the measure of development. A society of free individuals in which all, through their own work, contribute to the liberation and enrichment

of the lives of others, is the only environment in which an individual can really grow normally to his full stature (John Dewey, 1964, p. 15).

Brookline Massachusetts' School-Within-A-School (SWS) cannot be counted among Kohlbergian just community schools because Kohlberg served in an advisory capacity secondary to Ralph Mosher, chairman of the Counseling Division of Boston University. Mosher nurtured SWS from its beginning and long after Kohlberg became involved in other projects. For a period of time, however, Kohlberg met with the developing SWS teaching team and stimulated them to sharpen their thinking about cognitive development and a sense of community. An excellent introduction to Mosher's approach to the development of values can be found in Sprinthall and Mosher (1978). An extensive overview, enriched by Mosher's gift for finding the perfect metaphor, can be found in "Moral Education: A First Generation of Research and Development" (Mosher, 1980).

Mosher experienced his introduction to Kohlbergian moral development theory as a "gift" that led him and his colleagues to experience a paradigm shift. "No existing psychological theory, not humanism, behaviorism, or social learning theory, offered so explicit descriptions of the progressive logic-structure in children's and adolescents' thinking about a really wide range of phenomena in their school, home, and social lives" (Mosher, 1988, personal communication). He likened his relationship to Kohlberg as that of educational engineer to Kohlberg's architectural designs. Within the same metaphor, he characterized Edwin Fenton (1977, 1980, 1985) as the on-site construction chief.

Mosher saw his role as consultant to SWS differently from the way Kohlberg functioned vis-à-vis the just community schools. Kohlberg saw his consultant role as encompassing advocacy; Mosher believed that groups must decide their own destinies and that it was not the consultant's role to try to accelerate the institution's development. While Kohlberg's primary objective was fostering an orientation toward justice and fairness in individuals and within the school, Mosher subsumed these goals to what seemed to him the broader objective of school democracy.

According to Mosher, Kohlberg saw justice as the end and democracy as the means. To Mosher, education for democratic participation was a magnificent end in itself. "The democratic experiences of determining school policies, making decisions about collective life together, and adjudicating school norms were a remarkable prisim that refracted onto many emerging competencies. . . . Where democratic participation touched naturally on the moral core of school life it became a very powerful means of character building. To make the content of democratic debate insistently normative, however, was, I felt, a serious reductionism" (Mosher, 1988, unpublished manuscript).

Circumstances, as well as difference in theory and personality, undoubtedly also account for the differing emphases of Kohlberg versus Mosher. While SWS had problems similar to those of Cluster and the other just communities, SWS had

had a relatively stable existence for five years before moral development teaching strategies were introduced in a systematic way. In Brookline the student population was a mixture of students from many backgrounds; in the Cluster School a greater proportion of students came from homes in which they did not have a family model of community on which the school model of community could be built.

THE SCARSDALE ALTERNATIVE SCHOOL

I don't want to be making a testimonial and stuff; but it was a real civic education for me, and it just made clear the democratic system our society is built on. . . . It sort of makes me more accountable to make me think about what my obligations as a citizen are. I guess it has broadened my moral perspective, when I have to think about things like that (Edward Zalaznick, SAS student, *Moral Education Forum,* 6-4, p. 64).

The next alternative school with which Lawrence Kohlberg was actively involved was the Scarsdale Alternative School, known as SAS. SAS differed from the Cluster School in significant ways. It drew its student body from the Scarsdale, New York, high school, an upper-middle-class suburban school with high academic standards and a relatively homogeneous white student body, almost all of whose parents were successful professionals. Thus, SAS was much more like a typical private school than part of the public education system. Some of the students would have been highly successful within the traditional high school, some were in active rebellion against traditional authority. While violence, racial tension, and stealing were not significant issues; more subtle tensions related to autonomy and competition versus cooperation and commitment came to the fore.

In contrast to Cluster, SAS had already functioned as an alternative school for five years before it became a "just community school." It grew out of the climate of the 1960s that aimed to provide for individual freedom and the individual needs of students. That freedom was variously interpreted and this ambiguity ultimately led to a great deal of trouble. Organizational problems plagued SAS. Students had autonomy to choose their own courses of study, while at the same time they were asked to make decisions collectively for the good of the whole school. This combined individualistic and communitarian philosophy led to an informal, and precarious, governance structure.

The structures of our school put students in an untenable position. Students were told that they were individuals, free to grow and develop on their own; at the same time, they were told that they were responsible to a community. It was difficult for students to make sense of the two-fold ideology. . . . Week by week we found ourselves becoming increasingly exhausted. . . . We had to give our programs and our students some direction. . . .

Community Meeting had been an exciting part of our week, one that everyone attended. Then, toward the middle of the third year of our alternative school, attendance began to drop off. Those who continued to attend had to cope with the problems of others' lack of attendance, so they passed a rule requiring attendance. However, there was no way to enforce this rule; and attendance did not pick up. The school community then faced a conflict: Should there be no consequences for those who broke a community rule, or, since the school had embraced the philosophy of individual freedom, should student be allowed to attend these meetings, or not, as they wished?

In its fourth and fifth years of SAS the community experimented with different types of representation. . . . Still, decisions did not engage student much. . . . Students found the meetings dull. . . . The community component of our school began to flounder (Codding and Aranella, 1981, *Moral Education Forum*, 6-4, pp. 3-4).

It was during this period of disenchantment that the faculty of SAS became interested in Kohlberg's work. During the summer of 1977, three SAS staff members attended the summer institute at Harvard's Center for Moral Education and found that cognitive moral development theory provided a philosophical and psychological rationale for their goals; at the same time it provided a systematic means for understanding the conflicts and failures which had begun to "burn out" the staff and students.

The incorporation of moral development theory did not mean that SAS had to abandon any of its original goals:

- to create a sense of community where students and teachers could increasingly work together toward agreed-upon goals;
- to establish a workable, democratic school governance system;
- to emphasize community and cooperation while recognizing the individual needs and differences within the community;
- to increase students' freedom and responsibility in pursuing their own education;
- to heighten students' and teachers' awareness of, and attention to, process in the school without sacrificing product and content;
- to make the school less isolated from, and responsible to, the larger community outside its four walls (Codding and Aranella, 1981, *Moral Education Forum*, 6-4, p. 5).

Kohlberg's philosophy supported SAS teachers' advocacy of fairness, justice, and responsibility of all community members, within a framework of democratic decision making. With the weekly Community Meeting as the central feature of the just community, Kohlberg and the SAS team created a supporting structure of small Core Group meetings. In these small groups each student had a voice and a stake; Core Groups provided content, emotional support, as well as skill training in leadership for the Community Meetings. Kohlberg met with SAS staff before and after Community Meetings and took an active role in them. He helped to shapen the issues; his presence and respect for student ideas contributed to the students' respect for themselves and the process. Kohlberg's involvement with SAS was at its peak in the late 1970s and early 1980s, and as the program grew in strength, SAS faculty members became an integral part of the faculty of the summer institutes on just community offered by Harvard's Center for Moral Education.

THE IMPACT OF THE SAS PROGRAM ON STUDENT DEVELOPMENT

It is helpful to educators contemplating the democratization of their school governance structure to read how the Cluster School, Brookline's SWS, and the Scarsdale Alternative School evolved. It is perhaps even more illuminating to see such a school structure from a student perspective. The next chapter provides two student perspectives. William Kolber was a junior at SAS when he described his high-school experience; Edward Zalaznick was a senior who had the enviable good fortune to spend a high-school internship period at Harvard's Center for Moral Education. His dialogue with Lawrence Kohlberg, reprinted here in its edited version, took place at that time.

Last but not least, the observations and perspective of an experienced visiting teacher, who had many doubts about the just community approach, is included. Beverly Noia had been a traditional high-school teacher for seventeen years before she had the opportunity to explore alternative educational settings as part of a 1982-1983 Klingenstein fellowship. Noia's perspective is of special interest because it provides a vivid picture of discipline and locus of control during instances of "moral crisis" when the rules of SAS had been breached. It illustrates how a school based on moral development theory can continue to function and grow over time.

THE JUST COMMUNITY SCHOOLS IN THE BRONX AND MANHATTAN

In the Bronx project, the appeal of democratic community to students is less escape from the authority of teachers than their desire to end theft, intimidation, and isolation in the peer world itself (Lawrence Kohlberg, in Kurtines and Gewirtz, 1987, with grateful acknowledgment to John Wiley Press to quote from p. 126).

From 1985 to the end of his life, Kohlberg was totally committed to the creation of just communities in selected New York City high schools.

One hundred students were recruited for the Community School (RCS), a part-time alternate school within the larger Roosevelt High School. Seventy tenth to twelfth graders formed the experimental group, and two comparison or control groups were selected. Students were assessed annually for moral judgment stage and moral type. Newly constructed interviews tapping the perceived moral atmosphere of the school and the perception of the "moral self" were administered (Higgins, 1987, report to the W.T. Grant Foundation). School records on attendance, drug use, and arrests were included, as were student ratings on a school adjustment index. All Community Meetings were videotaped and a large proportion were transcribed.

Shortly after the inception of this program, a second group of one hundred students who were at high risk of becoming drop-outs were added to the project. This group was called Roosevelt Community Renaissance (RCR).

The prestigious Bronx High School of Science was the site for another just community project initiated in 1985. This project involved 100 experimental subjects and matching control groups, all of whom were to be assessed annually over a three-year period for moral judgment stage, moral atmosphere, school record data, teacher ratings and taped and selectively transcribed Community Meetings.

The start-up problems in the New York City schools were similar to those describing the Cluster School and SAS. Although the RCS and RCR students may not have had the linguistic skill and unusually developed maturity of the Scarsdale students, the self-awareness of their personal growth in the program, so vividly demonstrated by Kolber and Zalaznick (1981, *Moral Education Forum*), was similar. In each of the schools, the issues across the years and across socio-economic differences remained unfailingly the same: truancy, substance abuse, stealing, and cheating. In each of the schools the students experienced the same major difficulty in their growth toward creating a just community: the struggle to develop trust and the struggle to assume responsibility for enforcing the rules made by the community. Project descriptions can be found in Higgins (1989) The Just Community Approach to Moral Education: Evolution of the Idea and Recent Findings.

DISCIPLINE OR FAIRNESS COMMITTEES

In a community in which students are encouraged to make public their expectations of others, to debate proper behavioral norms, and to formalize these expectations through norms and rules, it is important to provide structures that will enable the community to determine fair consequences for those who do not abide by these rules (Chesbrough and Conrad, 1981, p. 12-13).

In any school, be it an alternative school or within the mainstream of education, taking responsibility for enforcing rules made by consensus is one of the most difficult developmental tasks for adolescents because their need to be liked and respected by their peers is so powerful.

   This rule-enforcing function is as crucial to the maintenance of a viable, democratic community as it is difficult to effectuate. Students relish participating in debates over standards even when such debates become difficult, complex, and controversial. However, such debates always remain, in a sense, theoretical. When individual students or teachers fail to live up to community rules, the question of fair consequences and/or punishment becomes less theoretical, because it involves real consequences for friends and other community members (Chesbrough and Conrad, 1981, p. 12-13).

   When a school community experiences a profound crisis, the whole student body and/or its representatives become—and from Kohlberg's view, must become—involved. However, schools would come to a standstill if every infraction of the rules had to be mediated by the whole student body. This is why a Fairness Committee becomes a necessity in any democratic school. Whether membership to a Fairness Committee is by election, selection, or volunteering is less important than that a Fairness Committee exists and is in a position to make decisions properly. The nature of a consequence is secondary to the inevitability of a consequence. If a school is too large to be served by a single Fairness Committee, grade-level committees need to be in place.
   Discipline or Fairness Committees are only one part of an optimal school governance structure at the secondary school level. On the basis of his experience in multiple just community school settings, Kohlberg and his colleagues suggested the organizational structure outlined in Table 7-1 (Kohlberg and Higgins, 1987, p. 108).
   Strictly speaking, a just community is itself a "Fairness Committee" and may have a "Discipline Committee" to enforce community rules. A high school that is too large to function as a community, and elects representatives to enforce school policy, can have a Fairness Committee. In practice, the more appealing name of "Fairness Committee" has been used both in just communities and in the large high school setting.
   Why are Fairness Committees so important for students' moral development? In their chapter on "School Democracy and Social Interaction," Kohlberg and Higgins elaborate on the multiple benefits of such committees for individual student development and for the moral climate of the school (Kohlberg and Higgins, 1987). Discipline or Fairness Committees depersonalize and demystify the relation between the process of rule making and rule enforcement. They force students to try to maintain a balance between loyalty to favorite peers and the school community as a whole. A Fairness Committee's roles and duties develop over time and tend to expand, so that by the second or third year of their existence they also tend to serve as a mediation board for interpersonal

Table 7-1: the Organizational Structure of a Just Community Program		
Institution	Members	Tasks
Agenda committee	8 to 12 students and 2 to 3 teachers	Deciding on issues: putting together the agenda
Advisory group	1 teacher/ advisor and 10 to 15 students	Creating an informal atmosphere for discussing personal problems; having a moral discussion on the 1 or 2 important agenda issues
Community meeting	All students and teachers	Discussing and resolving moral issues; making rules and appealing violations
Discipline committee	6 to 8 students and 2 teachers	Hearing cases of rules violations and interpersonal problems of disrespect; giving sanctions; enhancing interpersonal understanding

Kurtines, W. and Gewirtz, J. (Eds.), *Social Development and Social Interaction.* 1987, New York: John Wiley, p. 108

disputes. This function, too, has a significant effect of moral development.

It is not only the individuals brought before the committee whose capacity for perspective taking is enhanced by the process. Committee members also, perforce, expand in their capacity to understand multiple points of view. A phenomenon not specifically mentioned in the literature about Fairness Committees is that the process sometimes brings into dialogue students who are not part of the same friendship groups. Rule-abiding students prudently avoid "trouble-makers" in many high schools. Except for a Fairness Committee setting, "trouble-makers" may not get to hear the rationale for Stage 4 behavior from their peers. Conversely, the fact that preconventionally reasoning students nevertheless reason morally from their own perspective may not have been apparent to peers who simply saw their behavior as uncontrolled.

Consistently, each of the just community schools experienced its most profound crises when one or many students violated a norm that had been affirmed by the community as a whole. Students new to the moral atmosphere that faculty and experienced community members sought to foster were sometimes mystified by what seemed to them tempests in a teapot. Yes, they voted to ban the smoking of pot on the community retreat, but if some students still chose to bring pot to the retreat, it was their responsibility to do it unobtrusively so that faculty would not be in the unpleasant position of having to notice and take disciplinary measures. Yes, the community took a vote on attendance requirements, but the enforcements of these requirements was the school's responsibility. "Most adolescents are hesitant to accept responsibility for enforcing among their personal friends and classmates those rules that they believe should be enforced. . . . Observing a rule infraction, or being told about one in confidence, raises further conflicts about whether one should 'tell' on a colleague or whether it is really the business of the adult to ferret out infractions" (Chesbrough and Conrad, 1981, p. 13).

The enforcement of community standards by the community presented such a moral dilemma for many of the students in the various just community schools that this necessitated multiple Core Group and Community Meeting sessions from time to time. (Two such crises, one involving cheating and the other involving a decision on whether or not to expel a student, are presented in detail on pp. 137-145.)

THE MAINSTREAMING OF KOHLBERG'S "JUST COMMUNITY" IDEAS

The summer institutes offered at Harvard's Center for Moral Education influenced the secondary school teachers and administrators who attended them, but this influence has not been documented in terms of program shifts and program assessments. The exception is the work of Elsa Wasserman, who pioneered moral atmosphere research (Wasserman, 1977) and incorporated significant elements of the just community concept in her roles as Director of Guidance and subsequently as Acting Principal of Cambridge Rindge and Latin High School.

Wasserman faced the reality that committees in a large high school had to function as representative bodies and not as a community-as-a-whole. She has tried to keep the spirit of the just community school through combining decision making by representative committees with balloting of the whole student body on every important issue (personal communication).

Multiple strategies are used to encourage maximum student participation in democratic school governance. The public address system is used to identify and highlight issues, communicate committee decisions, and announce questions on which the student body will vote. On important issues there are likely to be a series of ballots that deal with component parts of the broad issue. Every student has access to the principal and to the various governing bodies of the school. The process of decision making is made explicit; students are informed about which individuals or groups make what kinds of decisions, and what the process of appeal is against rules that seem unfair.

The school not only has a Fairness Committee but allocates school time to teach the communication and reasoning skills needed to function in such committees. Participation in the life of the school is not left to chance. A full-time faculty position is allocated to coordinate a full-year, once-a-week program for all entering freshmen.

The in-house guides for teachers and students have been elaborated into general guidelines for secondary schools. Fenton and Wasserman collaborated on a Leader's Guide and a Participant's Manual for "Improving School Climate Through Implementing the Fairness Committee" (Fenton and Wasserman, 1985). This is the title of the second edition of the "Fairness Manual." Wasserman and colleagues developed a validated Title IV-C project that has published "A Teacher's Guide, Teacher Advisory Program (TAP): A Multi-Cultural Approach to High School Orientation and Support for Ninth Grade Students" (Wasserman et al., 1982).

In the preface to the Participants' Manual, Wasserman and Fenton note that is has grown out of nine years of experience with various forms of Fairness Committees in a variety of schools and that "literally hundreds of people have contributed to this work." Clearly, this was not a "Kohlberg project," but the authors "tip their hat" to Larry Kohlberg "who asked us hard questions and cheered many of our answers." The Teacher Advisory Program (TAP), of which Wasserman was the School Climate Project Manager, is the product of intensive collaboration of many professionals within the Cambridge Public School System. Again, there is no way one could call this a "Kohlberg project," but many team leaders and members of the resource team had integrated what they learned from Kohlberg and made it their own.

Alternative schools will always serve only a small proportion of the school population. If the "Kohlberg legacy" will have an impact on mainstream education, it is likely to be through the explicit ways in which complex ideas have been translated into warming-up exercises, games, role-playing opportunities, check lists, interviews, and discussion topics that help all students to become part of their school community and empower them to take part in the democratic process.

The task is to give the psychology of moral development and education away to as many teachers, administrators, parents, and interested others as possible. That will begin to make morality a common cause rather than the special mandate of moral educators (Mosher, 1980, p. 385).

FOSTERING MORAL DEVELOPMENT THROUGH TRADITIONAL CURRICULUM

The introduction of hypothetical dilemmas into the classroom and the attempt to transform the school through the "just community" concept had a direct impact on selected school settings during Lawrence Kohlberg's lifetime. His influence on curriculum in "regular" subjects was less direct. Kohlberg was not a curriculum writer, but his theories, research, and participation in educational interventions have implications for curriculum writers.

Three programs will be described in the following pages. "Ethical Issues in

Decision Making" is a one-semester literature course that received New York State and National Validation as an exemplary program. Two volumes called "Reasoning with Democratic Values" (Lockwood and Harris, 1985) are widely used texts in secondary school social studies. "Facing History and Ourselves: Holocaust and Human Behavior" is a unit of study that can be used in flexible ways, which also received National Validation for its excellence.

Literature and social studies are not the only programs that can have a moral development approach; curricula in mathematics, science, the arts, or physical education could equally well incorporate strategies designed to deliberately foster moral development. The three programs described here were developed by authors who were within Kohlberg's circle of students, colleagues, and friends. More importantly, it can be shown that the courses meet all criteria for subject content, at the same time that they deliberately foster cognitive dissonance and opportunities for role-taking and reflection.

ETHICAL ISSUES IN DECISION MAKING

"Ethical Issues and Decision Making" was developed within the context of the Scarsdale Alternative School's Just Community in cooperation with staff from the Mamaronek High School. Designed to be a one-semester course based on cognitive-developmental theory, each of the eight units in this literature program is centered around a different set of moral issues and calls on students to choose between conflicting values. The accompanying chart provides an overview, sample activities, as well as objectives and skills to be learned by the students.

Chart 7-1: *ETHICAL ISSUES IN DECISION-MAKING COURSE**

Unit title	Sample Activities	Objectives and Skills to be Learned
Unit I An Introduction to The Course	a) Read and discuss moral issues in the book *All My Sons* b) Read and discuss the article "Fisherman at Sea in Puget Sound" c) Discuss the moral issues involved in a legal decision by Commissioner Nyquist	a) Students should be able to locate and define universal moral issues which come into conflict in moral dilemma discussions b) Students should begin to identify the broader range of critical thinking discussion and reasoning skills which will be stressed throughout the course
Unit II Critical Thinking Skills: A Look at Logic and its Use in Moral Dilemma Discussions	a) Uncritical inference test b) Discussion guidelines for "On Being Logical" c) Discussion guidelines for "Analyzing Deductive Arguments"	a) Students should be familiar with criteria for drawing acceptable inferences b) Students should be able to identify certain formal fallacies of reasoning c) Students should be able to recognize and evaluate conditional arguments d) Students should be able to identify and evaluate syllogisms

Unit Title	Sample Activities	Objectives and Skills to be Learned
	d) Discussion guidelines for "conditional syllogisms"	e) Students should be able to distinguish between the concepts of truth and validity
Unit III Friends, Family, and Teacher: To Whom and How Am I Related?	a) Watch the film and discuss "When Parents Grow Old" b) Read and discuss the article "Judge Upholds Transplant Denial" c) View, discuss, and write about the film "No Man Is An Island"	a) Students should become aware of, and be able to identify, the individuals and groups to whom they are related b) Students should become aware of, and be able to identify, some of the duties and obligations they have toward individuals or groups to whom they are related c) Students should improve their ability to generate reasons in support of the positions they take in moral dilemmas
Unit IV Conflicting Loyalties	a) Read, discuss, and write about *A View from the Bridge,* by Arthur Miller b) *A Doll's House,* by Henrik Ibsen c) Watch the film and discuss "Am I Wife, Mother, or Me?" d) Read and discuss the article "Long Marriage on the Rise" e) Watch and discuss the film "Illegal Aliens: Invasion out of Control?"	a) Students should improve their ability to define the duties and obligations they have toward individuals and groups to whom they are related b) Students should be able to identify a variety of situations in which they face dilemmas of conflicting loyalty c) Students should better understand how they might resolve dilemmas of conflicting loyalties d) Students should improve their ability to generate reasons which support positions opposed to the ones they hold in moral dilemmas e) Students should improve their capacity to take the social perspective of others
Unit V Problem Solving and Decision Making	a) Take part in group problem-solving activities, such as "Blind Square" and "The Knot" b) Read and discuss "Mr Peterson's Dilemma" c) View the sound slide program "The Science and Ethics of Population: An Overburdened Earth?"	a) Students should improve their abilities to define problems b) Students should improve their abilities to generate alternative solutions to problems c) Students should improve their ability to choose critically among alternative solutions d) Students should be familiar with several problem-solving and decision-making models
Unit VI Ethical Issues in Conflict	a) Read, discuss, and write about *Enemy of the People,* by Henrik Ibsen b) View and discuss the film "Lovejoy's Nuclear War"	a) Students should improve their ability to delineate their obligations to groups other than their families b) Students should better understand their obligations to law, truth, and principles c) Students should better understand situations in which others have faced dilemmas of conflicting loyalties

Unit title	Sample Activities	Objectives and Skills to be Learned
	c) Read and discuss the dilemma "John Adams and the Boston Massacre" d) View and react to the film "Bill of Rights in Action: Freedom of Speech"	d) Students should improve their awareness of and ability to take the social perspective of others
Unit VII Moral Thought and Moral Action	a) View and use discussion outlines (Lord of the Flies) b) Discuss Josh's Dilemma c) View and use discussion guidelines for "The Milgram Experiment"	a) Students should more clearly recognize the distinction between moral thought and moral action in both theory and practice b) Students should become familiar with the theories that this disparity raises c) Students should become more aware of the issue of obedience to authority as it raises conflicts between individuals and the demands of the community
Unit VIII Theory, Philosophy, and Reflection on the Course	a) Students will read about moral development theory b) Evaluation of the course	a) Students should have some familiarity with developmental psychological theory b) Students should have raised broad and philosophical questions, such as what is right? and what is good?

Reprinted from Codding and Aranella (1981). *Moral Education Forum*, 6-4, pp. 20-21

Discussion guidelines for the teacher provide a page reference and spell out the dilemma and suggested questions for each reading. A few samples from the discussion guide accompanying *A View from the Bridge* by Arthur Miller are illustrative:

Chart 7-3: PROBE QUESTIONS FOR "A VIEW FROM THE BRIDGE"

Page	Dilemma	Suggested Questions
7	Should the Carbone family be housing two illegal immigrants?	1) Does it make any difference that are cousins? Why or why not? 2) Does the fact that conditions are bad in Italy make any difference: Why or why not?
11	Should Catherine turn down her job offer and finish high school?	1) Does Eddie have the right to tell her what to do? Why or why not?

		2) Is Catherine's obligation to obey Eddie more important than her need to begin to support herself? Why?
14	Should Eddie be telling 17-year-old Catherine how to dress, who to talk to, and what kind of job to take?	1) What obligation does Eddie have to protect Catherine. Why?
		2) What obligation does Beatrice have to protect Catherine. Why?
		3) What obligation does Catherine have to herself? Why?
		4) Should it make any difference that Eddie has worked hard to take care of Catherine? Why or why not?
		5) Should it make any difference that Catherine is Eddie's niece, not daughter? Why?
37	Should Eddie forbid Catherine to marry Rodolpho?	1) Should the fact that Eddie feels that Catherine is going to be "used" change his advice to her? Her response to him? Why or why not?
		2) Should parents always be obeyed? Why or why not?
		3) At what age should children be allowed to make their own deci sions? Why?

Reprinted from Codding and Aranella (1981). *Moral Education Forum*, 6-4, pp. 22-23

Discussion is not the only means for coming to grips with the dilemmas posed by the reading. All students are given a format—called a "brief"—for spelling out their positions in writing. Such a format, rather than a general essay, assures that each major issue is addressed. It is not only helpful in evaluating individual student progress along a developmental continuum, but also makes comparison among students possible.

REASONING WITH DEMOCRATIC VALUES

"Reasoning with Democratic Values: Ethical Problems in United States History" consists of a series of short essays about historical figures caught in a

Chart 7-2: *HOW WRITE A BRIEF*

Frequently throughout this course, you will be asked to write a "brief" (a legal term for a short analytical paper about a case. In this course, it will be a summary of your thinking about dilemmas) about the moral dilemma that you are discussing. A well-written brief should consist of the following:

1. A clear statement of the *dilemma* or action choice faced by a character, and a statement of the *moral issues* that are in conflict. Example: "Sharon must decide whether or not to give her friend's name to the security guard. Sharon's dilemma raises questions about the obligation one has to friends versus obligations we have to the law."

2. A clear statement of your *position* or *decision* about this moral dilemma. Example: "I think Sharon should not tell on her friend—obligations to friends are more important than those to the law."

3. A clear statement of the best *reasons* that support your decision. Example: "Obligations to one's friends must always be kept because trust between people is the most important thing we have."

4. A clear statement of the best reasons that would support the decision that would be the direct *opposite* of yours. Example: "Of course, there are people who would argue that the obligation to obey the law is more important because we need to count on people to act in certain ways."

5. A *summation* in which you clearly state why the reasons which support the decision you have made are better, or more important, reasons than those which support the opposing position. Example: "Even though I feel that it is important to obey the law in most instances, I don't feel that this obligation outweighs the obligation to protect your friend because friendship and trust are the most important things in the world."

Reprinted from Codding and Aranelle (1981), *Moral Education Forum*, 6-4, p. 21.

dilemma of their time. There are seven essays each in the Colonial Era (1607-1776), the New Nation (1777-1850), A House Divided (1850-1876), Expansion and Reform (1877-1918), Normalcy and Depression (1919-1940), Hot and Cold War (1941-1960), and Searching for Consensus (1961 to the present). The essays have snappy titles, clear and unambiguous vocabulary, and put the divergent views of the people of that time into historical and psychological perspective. The format for follow-up activities is consistent. Each essay is followed by questions tapping historical understanding and reviewing the facts of the case.

What might have been no more or less than an excellent text for secondary school students then incorporates activities that specifically encourage moral reasoning. Each essay has a section labeled "Analyzing Ethical Issues" and one labeled "Expressing Your Reasoning."

A few clarifying ideas precede the questions about ethical issues. For example, before posing questions about John Adams and the defense of the Red Coats, the authors write: "There is agreement on the answer to some questions. For other questions there is disagreement about the answer. We call these questions issues. Issues can be categorized as factual or ethical. . . . An ethical issue asks whether something is right or wrong, fair or unfair. Factual issues ask what *is*, ethical issues ask what *ought* to be" (Lockwood and Harris, 1985, Vol. I, p. 41). Students then decide whether each of the issues listed is factual or ethical.

"Expressing Your Reasoning" skillfully poses questions so that there are only two alternative choices about what the protagonist(s) should or should not have done. Referring to John Adam's legal defense, question number 1 asks: "Should John Adams have accepted the job of defending the British soldiers? State the best reason you have in support of your position" (Lockwood and Harris, 1985, Vol. 2, p. 42). Adams did take the case. Question number 2 supposes that Adams might not have done so and gives six plausible reasons why he might have refused. Without ever mentioning stages of moral reasoning, each of the reasons is from the perspective of a different moral stage.

After presenting the story of the Iranian hostages, the authors list and define the values involved in this story. "AUTHORITY: a value concerning what rules or people should be obeyed and the consequences for disobedience. PROPERTY: a value concerning what people should be allowed to own and how they should be allowed to use it. LIBERTY: a value concerning what freedoms people should have and the limits that may justifiably be placed upon those freedoms. LIFE: a value concerning when, if ever, it is justifiable to threaten or take the life of another. LOYALTY: a value concerning obligations to the people, traditions, ideas and organizations of importance in one's own life" (Lockwood and Harris, 1985, Vol. 2, p. 318). Students are then asked whether President Carter should have allowed the Shah of Iran into the United States, whether Carter should have traded the Shah for the hostages, and whether he should have ordered a military rescue attempt or not.

The name "Kohlberg" and the word "moral" never appear in these texts. However, the superlative nature and sequence of questions about ethical issues are totally "Kohlbergian" and show how seamlessly moral development research can be integrated into the teaching strategies of the educator.

FACING HISTORY AND OURSELVES

"Facing History and Ourselves" (FHAO) had its grassroots beginnings in a course developed by two social-studies teachers, Margot Stern-Strom and William Parsons Jr. in a Brookline, Massachusetts, school. With the participation of the social studies director and a small group of dedicated teachers the program took root in the district and within a few years had seeded itself into numerous communities and had earned National Validation as a program of excellence. FHAO has since become an independent nonprofit organization.

Kohlberg's tie to the program was peripheral. Strom took one of his courses, but Kohlberg used to say that she did not need his or anyone else's course; she understood moral development long before she came into his classroom (personal communication). Kohlberg, with and through his colleague, Marcus Lieberman of the Center for Moral Education, evaluated student growth in the FHAO program. Put in its simplest terms, an eight-week unit of FHAO created as much stage change as a year in one of the alternative schools (Lieberman, 1981).

FHAO (Strom and Parson, 1982) grows out of the developmental needs of adolescents; the universal questions of morality and the lessons to be learned from a history of totalitarianism, racism, and dehumanization are not unique to the Holocaust. The early sessions draw students' attention to the power of peer pressure and scapegoating. The education of Nazi youth adds insights about the power of propaganda in a totalitarian state. The program shows how a gradual dehumanization of the victims and the acquiescence of bystanders makes a "final solution" possible. Remarkably, when this unit is taught in a developmental way, its effect is not demoralizing or depressing. Young people are grateful for the opportunity to share with adults the most basic questions about good and evil, human motivation, and the meaning of life. They are energized to participate in the democratic process in their own time and community.

Chapter 8

The Impact of a Just Community Experience on Student Development: Three Views from the Scarsdale Alternative School

LIVING IN A "JUST COMMUNITY": A STUDENT PERSPECTIVE

William Kolber

Alternate Schools have often been considered alternatives for both the unsuccessful or extremely gifted students who, for academic, attitudinal, or social reasons do not function well in traditional high-school settings. Although these students' needs may be well met by alternative schools, those needs do not exhaust the resources of a well-organized alternative school. Indeed, such programs are capable of providing a more enriching and enlivening educational experience, beyond the scope of the traditional high-school curriculum, to a much broader range of students, including the student who is well-adjusted in a typical high school.

Although Scarsdale High School is not a typical high school in all respects, it strives to provide a traditional high-school education. As a freshman at Scarsdale High School, I was successful and well-adjusted in all respects. Now, as a senior and in my third year at the Scarsdale Alternative School, a school that is best described as a subsidiary of Scarsdale High School, I am proof that an alternative high school can be a more fulfilling and productive experience for students in today's society, even for those students who, by traditional barometers, are successful and well-adjusted.

Living in a Just Community Means Living Together

People should learn to live together peacefully, productively, and happily. Although it would be difficult to find a high-school teacher or administrator who disagreed with this idealistic statement, it is nearly as difficult to find a school that is actively committed to that ideal. The Scarsdale Alternative School is such a school. At SAS students and teachers work together creating school structures that allow everyone in the school community to take ownership of the educational process. The structures of the SAS do more than prepare us for "the future," when we will have to interact with others, meet expectations, and make decisions about our own lives. These structures help us now, with the situations we are facing in high school and outside of school at the present. While we learn to be members of a community by living in one, our high-school experience also becomes a fairer and happier one for ourselves and our teachers. As a student at SAS I have not felt that high school was a stepping stone to a distant goal; I have felt a part of our school structure, not a victim of it. By having forums for students to confront each other or to confront teachers, I am able to work out my problems with issues ranging from homework to peer pressure and generally feel that we achieve constructive resolutions.

In Community Meetings, students and faculty ask themselves, "Why are we here?" "What are our responsibilities, capabilities, and aspirations, individually and as a group?" "How are we going to decide which goals we must/should/can meet?" and, "How are we going to meet those goals?" These are general questions that the community addresses with specific discussions on topics such as scheduling, what we as a community have a right to expect of each other, what academic requirements we should set for ourselves in addition to those legally required, how we should deal with someone who breaks a community rule, and whether and why we need rules. In the discussion process, we are exposed to different points of view, different kinds of reasoning, and different solutions or resolutions. We learn to speak, listen, and reason more effectively. If I were to think that four years of math was an unreasonable academic requirement, we could discuss it as a community. Even if we were to retain the requirement without any amendment, I would respect its justification more than I would a dictatorial "because it is important." I would respect the faculty more for having presented their justification and for having listened to mine—for being open to change.

Last year, the SAS community adopted a ten-minute lock-out rule to combat increasing instances of lateness. We later rescinded that decision because it seemed to us that the injustices done to students who were justifiably late were greater than the benefits of increased promptness. Only by confronting student issues ("sometimes I'm late for a good reason"; "other kids walking into a class late is distracting") and confronting faculty issues ("I don't want kids missing class time because they're late or because I have to lock them out") could we get the perspective to help us find solutions.

We have discussed social problems such as exclusion of some students by cliques, or the disappearance of personal property, in similar open discussions. The process is one that makes our daily interaction more comfortable and pleasant. We have learned enough about the rationale for a "just community" to accept that. This process makes sense as an educational tool in a developmental framework. More importantly, this process makes us feel responsible for, and part of, our education and our school community. In a school like ours, we do more than "take classes" or "teach classes." Our education is not defined as the simple transference of factual knowledge. In our school, individuals are responsible for more than just their own needs. Our school structure transcends the me-ism and separateness that threaten the ideals of humanity and justice that education is intended to serve.

While these praises may seem to be overstated, or a lofty appraisal of a process that is, at times, evaluated by its participants as frustrating, burdensome, even unproductive, the structures created by students and faculty in community meeting give credence to the intent of the process, the ability of the process to carry out that intent, and the commitment of individuals to that process.

Living in a Just Community Means Living Fairly

Issues of fairness are inherent in a school community, just as they are in any group of people with different interests, opinions, and perspectives. How we treat one another, how we perform in our roles as teacher or student, and how we decide who is entitled to what are the specific issues from which we develop principles of fairness and justice. Without a structure for dealing with conflict, issues between students are relegated to schoolyard battles, and issues between faculty are sheltered from student awareness, perpetuating the "teachers aren't human" myth. When issues between students and faculty are handled in a dictatorial fashion, it leaves students feeling frustrated and angry and faculty feeling incapable of constructive resolutions.

The fairness committee constructed at SAS consists of students and faculty together who make decisions or suggestions for resolutions to issues of fairness in all domains, whether that be by setting consequences for rule infractions, by presiding as a jury over debated facts, or by helping to work out an amicable agreement in an interpersonal dispute. This structure gives a student the guarantee that he will be treated fairly, while still being held accountable for his actions, and the goal that students and faculty are equally responsible for upholding the rules of the community. The teacher is relieved from the burden of playing police officer, jury, judge, and jail warden. If I disagree with my advisor as to whether the reasons for my absence from class were legitimate ones, we can bring this issue to the fairness committee. I know that if I see someone breaking the drug rule on an outing, I have the same obligation to bring that to the community as a teacher would, even though I do not have the same legal responsibility. All community members have a greater sense of ownership for the rules they make and enforce. This ownership translates into reasons for not breaking rules that are rational and agreeable. For two years in a row, SAS had an orientation outing that was completely drug free. This was an outstanding achievement for students and faculty alike, in a school district where all other outings have been prohibited because of dangerously high levels of drug use.

The broadest and most serious of administrative issues are manageable when confronted openly. Drug use is just one such issue we have dealt with at SAS. We have dealt with affirmative action, academic requirements and standards, and evaluation methods. A school cannot set a policy concerning affirmative action admissions, for instance, without considering how that policy would affect students. "How does it feel to be in a disproportionate minority?" "How would it feel to know you were admitted to a school just because you are a minority student?" are questions that can only be answered by students. It is the type of issue that, while viewed differently by students than faculty, is one that students struggle with as much as faculty, and one that our school is not yet finished confronting. The process is one, however, that everyone can feel good about.

Living in a Just Community Means Building a Sense of Community

Within a school community itself, this means fighting the same insensitivity and ethnocentricity that is all too often confronted in a high-school setting when talking about "other cultures" but is completely ignored on a schoolwide level. Even in a community as homogeneous as Scarsdale, there are students and faculty from different backgrounds, with different religions, skin colors, attitudes, values, and interests. The small groups at SAS are successful in creating amicable relationships between students and faculty where hostile voids might otherwise exist. Small groups are formed both on an academic plane where the small classroom setting is an equalizer and on a nonacademic plane where interaction can be both more personal and less threatening. This occurs initially at the beginning of the year on a three-day outing, where students and faculty eat, work, and play together in both small and larger groups. We learn about each other's interests, talents, and fears. Shared experiences transcend diversity and form bonds between people who, in a traditional high-school setting, might have dismissed each other summarily without having even tried to start a conversation.

Building a sense of community at a "just community" school does not stop at the schoolyard. We are members of many increasingly larger communities and have obligations to those communities, not just as individuals, but as a school. Task groups at SAS examine the relationship between SAS and Scarsdale High

School. They explain SAS to prospective students and make sure that Alternative School students have the opportunity to participate in high-school sports and in other extracurricular activities. These connections between the Alternative School and the high school alleviate some of the feelings of alienation and confinement that occur in small schools. The career internship program at SAS enables students to experience different occupational possibilities. We learn about a particular profession, the daily responsibilities, educational requirements, placement opportunities, and salary ranges; and we learn about ourselves and whether that profession is one we might later want to pursue. If I wanted to enter a job immediately after high school, this would be a very practical experience, making sure that I understood the implications of my choice and possibly giving me some experience that could help me as a job applicant. If I wanted to pursue a profession after higher education, this experience enables me to better plan a productive course of study or to rule out a course of study that might lead to a professional field in which I would ultimately be unhappy. The Career Internship Program also removes barriers that insulate schools from the outside community. The lack of common understanding that exists between the adult culture and the teenage culture is one that stems from the absence of interaction between students and adults. This interaction, while a secondary goal of the Career Internship Program, is the primary goal of the newly proposed Community Service Program at SAS. The Community Service Program will require students and teachers to perform some form of other-directed service for a given number of hours per semester, for some needy organization or individual in the community. This program, pending community approval, will show our commitment to that noninsulative interaction and our commitment to what we feel is a growing obligation to our society.

THE JUST COMMUNITY SCHOOL:
A STUDENT PERSPECTIVE

Edward Zalaznick

Editor's Note: Zalaznick was a student at the Scarsdale Alternative School. During his senior year he spent three months as an intern at Harvard University's Center for Moral Education. Near the end of his stay he and Kohlberg reflected together about the just community school experience.

A brief sketch of the Alternative School will illustrate the functions and character of the various elements of the Just Community Program. The Scarsdale Alternative School is a self-contained program operating independently of the high-school curriculum. The school has seventy students, seven teachers, and is housed in a separate building adjacent to the main campus.

The central forum of the Alternative School's democracy structure is the community meeting, in which all important issues involving the school are discussed by all the students and teachers who make up the community. Decisions are reached by a majority vote and may be changed by the community at a later meeting by the same process. Any member of the community can bring an issue to the community by attending the weekly agenda meeting. The agenda meeting is open to all community members who, along with the chairpersons for that week, will decide the agenda for the community meeting. Chairpersons rotate each week, and all students are encouraged to try chairing or co-chairing a community meeting. One of the first issues voted on this year was that attendance at community meetings would be mandatory for all community members.

The other formal structure for executing the community's business is the fairness community, a smaller forum for dealing with issues of justice that are more appropriate for discussion in a smaller group than the community meeting. The fairness committee usually handles infractions by community members and recommends punishments to be approved by the larger group.

Core groups are smaller subgroups within the community, and one of their functions is to elect one student and a rotating faculty member to the fairness committee. Students choose a faculty advisor at the beginning of the year and meet with that faculty member once a week at the home of a student to discuss academic and social issues. Over the year, this arrangement develops into a close working arrangement that usually extends beyond school issues. As a student, I can attest to the value for adolescents in having such close, personal contacts. Core groups are cohesive entities within the community that are represented on the various school committees, make recommendations and proposals to the larger group, and rotate the chairmanship of community meetings.

Individual classes, generally consisting of five to ten students, also provide a context for promoting discussion and action on moral development. Just Community classes are unique because they are run democratically and maintain fairness as an educational goal. The grading system also reflects this orientation. Students receive written evaluations instead of letter grades, and these evaluations are discussed by students and teachers together. Teachers have the final say; but if a student disagrees with a teacher's evaluation, he or she can record that statement in the final transcript of the year.

Incorporated into all these activities is what Kohlberg calls the "hidden curriculum," or the moral atmosphere of the school. Ideally, the interactions and discussions that take place in the meetings and classes, which concentrate on issues of fairness and morality, will all develop the moral atmosphere of the school. This is important for the theorists who see the collective normative values of the community as being directly linked to students' moral reasoning and behavior. Thus, in the course of raising the stages and "phases" of the community's collective normative values the moral atmosphere is being developed. Individual student development should occur as long as the sense of community is strong and students adopt its normative values as their own. This is why community building activities to strengthen the bonds individuals feel toward the group are a major concern of the Just Community School. In addition to its regular daily interactions, retreats, field trips, and parties are some of the ways the Alternative School built up its sense of community.

Let me begin my critique of the Just Community *in practice* by relating the process I went through in evaluating the program. I first discussed with my fellow students what their impressions of the year were. Next, I studied the theoretical explanations of what was supposed to be happening and why. Finally, I combined the experience and impressions of my fellow students and myself to formulate a general overview of the trends and norms of the community through the year.

First and foremost, let me emphasize the overwhelming consensus regarding the program of the people involved—the Just Community Approach to high-school education is an exciting, stimulating, and mutually beneficial experience for students and teachers alike. What the theorists say about the positive influences of fairness in schools, affiliation with a caring community of one's peers and teachers, an informal school setting and participation in an intensive and personalized education program are, by and large, true. Yet, these characteristics are not unappealing on their own, divorced from a concern for moral and civic development. The all-around positive attitude toward the program by its participants is not to be underestimated, for even if no stage development occurs, most would agree the program is effective educationally and appealing socially. Whether moral reasoning and moral behavior were affected positively is a different question that I will now begin to discuss.

A discussion of some of the elements of the Alternative School's moral atmosphere will, I believe, illustrate the increased sense of community and concern for adhering to its norms that the students developed gradually during the year. At the beginning of the year, the community planned a retreat and community meetings focused on the planning and making of rules for the outing. The staff raised the question of a drug rule, a major concern in past years because of traditional use of alcohol and marijuana by students on such outings. At first the community was content with making a rule and letting it go at that; but the staff raised the question of who would be responsible for enforcing the rule. The ensuing discussion centered on the group's commitment to uphold the rule and come to a decision that would realistically ensure its enforcement, if there was to be an outing at all. Most students voiced their belief that they had a right to smoke on the outing, as long as it did not interfere with anyone else. Others argued that it affected the whole community if anyone was getting high. Clearly, at this point in the year the norm of the group was that it was OK to get high, as long as you did not get caught. The community agreed that it was unfair to expect the teachers to assume the burden for enforcing the rule; yet, when a vote was taken between two choices, whether both students and teachers should and *would* enforce the no-smoking rule, or whether only teachers should and would enforce the rule, the second alternative won by a close margin. Students felt that even though they *should* turn in other students that they probably could not and that the teachers would have to assume the responsibility. At this early stage in the year, the community clearly placed friendship over group commitment.

The beginning of collective growth of group norms began shortly after the outing though, when violaters of the drug rule were asked to confess in community meeting because various students voiced their anger that the community rule had been broken. Students claimed that they had seen or heard of violations on the retreat but were not willing to turn anyone in. These students expressed a Stage 4 concern for community's responsibility to uphold the rules it makes for the sake of the entire community. Eventually, a large group of students confessed and were given the punishment of losing their vote for one week. At that time in the year, when important scheduling and policy decisions were being made for the rest of the year, this was a serious penalty. More importantly, the discussion about why it was important for the community to take responsibility for enforcing its own rules and punishing members who violate them began to show signs of a Stage 4 concept of community evolving and a real sense of ownership on the part of the students. Responsibility to the group was shifting from a simple notion of giving a little in return for something, to a commitment to being a good community member and upholding the group's normative values. These meetings also displayed a healthy quantity of heterogeneous reasoning that made for productive moral discussions.

Toward the middle of the year, another heated issue came up regarding a well-liked student, who, because of his consistent failure to meet his obligations in classes, was up for expulsion. The staff had recommended that he leave the school, and the issue was handed over to the community. The student requested that his case be heard in front of the whole community instead of the fairness committee; and a series of four community meetings ensued before a decision was reached by the group. After long discussion on the minimum obligations for remaining in the community and whether a student should be allowed to fail courses and remain in the community, the community finally agreed that the student would have to leave the school that year, but with the option to return and make up the year the following year. The community, in these discussions, made every possible attempt to work out alternatives for the student, including probation agreements which that student subsequently failed to meet. Obviously, the group had a great deal of trouble in judging one of their peers, especially a well-liked student, who just could not meet the responsibilities and obligations that the community had agreed upon. The process we (they) went through in judging his case, however, showed two elements of the community's moral atmosphere: an overriding concern to treat the individual fairly (although we cannot tell if an unpopular student would have received the same treatment), and a basic priority for keeping the group's concerns above any one individual's.

Clearly, the caring element of the community came across in this episode; but we continued to ask ourselves if there was any justification for asking a student to leave a school which supposedly is interested in educating individuals about how to live with authority and develop a sense of responsibility and social obligations. Also, do the individual's interests have a lower priority than the group's in the Just Community?

During my Harvard internship, I visited SWS, the School-Within-A-School at Brookline High School, several times. I found that the students at SWS had the same problem as the Scarsdale students judging their peers. Their system of peer review, from what I could see and what students in that program have said, has not worked very well. Students were consistently unwilling to punish their peers. This suggests that the moral conception of the community had not yet developed a stage conception of community higher than individual affiliation.

What happened to the individuals within the program? My view is generally positive, but we know that no classroom experience could possibly address every individual's needs; and it is inevitable that some students will take little or nothing from a program involving up to seventy students. One must be concerned with the majority, and it is the majority of students that I speak of when I say that individual development did occur in the Alternative School, to the best of my knowledge. This does not mean, however, that the group should come before any one individual in the program. It is to this concern, the right of each individual to enjoy the same opportunities for growth and edification, that I address the concerns I have regarding what happened in our school. These issues which I will attempt to explain and possibly offer solutions to, are: moral intimidation, abuse of the stage hierarchy, and the negative effects of the "halo effect" in moral stage development.

Moral intimidation was a major issue in the Alternative School in my senior year. Some of the most hotly contested and emotional community meetings attempted to deal with this issue. It surfaced in the first half of the year, in response to Dr. Kohlberg's presence and the entire atmosphere of MORALITY. Students were concerned about being treated like guinea pigs that were part of an experiment to see if moral stage development could be prompted by Kohlberg's methods. Students were angered because they saw the school curriculum and the actions of all the teachers as planned to reach a certain moral goal. There was a widespread sentiment that the school no longer belonged to the students and that the year was planned out beyond their ability to affect it.

Dr. Kohlberg was asked to explain his theory and exactly what he was attempting to do at our school to the students. He agreed to do this, but I think he would agree that his message was not clearly understood by most of us. The hostility toward this covert attempt to "make us moral" continued, prompted some attitudes to the effect of "I'm Stage 2 and proud of it." But these people were clearly not proud of it, and many were intimidated by the fact that the faculty and some students were obviously aware of some "higher" morality which was better than theirs. Kohlberg and the moral educators would agree that this is true and needs to be, so that they can work toward improving those at the lower stages. However, this was never explained to students; and theoretically, even if it was, most students would not be at a stage where they could really understand it anyway. The feeling of being pushed toward "higher stages" was very intimidating to many students. They perceived that every issue was presented with a "right" and a "wrong" side and that there was tremendous pressure to choose the "right" side, despite what they really thought. This I see as a major problem to avoid in education, despite the theorists' claim that this is a positive impetus for students to begin the process of cognitive reorganization. Some compromise must be established so students are not afraid of morality, or feel forced into it, for I see this as reverting back to indoctrination. Here is where the bridge between thought and action would surely collapse and is therefore of little use to the individual.

A way to approach this problem is, first, to establish an understanding with the students as to what the moral development approach is all about and how development supposedly occurs. In speaking with students in my school, I found that many never had a clear idea of what the Kohlberg model was all about and were worried about their performance in it as a result. Also, teachers must be sensitive to how they approach the process, to avoid "preaching." After all, the teacher figure is respected by the adolescent; and having the students accept these ideas merely because they perceive them as the teachers' "bag of virtues," is not effective. This I saw happening in our school especially, with a big-shot Harvard professor in addition to the entire staff supporting certain ideas which they called better.

Directly related to this issue of moral intimidation is the problem of abuse of the stage hierarchy, or the use of the stages as a weapon. With the notion that there exists a hierarchy of reasoning and values in the air, the idea of better and worse is always on the minds of students. Kohlberg claims that there is a better way to construct reasoning using certain universally acceptable principles. Students can, and do, interpret this to mean that not only are there better "contents" than others but that there are better or smarter students, depending on their stage of development. This is impossible to understand for the student who has a vague idea of what a higher stage is but, because he has not reached it, cannot see that it is a more adequate system. He believes he is wrong but does not understand why. This is the root of the negative aspects of the "halo effect," as well as the way certain students, who may not even be reasoning adequately at a higher stage, can adopt a position on an issue and seem to have "right" on their side. This turns discussion of real issues into battles of who is right and who is wrong, based on stages.

This was usually not a major problem in our school because our emphasis was on justice, not stage development. Fortunately, the concern about stages began to drift into the background when a "real" issue, concerning the students directly, was being discussed. But again, because this problem did not happen to the majority of students does not mean that it should be ignored. It is a problem for both the user of the weapon and the victim, for neither have engaged in a real discussion of the issues. Teachers should be sensitive to this possibility and be able to direct the discussion in a way that challenges the faculty reasoning or aggressive tactics of the attacker and elicit the real reasoning of the other. In general, emphasizing a discussion of the issues as to their fairness and justice is the only way I can see of keeping the stages out of the discussion.

If teachers or some students were to see other students with a "negative halo-effect" by giving the impression that they thought of them as lower-stage and with little potential, this could freeze such students developmentally. Especially in a Just Community School, where lower stages carry a negative connotation, it is important to deemphasize the discussion of stages. At the same time, teachers need to show students that they can help each other in more direct ways than by confronting each other in discussion. Teachers need to convince the more aggressive students that it is more important to help a peer than to overwhelm him or her with superior debating skills.

These are some of the more prominent concerns that I have noted from my experience. There are others, such as frustration that students feel from having to deal with issue after issue that they may feel is irrelevant and only being raised for the sake of moral development. This is a real concern but something each school has to work out on its own. Despite such issues and problems in Just Communities, I believe they provide the most logical and reasonable approach to educating students.

DIALOGUE: LAWRENCE KOHLBERG AND EDWARD ZALAZNICK (EXCERPTS FROM A RECORDING MADE IN MARCH 1980)

Lawrence Kohlberg: Could you tell us how you felt about the A-school in comparison to the regular high school, what you saw as the differences?

Edward Zalaznick: Well, . . . the most striking example of a difference was that the people in the school were forced in a sense to confront each other more often, especially on nonacademic subjects, which made the functioning of the school and the relationships in the school more constructive, and students' needs educationally were more directly addressed. Socially, from the start we started to become a community; we had various community-building activities, and there was a general feeling in the school that a community would be a desirable thing, that people felt friendly toward each other. There was a pressure, almost, to work toward fostering the group.

You felt like you belonged at the school and that was what created the pressure, the energy of working to build as opposed to destroy, this feeling of, you know, everyone wants to be part of the group. In a sense it was a comfort and a shelter that people would gravitate toward the school, and you sort of felt unique. It was sort of one big clique apart from the large high school and we did, we had an identity and everything; it was something that built up naturally and became quite strong.

I want to make the point that in the regular high school a lot of people were so distracted by the need to worry about what everyone else was doing and how they stacked up in terms of the competition, whereas in the alternative school, that competitive factor really wasn't there, or grades, or status in terms of academics. It was more. . . . status was measured more in terms of your merit as a community member; and so academically, a majority of the people there felt like this was a better atmosphere for them to work in, and so they could get more done.

LK: But wasn't there then the same kind of competition in the A-school about being a good community member, as there was academic competition in the regular high school?

EZ: In a sense, especially for standing in the teachers' eyes. I think that's something students worried about. There was a big division in the school, a definite division of "the teachers' side" and "not the teachers' side" on almost every issue; and the students who argued on the teachers' side were sometimes doing that just to be doing the right thing—what they thought was the right thing; and students who argued against the teachers' side, I think, were concerned about what the teachers were thinking.

LK: Did you sometimes have the feeling of being intimidated?

EZ: Well, I did, but in a sense I was one of the moral intimidators; and the moral intimidation came in because we, in a sense, forced kids at the lower stages to become aware and to have to deal with higher stages. The people who were aware of the higher stages, who were at the higher stages, now had a weapon. When there would be a split on an issue, and it would seem to be a stage split, almost, there was now this kind of weapon. A lot of times we would have to stop our discussions that were getting nowhere and say "the people that are on the two sides of this issue are like two ships passing in the night," they're not addressing each other anymore, they're not communicating. When we would be talking on the drug rule, for instance, some people would say we have to make rules, and it's good for the whole school that everyone live up to the rule, while other people would be saying, this is a rule that is unfair because getting high is something that doesn't hurt the rest of the group. It's something that I do and it doesn't hurt the rest of the group, so I should be able to do it. When there were two sides and one side wasn't seeing the other's point, there was this kind of feeling that the side that the teachers took was another stage higher, was a more moral thing to say, and that "I *must* be wrong because I'm a lower stage, even though this is what I really believe and what I see as being true. Larry Kohlberg says that we don't always understand a more better or more moral thing, and so I obviously just don't understand the better thing to be doing at this point of view, so therefore I'm less right." That was really intimidating to a lot of students, and I think it caused a lot of them to go along with decisions that they weren't really sure they could live with.

LK: Did you feel you were exposed to "moral teaching" or "moral indoctrination"?

EZ: Hmm. Well, when you talk about teaching morals, I would assume you meant teaching a higher stage, a higher perspective of justice—you know, a more universal concern. Well, I think there was an attempt to teach that, and it was agreed upon by everyone that we would try to be as universally just in all our actions as possible and that the teachers would stimulate discussion to get the most universally just decisions out of the group as we could come up with. We were never indoctrinated in the sense that someone would come up with "this is the situation, and this is the most fair thing to do, and can you all see that now." It was more like "we have this focus and we're gonna work on it and so let's talk about the issue with that in mind"; and so we all had to teach ourselves the experience.

LK: You said that everyone agreed on an idea of justice as being important in the school. How did that agreement come about? Was that something the teachers laid on the kids?

EZ: Well, no, the first agreement that we made on that system was in coming to the Alternative School, which we knew was run so that everyone could contribute. So everyone knew that this was a system which tried to be fair to everyone by letting them speak up. And so we came into the school with that foundation. We always came back to the idea of fairness as a central idea of the school.

LK: Even more important than the idea of community?

EZ: (Long pause). I think no one would have said that, although I don't think the two ideas are that separated because they would be sort of interchanged with each other. "Community is the most important thing." "Fairness is the most important thing." People tried to view it equally. They were part of each other. When we had graduation, we originally had decided to have the party at a girl's house. . . . the party was on a Friday night, and the girl's parents got back and said "You can't have the party here on the Sabbath." Then we had to all work out well, what are we going to do? Are we going to change the date of graduation because some parents aren't going to come? And so. . . . and in our discussion, all our alternatives were ordered in how fair they were to everyone. And that was something that went on throughout the year.

We all wanted to guarantee that we would stick to being fair; that there would be no breakdown where teachers could suddenly usurp power and do something underhanded or unfair, and so we decided that everything that we do should be done with the priority of fairness and democracy—and majority rule went along with that. We all said, "Well, sometimes we're not going to be completely fair, some people aren't going to get their way." So in a sense we arrived at a just community on our own. I think that we never really called ourselves the Just Community School in an official way, but we sort of structured our school to be one. When we were given alternatives and we talked about the different ways our school could be set up, it turned out to be a Just Community School.

LK: What did you feel you got out of this?

EZ: I got out of the school a feeling that I had learned to work constructively toward resolving problems, as opposed to complaining about problems in school and in relationships with other people. I thought it was beneficial for students to be allowed to try to run a school by themselves. We all became aware of the problems of other people because we were forced to come out of our own perspective in looking at a situation and a problem. I think everyone had to do that. It also just made us more responsible because we had to live up to strong expectations that mattered. The teachers' expectations are not that important, but your peers' expectations are very important; and so we learned to be more accountable. It helped me in terms of academics, and it helped a lot of other kids in terms of academics because they felt like they had to come to class, not just to get a good grade, but because they didn't want to look like they were bad students or bad community members in front of their friends and peers. There were positive norms created by the students in this situation, as opposed to negative norms created in the high-school situation. The norm of the students in the high school is to create trouble and to get away with as much as you can and to get by with as little work as possible; and all those sorts of negative norms were really converted into positive norms now because that whole thing was that the students were not helpless against the system; they *were* the system, so they were forced to take on some responsibility. It was good for us to have some responsibility and not just talk about *wanting* to have responsibility.

LK: Well, now you're going to college and are working and are no longer living in this Just Community, and so on. Do you think the last year has had any effect on you?

EZ: Well, again, I don't want to be making a testimonial and stuff; but it was a real civic education for me, and it just made clear the democratic system the society is built on and how we all have to act accordingly; form our attitudes and opinions in the larger society as if we really were part of that group; that we all have some common agreement. You know, we are all in a sense a just community out in the real world in the United States. It sort of makes me more accountable to make me think about what my obligations as a citizen are. I guess it has broadened my moral perspective, when I have to think about things like that.

LK: Does it seem at all real that the United States is a democratic community?

EZ: Yes, it does; and it gives me also a weapon, to talk to people who are not living up to those obligations. When you discuss issues of the day with people who are addressing the issues from a very chauvinistic point of view from their own group, you can confront them with this and. . . . this kind of logic will prevail. So the exercises in debating or in policy making or issue making that went on in the school were really based upon the same principles that the society is. Those discussions out in the real world would have to take the same. . . . *can* take the same format.

CHEATING AND TRUANCY: DISCIPLINE AND LOCUS OF CONTROL IN A "JUST COMMUNITY" SCHOOL

Beverly Noia

As part of the effort to increase my understanding of moral development and education, I spent considerable time during my Klingenstein fellowship year visiting schools of contrasting philosophies. Among these schools was the Scarsdale Alternative School, a high school which is designed to function as a "Just Community." Coming from a fairly traditional school, I approached the Alternative School with certain preconceptions, most of them negative. Here are some:

- Kids need adults to tell them what to do; this kind of school will fail in that.
- If kids are asked to be judges, they'll be unfair or cruel or both; adults shouldn't abdicate this responsibility.
- If you involve kids in making the rules, you'll have a sloppy ship.

• You shouldn't lead kids into binds they don't have the maturity to face, but this school will do that. And so forth.

So it was with some degree of trepidation, if not actual antagonism, that I undertook visiting the A-School. Two particular cases, one dealing with cheating and one with possible expulsion, served to challenge the preconceptions I had harbored. We traditionalists are challenged, as the reflections interspersed within the narration of the cases make clear.

* * *

The Scarsdale Alternative School is a public high school (grades 10-12) of under a hundred students, six full-time faculty members, and several part-time teachers. Students who elect to attend this alternative to the more traditional Scarsdale High School understand that it is run on the democratic principles of Kohlberg's Just Community model. Faculty and students discuss what the behavioral norms for the community should be, vote on what rules to adopt, and how these rules should be enforced.

Core groups, consisting of ten or twelve students and two teachers, meet weekly in an informal, home environment, to build close and trusting bonds and to provide a forum for discussion of issues, large or small. Often matters to be handled in the full community meeting which follows core group are dealt with preliminarily here. There is a fairness committee consisting of both students and faculty members; this committee deals with students and teachers who are brought before it by other members of the community who consider them to be in some way failing in their responsibilities to the community. Very serious cases might be brought before the entire community for discussion and decision. The emphasis on student involvement in all aspects of the school—including those of rule setting and discipline often reserved to the faculty and administrators in more traditional schools—reflects the principle that moral development can be encouraged and hastened when one is required to make truly important decisions and to accept responsibility publicly for one's judgments and actions. I felt fortunate to have been present when the community grappled with two problems that beset many schools: cheating and truancy.

Admitting to Cheating: Hypocricy or Meaningful Dissonance?

Early in the school year, the A-School discussed the concept of cheating and achieved some consensus that it should be discouraged in the community. By democratic vote they had decided to make a rule against cheating and to have both students and teachers responsible for enforcing the rule. If a student should see another cheating, it would be his/her responsibility to tell that student to report himself or herself; if that student did not do so, then the one who had seen the incident should report it to the community. The infraction would then be handled by the fairness committee.

At the core group meeting I attended, the discussion focused at first on whether, in fact, cheating had stopped at the A-School—since no cases had been brought up since the procedures had been established—or whether there were instances that were not being reported. One student, whom I will call Susan, became uneasy, saying that she had witnessed a friend copying homework but had not confronted him. She had not believed that the student would either accept the confrontation or report himself; since it seemed pointless and only painful to act, Susan had done nothing. Now she regretted her decision because, she said, she believed she had hurt the greater community by her silence, her failure to do as she, a member of a democratically constructed society, had agreed to do.

While I was impressed with Susan's concern for the community and for her own responsibility, I was also uneasy at this point: Should we, in fact, be allowing adolescents to be caught in a bind of peer pressure, fear and friendship, and idealistic responsibilities? Were we expecting too much of them? Were we asking them to behave in manners appropriate to people more mature, or in Kohlbergian terms, of a "higher stage"? Was that good or bad?

The core group discussion continued. The students urged Susan to confront her friend, but she said that she knew what the response would be; there was no point in trying. Suddenly she decided that she *would* name the cheater: the person who had copied homework (Peter, I'll call him) was someone in a different core group; but the person whose paper he had copied was in the present group. The tension was immediate; the girl whose paper had been copied was asked whether she wanted to say anything—"No." Other students began expressing their judgments about what was occurring. There was some sense that the girl should not have named the cheaters, since she had not spoken to them; she became upset that she had tried to do what was right and had apparently only caused more trouble.

Should youngsters have to go through this kind of confusion and distress, I wondered. And what of the old value on privacy? And yes, the community *might be helped by sessions like this, but were* individuals *being sacrificed somehow?*

The discussion continued, with some wise and helpful contributions on the parts of the two adults in the group. I was pleased to see that while the adults and students lived in this community as equals, the adults had not abdicated their responsibilities by simply leaving everything to the students. No, the adults added their insights and gave their advice, not imposing these, but offering them for consideration. By the end of the core group session, it had been decided that the girl whose paper had been copied should speak to the copier, and that they should then report themselves to the community. One of the student members of the group suggested that all members should agree to say nothing of this issue until those directly involved had had a chance to handle it properly; the group agreed to keep the issue private.

Could they, really, I wondered. So few people, adults included, can resist telling a secret — should the students be promising something (silence for a week) that they most probably couldn't manage? Were they not being set up for failure? Wouldn't the failure eventuate a tendency to conceal the failure— wasn't inauthenticity being courted?

The core group meeting broke up, and the entire community reconvened back at the school. Once the whole-group community meeting was called to order by a student leader, Peter raised his hand, and was called on. "I have a confession to make," he began. "I cheated. I copied someone's homework, and I'm ready to pay the penalty for hurting the community." He laughed a little, and members of the group laughed, too, making "shame on you" gestures that suggested they really didn't find the issue all that serious. The meeting moved on to other things.

So, keeping the matter private for a week would be no problem — it was out in the open already. But how sincere was that confession/apology? And what was the meaning of the students' responses? Actually, nothing else really could have happened, could it? Peter had HAD to confess, since the facts were out anyway. And the tittering among his fellow students probably was basically from their nervousness or embarrassment, not really an expression of not taking cheating seriously. But hadn't some sort of social pressure practically necessitated inauthentic behavior? Something I had wondered about as I had read about schools like this one finally took clear form for me: was a danger of this approach that it forced youngsters to behave in ways that were not expressive of their real values but were in response to group expectations? *Might it be that instead of helping youngsters develop beyond Stage 2 or 3 such a system might "freeze" them at a level of doing the pragmatic thing, acting in ways that would gain the group's approval?*

In conversation after the community meeting, I raised this question with the school's director, Judith Codding. The response I received forced me to reconsider the condemnation I had began to harbor. Codding (called "Judy" within the community) agreed that the boy's "confession" had been under duress and had not resulted from his having reached an inner conviction that what he had done was wrong and that he owed it to the community and himself to admit his error and accept the consequences. Nonetheless, the director maintained, this would not be simply an event of forced inauthenticity; *the dissonance between what Peter felt and what he did would, as it were, rankle inside him, and through living through the conflict and confusion and suffering, he would be put in the position of having to examine, reconsider, and simply grow.* One instance like this one might not by itself cause stage development; but repeated instances of having to resolve internal conflict should ultimately lead to such growth.

* * *

Reflecting on what I had seen and felt and heard, I left the A-School that day uncertain about the relative values of the community's right to monitor its voluntary members and an individual's right to privacy. I had seen some disturbing events; but in light of the director's explanation, I could not simply say that since they were disturbing to me and painful to the participants they should not have happened or that a school should not be so constructed as to facilitate them. No, if indeed a grain of sand can irritate an oyster into forming a pearl, then perhaps the A-School was approaching moral development with wisdom.

One effect of that first visit to Scarsdale was that it made me reconsider the negative prejudice with which I had approached the school's processes. Another effect was that I was forced to reconsider the "positive prejudice" I had held for the way my own school operates. What misgivings might an observer validly entertain were he to observe how I deal with cheating? At the beginning of a school year, I inform my classes that cheating is not acceptable. I give the students some moral reasons and some pragmatic reasons. I tell them that I will tear up the paper of any student I find cheating, enter a zero in the grade book, and communicate with his parents and the school administration about the incident. Usually once, early in the year, I "catch" one student, dramatically tear up his paper, let him sit there until class is over, then confer with his parents and the school head. Rarely does another instance of cheating happen. The control is sufficient. But even as I have been writing this, I have been cringing: in the past I have been proud of the "fine discipline" I have in my classes and of how well my students do as I direct them. *But have I considered whether my total control of the situation is ultimately beneficial for their development of moral values?* No, not until this year's research and particularly my experience at Scarsdale forced me to reevaluate what I do. Can it not be said that I deny the students the opportunity to develop and internalize a value about honesty when I simply tell them how to behave? Can it not be argued that I force inauthenticity by making them behave as I want them to, or pay a too-heavy penalty? Can it not be seen that my tearing up a student's paper in front of his peers is at least as much a violation of privacy as the community meeting I took exception to at the A-School? Could it not be true that by taking most of the responsibility for enforcing the rule on cheating, I am denying the students their grain of sand for pearl-making?

Facing Expulsion for Truancy: Last Straw or Foundation Stone?

One of the major reservations I brought to my consideration of Just Community schools is their practice of having discipline issues handled by a fairness committee or, sometimes, the entire community. It seemed clear to me that problems of behavior or achievement should be dealt with in private by the "constituted authorities"—teachers, department chairpersons, or administrators who presumably have the maturity and experience to make wise and fair decisions. This assumption on my part made my last visit to Scarsdale one I dreaded: I was to attend a community meeting in which the question of whether a certain student (whom I shall call Martha) should be expelled. This would be decided by a vote of the students and faculty together.

I had attended the faculty meeting a week prior to this and had heard the teachers and director of the school discuss the details of Martha's situation. Martha was a sophomore, new to the school that year, and had had little success of any kind. She frequently cut classes, rarely did her academic work, and often was rude, particularly when adults tried to correct her. The teachers and director had tried repeatedly to convince her to change and had been unsuccessful. She was taking an inordinate amount of teacher time and hence was hurting the community. Her outbursts of temper were wearing on the people who had to deal with her. The faculty decision was unanimous: She should be expelled.

In my more traditional school, at this point the student *would* have been expelled. But would this point have been reached, really? I had doubts. If intermediary counseling and disciplinary steps had been taken after one or two cuts, after one or two missed assignments, would it have had to come to this point? I understood that at the A-School Martha was indeed confronted for her various unacceptable activities and that her parents were involved; but there seemed to have been little, if any, positive effect. Occasionally she would be a bit more regular about attending classes — for a week, perhaps. But then the old behaviors would return.

At the A-School, while students know what is expected, their behavior can be in direct confrontation with expectations for a considerable amount of time, apparently, before external controls are imposed. The students are given more opportunities to err and correct themselves before authority steps in to direct them. Some observers would say, "the kids are allowed to dig their own graves." Others would say, "the kids are allowed to learn experientially the value of obeying certain rules, and the consequences of disobeying them. These consequences are integral (e.g., if you cut class, you get behind and then can't catch up) instead of superimposed (e.g., if you cut class, you get detention). Thus, the students are given the chance for not mere obedience but actual maturation."

Which procedure is better?

One must ask, "Better for *what*?"

There is a certain value to the more traditional approach: Students know what is expected, and they know the penalties, and they generally make what we adults would call the "right" decisions. The school runs smoothly, the students benefit immensely from consistent class attendance and academic preparedness, and the atmosphere is generally pleasant and positive. Very few behavior or discipline problems arise; students and faculty alike are generally mutually respectful and enjoy each other.

In retrospect, perhaps the high school from which Martha came operated this way. Perhaps her transfer into the A-School was already an acknowledgement that the traditional approach was not working with her. For Martha, perhaps, the A-School was, already, a "last resort." And now Martha was facing expulsion. What would happen to Martha now? Would she, as I anticipated, end up expelled, but only after paying the gruelling price of public humiliation?

The student moderators called the community meeting to order, and Martha's advisor, a teacher, presented the fact to the community. It was made clear that while there were some bright moments in Martha's time at the A-School, they did not offset the fact that she seemed intransigent, or perhaps unable to improve. The faculty consensus that Martha should be expelled was announced. Martha was asked to present her "defense"; she had very little to say. Her main point was that although she recognized that she cut classes too often, still she felt that she had made some improvement since coming to the A-School, for in fact the previous year she had been in full attendance at her school for only six days. She expressed a desire to stay at the A-School and a willingness to try harder to meet her responsibilities.

Perhaps if they had lowered the boom earlier, I thought to myself, she would have seen the seriousness of the matter sooner and have taken herself in hand with much less suffering all around. This— the facing of expulsion—seemed to be the first time she had been forced to do some deep thinking and make some hard decisions and commitments. Would it have been less helpful, for her moral development, to have acted sooner?

The members of the community, students and teachers alike, began to ask Martha questions, seeking to understand why she had behaved as she had. It became clear that Martha saw that what she had been doing was not good for the community and that it was hurting her as well. She seemed genuinely to want to change but also to recognize that she had what she called "sort of an addiction." The more she cut classes, the less she could do the work; and the less she could work successfully, the more she cut classes. But she was convinced that she had the capability of doing the academic work expected of her, if she could only break that vicious cycle. How might she? She had tried before and failed. What was there to suggest that another chance to try would end any differently? "I've never been so scared before," she answered. "Now I know I have to do it."

Again I wondered whether this child had been done a disservice by being given too much freedom— too much rope, to hang herself, some would put it. The primary motivations seemed to be fear *(of being sent back to her former school— where she would have been freer to do the things she was now in trouble for doing!) and* desire *(to remain at the A-School—even though it asked of her behavior she found so difficult). Shouldn't these motivations have been brought to bear earlier and have spared the child, the faculty, and the whole community much stress and this current distress?*

As the discussion continued, something I had not anticipated began to occur: The community drew together seeking not simply justice (which would have been served had the student been expelled) but something else: the good of the student and of the wider community. One student suggested that interested students might volunteer to be a "support group" for Martha: call her at home in the evenings to see if she'd done her homework and offer to help if she needed that; say, "Hey, you coming to class?" when they might see her lounging outside just before class; or simply be around to offer encouragement and appreciation. There was enthusiasm evident among Martha's peers as they realized they might be able to help her, and she herself seemed somewhat surprised at their caring, and grateful to accept their involvement. She wisely, though, would not pretend that her fate would be in their hands. "I've got to do this myself," she said repeatedly. She also knew that her tendency to flare up at adults when they "nagged" her might also apply to her peers, and she asked that the support group "not be on my back all the time."

What I was witnessing here was, to me, something both remarkable and beautiful: Some sort of transformation was happening, not only for the student but for the whole community. The metaphor of antibodies rushing to a wound to help both cure it and restore the health of the whole organism seemed somehow appropriate. In my prejudice, I had anticipated some sort of "crucify her!" scene; but I had underestimated the degree of caring, of maturity, and of willingness to share responsibility that existed in this group of adolescents.

The time came for making a decision. Four alternatives were proposed. 1) Martha could stay on, with no conditions. 2) She could stay at the A-School but on probation, with realistic terms to be set by a group including herself, the school director, and her advisor. 3) She could be sent back to her original school; and if her behavior improved there, she could return to the A-School the next fall. 4) Or, she could simply be expelled, with no opportunity to return. Martha asked permission to leave while the vote was taken, but the director convinced her to remain.

Should a fragile youngster be asked to stay while her fate is decided? Should adolescents be asked to vote on the fate of a peer, in her presence? The secret ballot is a long-standing tradition—why submit this girl to further suffering, or her classmates and teachers to the pressure of showing her exactly how they judged her? I was most uneasy.

The vote was taken: No one voted that she stay at the A-School unconditionally. No one voted that she be expelled with no chance to return. Roughly 95 percent of the community (including the *entire faculty*) voted that she be permitted to remain on probation. A few hands were raised for the expulsion-on-probation option. The mood was immediately one of rejoicing—faculty and students alike seemed to share some sense that goodness had been done: They hadn't given up on one of their community members, nor had they ignored inappropriate behavior, and most of all everyone had come together to find a way to make things good.

I was glad Martha had seen the vote; it had to say something very important to her about the community's caring for her, and that in itself might be the key to her finally freeing herself from her "addiction." The overwhelming statement of support from her community was surely as important as the actual outcome (not being expelled), both for her development and for theirs.

Were the qualities of care, responsibility, and general moral maturity in this community higher than they would have been in a school not run on the Just Community model? I do not feel qualified to judge that, but I do believe that their experience in expressing their values and judgments and their opportunity to make decisions that mattered, played a vital role in their capacity to handle this issue of truancy and potential expulsion with such moral maturity.

Chapter 9

Assessing the Moral Culture of the School

Lisa Kuhmerker

We have stressed that one way of conceptualizing democratic social interaction as contributing to moral development is to see such interaction as interindividual dialogue, reciprocity, and cooperation among peers, the view stressed by Piaget. A second way of conceptualizing democratic social interaction is as the egalitarian building of a moral culture or moral group through the creation of shared moral norms. In our view, this moral culture is required not only to create the conditions of interindividual cooperation and dialogue but to build a general moral self, a development function of the adolescent years (Lawrence Kohlberg, in Kurtines and Gewirtz, 1987, p. 128, quoted with permission of John Wiley Press).

INDIVIDUAL VERSUS GROUP NORMS

Institutions aren't moral or immoral, individuals are; but individuals are affected for better or worse by the moral climate of the institutional setting in which they find themselves, and individuals *in interaction* can affect and change the moral climate of the institution.

Kohlberg's research career began with the study of individual moral development, but as soon as he and his colleagues studied and began to engage in educational interventions they became aware of the stultifying or liberating effect of the institutional environment on the moral development of their subjects. When Kohlberg and his associates became involved in educational interven-

146

tions in urban high-school settings, the possible relationship between individual moral development and the moral atmosphere or culture of the school became more than a major research problem. The establishment and assessment of the relation became part of the rationale for seeking funding from foundations and writing up project reports.

In the 1970s Scharf (1973), Reimer (1977), Wasserman (1977), and Jennings (1979) postulated a relationship between institutional climate or moral atmosphere and individual moral development. In their view, moral atmosphere influenced moral development insofar as it provided certain conditions for moral growth. While the number and description of conditions varied somewhat according to the author, they all agreed that the conditions included those present in good moral discussions and others specifically related to democracy and community (Power, Higgins, and Kohlberg, 1989, p. 99).

Scharf's (1973) research in the creation of a just community in a prison provided powerful confirmation of the negative effect an institution could have on individual moral development. Most inmates reasoned between Stage 2 and 2/3, but the traditional custodial prison administration tended to function primarily in terms rewards and punishment, Stage 1, and the treatment by guards was often harsh and demeaning. "The inmate culture was no better—as inmates often abused each other and formed relationships more for mutual protection and instrumental gain than for friendship" (Power, Higgins, and Kohlberg, 1989, p. 100).

Kohlberg witnessed the powerful effect that the moral culture of an institution can have on individual development when he visited an Israeli kibbutz in the summer of 1969. Educating its children to sustain the life of the collective settlement is a major goal of every kibbutz. This kibbutz was unusual in having established a high-school program that had as its main objective bringing lower-class adolescents from the cities and educating them alongside the smaller number of youngsters born to the parents in the collective. Kohlberg's observations and conversations with the Madrich (educational leader) so impressed him that throughout his subsequent publications Kohlberg credited his kibbutz encounters with inspiring him to create just community schools at home.

Research confirmation of the positive effect that a community setting could have on individual moral development was shown by Reimer (1977) who analyzed the effect of kibbutz living on the moral judgments of adolescents. When the moral reasoning of the adolescents was tested, the urban newcomers scored markedly lower than the resident adolescents. Within two years, however, the difference was erased and both groups scored high for their age on the Moral Judgment Interview. Test scores alone could not reflect the quality of the interaction and the reality of what later came to be called "group norms."

How might one "capture" and assess group norms? Wasserman (1977) was the first to examine the conditions for moral growth from a Kohlbergian perspective. She analyzed the community meeting transcripts of the first two years of the Cluster School program, looking at moral concerns in agenda items, the existence of moral conflict, the opportunity for role-taking, and the proportion of student versus staff participation. Power (1979) analyzed overlapping and similar data in the four-year longitudinal study of the moral atmosphere of a just community school that constituted his doctoral dissertation. Wasserman (1979) moved from this initial involvement in a just community school to the adaptation of some of its best features to mainstream high-school education. Kohlberg's research focus on moral atmosphere and moral culture is sustained and extended by Power and Higgins (Power, Higgins, and Kohlberg, 1989).

While community meetings are an important source for perceptions about a moral culture, the data they provide are limited. People get cut off, statements may be difficult to interpret, only a portion of the attendees choose to participate or get a chance to have their say. To supplement and complement the data from community meetings, an ethnographic moral atmosphere interview and a school dilemma interview were developed. The ethnographic interview asks very general questions about participation in decision making and the fairness of school rules and discipline (Power and Kohlberg, 1984). The school dilemma interview asks students about particular problems, like drug use or stealing, that are common to many high-school settings.

An elaborate scheme for categorizing responses to the two interviews has been developed (Power and Kohlberg, 1984). The scheme has been extrapolated from the ethnographic and school dilemma interviews but is not dependent on them. Researchers or staff members of a school can pose questions and invent dilemmas that are best suited to the issues they want to explore and still use the developmental sequence of this scheme. This is in contrast to the assessment of individual stage of moral development, as tested by the Moral Judgment Interview, which has validity only if administered strictly according to protocol and assessed by matching to criterion judgments.

THE SCHOOL CLIMATE QUESTIONNAIRE

The School Climate Questionnaire (SCQ), designed by Higgins and Kohlberg, is a group-administered instrument consisting of sixty-eight items that can be completed in about thirty minutes. The first part of the SCQ focuses on student perceptions of the social, moral, and academic atmosphere of the school. Students rate items about rules and typical kinds of social relationships, as they believe they are perceived by most of the student body, on a five-point scale from false to true. An advantage of the questionnaire is that it is simple to administer and score. The summing of scores from students within a particular school can be contrasted with the scores from students in other schools and differences in perceived school climate emerge clearly. The weakness of the questionnaire is that it fails to probe beneath the surface of student impressions; therefore it is an adjunct to, rather than a substitute for, more fine-grained measures.

THE MORAL CULTURE SURVEY

The Moral Culture Survey (MCS) designed by Power as a follow-up to the SCQ, consists of "practical school dilemmas" (Power, Higgins, and Kohlberg, 1989, pp. 246-247). The dilemmas were extrapolated from recurrent crises in the various just community schools and deal with issues of cheating, stealing, fighting, drugs, and alcohol. Each dilemma takes about twenty minutes to complete and can be administered individually or to a group. It is more difficult to complete than the SCQ and requires more supervision.

> Each questionnaire consists of the same general pattern of items. It begins with a series of general items about a particular rule or expectation. . . . These items assess whether the teachers enforce the rule conscientiously, fairly, and consistently and the extent to which students comply with the rule or expectation. The next two sections of the questionnaire deal with what we call the phase or strength of the norm. Both sections consist of the same items. The students first respond whether the items are true or false for them personally. They indicate for how many others (none or very few, some, many, most, or all) those items are true. These scales indicate the extent to which students are committed to uphold the norms and rules of their program or school. Students are initially asked whether they or others even care about the rule in question, and finally whether they or others would be willing to report the violator of the rule (Power, 1988, pp. 7-8).

The last section of the MCS asks students to justify the reasons for rules, and this makes it possible to look specifically at the stage of reasoning students use in elaborating the two specifically moral value orientations; those dealing with fairness and community. "Because you might get caught and punished" is clearly a Stage 1 response, "because the teachers will feel let down" is a Stage 3 response, etc.

Why did Kohlberg, Higgins, and Power decide to use a moral culture survey instead of the MJI or the widely used DIT of James Rest? Their research indicated that an aggregate of individual norms was not the same as a group norm. Students generally reason below their individual intellectual competence when dealing with school-related issues (Power, Higgins, and Kohlberg, 1989). Just community programs were designed to bridge the judgment-performance gap. In the just community programs the development of moral reasoning competence (as measured by the MJI) often follows upon the development of performance-related reasoning (Power, 1988, p. 10). Despite the way group norms are reflected in individual interviews about the moral culture of the school, when the actual statements made by students in Class Meetings are analyzed, the group norms reflected in these statements more closely resembles the thinking of higher-stage students than it does a class average of individual scores.

The categorization of responses, reflecting the perceived moral culture of the school during community meetings and on questionnaires, is complex. In the Kohlberg et al. scheme described by Power, Higgins, and Kohlberg (1989), just community norms are analyzed according to their degree of collectiveness, their phase, and their stage. Just community values are analyzed in terms of institutional valuing and the stage of institutional valuing. Unless one is engaged in basic research—or has to report in detail to a funding agency—school personnel is not likely to need so fine-grained an analytic structure.

Table 9-1
The Degrees of the Collectiveness of Norms

Individual-Based Norms or Descriptions of Lack of Collective Norm

1. I—Rejection:	No one can make a rule or agreement in this school which would be followed or taken seriously. No group constituency. I as an individual. Descriptive.
2. I—Conscience:	An action in accordance with the norm should not be expected or demanded by the group because it should be left to each individual's free choice. No group constituency. I as an individual. Prescriptive or possibly descriptive.
3. I—No awareness:	Does not perceive the existence of a shared norm concerning this issue and does not take a position pro or con about the group's developing such a norm. Also does not have an individual norm concerning this issue. No group constituency. I as an individual. Descriptive.
4. I—Individual:	An action should be performed which is in accordance with the norm where this action is not defined or implied by membership in the group. There is no suggestion that the task of the group is or should be to develop or promote the norm. Universal constituency applied to people in the group as much as to people outside the group. I as an individual. Prescriptive.
5. I—Individual ambiguous:	An action should be performed which is in accordance with the norm where this action is implied by membership in the group. Ambiguous constituency but seems to apply to people in the group more than to those outside. I as an individual. Prescriptive.

Authority Norms

6. Authority:	An action should be performed because it is expressed or

demanded by the teacher or administrator whose authority derives from his/her status or the law which makes the teacher a superior member of the group. Group constituency. Teacher as authority. Prescriptive or descriptive.

7. Authority—acceptance:	An action should be performed because it is expected by authority or law with the clear implication that the group accepts this authority and thinks promoting and upholding the norm is in the interest of the group's welfare. Group constituency. Teacher as authority. Prescriptive.

Aggregate Norms

8. They—aggregate (I disagree):	They, the group or a substantial subgroup, have a tendency to act in accordance with a norm in a way that the individual speaker does not share or disagrees with. Group constituency. I as a member of the group. Prescriptive or descriptive.
9. I and they—aggregate	They and I have a tendency to act in the same way in accordance with a norm. Group constituency. I and they as members of the group. Prescriptive or descriptive.

Collective Norms

10. Limiting or proposing I:	The speaker thinks the group or all members of the group should follow or uphold this norm better or should have this new norm. (This category overlaps with phase I.) Group constituency. I as a member of the group. Prescriptive.
11. Spontaneous—collective:	They or they and I think that group members should act in accordance with the norm *because* they feel naturally motivated to do so as a result of the sense of belonging to the group. Group constituency. They and I as members of the group. Descriptive.
12. They—limited collective:	They think that group members should act in accordance with the norm without the speaker identifying her/himself with that normative expectation. The speaker differentiates her/his own normative perspective. Group constituency. They as members of the group. Prescriptive.
13. I and they—limited collective:	Both I and they, as members of the group, think that group members should act in accordance with the norm. Group constituency. I and they as members of the group. Perscriptive.

14. Implicit—we collective:	The members of this group think that all of us should act in accordance with the norm. Group constituency. We (implicit) as members of the group. Perscriptive.
15. We explicit— collective:	We, the members of this group, think that we should act in accordance with the norm. Group constituency. We (explicit) as members of the group. Perscriptive.

Reprinted from Power, Higgins, and Kohlberg (1989), pp. 121-123.

STAGING GROUP NORMS

The scale for institutional valuing rises from 0) rejection; the school is not valued), through 1) instrumental-extrinsic; the school is valued as an institution that helps individuals meet their own needs; 2) enthusiastic identification; as at special moments, as when a team wins a victory; 3) spontaneous community; where members feel close and ready to help each other; and 4) normative community; where the community is valued for its own sake and expects members to uphold group norms and responsibilities (Power, Higgins, and Kohlberg, 1989, pp. 117-118). This is not a developmental scale; it is a scale based upon a subjective value orientation. It is a value orientation that many educators may seek and share, but one would not—and perhaps should not—expect all social institutions to aim toward, or achieve, a "4" on this scale. Thus, one would wish that the primary school or work affiliation be characterized by democracy and affiliation, but music schools, ski clubs, and many other social/educational institutions may legitimately aspire to a "1" or "2" on this scale.

The sense of community valuing can be "staged." Thus at Stage 2, there is no clear sense of community apart from exchanges among group members designed to meet their individual or overlapping needs. At Stage 3, the group is valued for the friendliness of its members. At Stage 4, membership in the community is understood in terms of entering a social contract to respect the norms and ideals of the group (Power, Higgins, and Kohlberg, 1989, pp. 119-120).

"Listening with the third ear" for the *collectiveness* of group norms during class discussions is instructive. The fifteen-point scale is complex but ultimately illuminating. If the researcher wishes, instead of looking at all fifteen categories on the scale, the degree of collectiveness can be analyzed according to the four major categories under which the fifteen are grouped. They are 1) individual-based norms or descriptions of lack of collective norm, 2) authority norms, 3) aggregate norms, and 4) collective norms. Criteria can be considered in terms of 1) affiliative constituency, b) speaker perspective, and 3) prescriptivity. Listening for the collectiveness of group norms is important when educators feel that it is not sufficient that students have high standards as individuals, but that the school as a whole needs collective standards. Schools in which violence and drug use are pervasive need to look at the school culture through this lens.

Collective norms can be viewed in terms of *phases,* starting with Phase 0, where no collective norm exists or is proposed (Power, Higgins, and Kohlberg, 1989, pp. 129-132). In Phase 1, collective norms are proposed for group acceptance; in Phase 2, they are accepted as a group ideal but not expected as behavior; in Phase 3, the collective norm is accepted and agreed to but not (yet) expected as behavior. Collective norm expectation is naively accepted in Phase 4, and accepted but not followed in Phase 5. By Phase 6, collective norms are expected and upheld through persuasion, and in Phase 7, collective norms are expected and upheld through reporting. Phases are helpful ways of viewing the difficulties adolescents encounter in upholding group standards when they interfere with friendships and group loyalty.

Norms prescribe a particular value, for example, trust, care or respect for property, and *elements* refer to terminal values justifying the upholding of a norm, such as group harmony or community welfare (Power, Higgins, and Kohlberg, 1989, p. 115). The most conceptually difficult problem in the Kohlberg et al. methodology concerns the sense in which it is possible to speak about a stage structure of shared expectations and values that is distinct from an individual stage structure.

Although we refer to collective norms and elements as having a stage, we do not wish to imply that collective stages are the same as Kohlberg's stages of moral reasoning. . . . First of all, only individuals think. We do not believe in a "group mind," even though we do maintain that individuals interacting in groups construct common norms, which in turn influence their thinking in the group. The construction of such common norms reflect reasoning performance not moral reasoning competence. Collective stages are not derived immediately from the moral reasoning of individual group members but through their actual interactions or performance in group contexts (Power, Higgins, and Kohlberg, 1989, p. 137).

While individual development is traced from Stage 0 or 1, the starting point for collective development depends both on individual development and institutional interaction. Individual stages may set an upper limit but not a lower limit for the collective stage. For example, in a school with students reasoning at Stage 3 and 4, the collective stage may be as low as Stage 1 or 2, but not higher than Stage 4. Collective stages may regress because, unlike competencies, performances may fluctuate, and because each year's graduates are replaced with a younger and generally less-developed freshman class (Power, Higgins, and Kohlberg, 1989, p. 137).

Are collective stages really logical structures or are they contents that change in a sequence analogous to the structural development of the individual stages? Research still to come should lead to greater confidence in addressing this question. In the meanwhile, the state of the art in analyzing the moral culture of the school, and assessing collective versus individual moral development, can be a boon to school reform and school transformation.

PART III

KOHLBERG FOR THE RELIGIOUS
EDUCATION PRACTITIONER

Chapter 10

The Kohlberg Perspective on the Influence of Religious Education on Moral Development

Lisa Kuhmerker

INTRODUCTION

Lawrence Kohlberg devoted his professional life to three monumental concerns: 1) the study of the sequential development of the capacity to reason about issues of justice, 2) the assessment of the structure of thinking about issues of justice that are at the root of making moral judgments, and 3) the bridge from theory and research to the creation and encouragement of moral education programs.

Kohlberg focused on the *structure* of thinking about moral issues and saw religious beliefs as part of the *content* of thinking about moral issues. His view was consonant with the principles of our constitutional government—that it is the public school's role to foster the capacity to reason about moral issues, without "teaching" the belief system of any organized group, whether or not all or most of the parents in the community, state, or nation held to a specific set of beliefs.

This does not mean that Kohlberg's research findings and suggested teaching strategies cannot be used by religious educators. As a matter of fact, it is Kohlberg's focus on the *structure* of the developing capacity for reasoning about social justice, rather than upon its *content,* that has made his work so relevant to theologians and religious educators of widely divergent points of view.

MORAL EDUCATION AND RELIGIOUS INSTRUCTION

Religious instruction has multiple goals, involving the transmission of traditional cultural values as well as precepts for human behavior. Moral education as education for justice, which is the way Kohlberg viewed it, is *one* of these multiple goals. Moral education in this sense is "content-free," and thus acceptable within the context of any religious denomination. While religious denominations vary in the emphasis they put on rote learning versus discussion of moral issues, during Kohlberg's lifetime many religious educators coming from Catholic, Protestant, and Jewish institutions adopted his strategy for using dilemma discussions for sharpening awareness of justice issues.

During the 1960s and 1970s Kohlberg defined the aim of moral education as stimulating movement to the next stage of moral development and saw dilemma discussions as the process for stimulating this movement. He saw this approach as going beyond the relativism of the value clarification approach because it stressed that there is an order of adequacy in moral reasoning, while at the same time it is not indoctrinative because it does not directly teach or impose particular values to students (Kohlberg, 1974, p. 10).

Kohlberg believed that a philosophic basis for moral education is to be found in natural law statements of moral philosophy and theology. "The natural law perspective holds that there are universal or natural principles of justice which should guide all societies and which are known to man by reason and independent of specific religious revelation" (Kohlberg, 1974, p. 5).

Kohlberg emphasized that we need to stress the natural sense of justice in the child because of the social scientific popularity of the opposite doctrine, claiming that the child's values come from outside himself, from his parents and his culture through processes of indoctrination, modeling, reward and punishment (Kohlberg, 1974, p. 8).

Kohlberg then used as example his son's decision at age four that it was wrong to kill animals and that, therefore, everyone should be a vegetarian (which was not a belief consonant with the eating patterns of the Kohlberg family at that time) to illustrate that children often generate their own moral values and maintain them in the face of cultural training and that these values have universal roots.

Again and again, Kohlberg stressed that while the child is a moral philosopher with his own sense of justice, the child's view is very different from our adult principles of justice. "This difference is a qualitative difference in thinking, it is not just a difference in degree of knowledge or sophistication. This is basically what the theory of moral stages means, that the thinking of children is qualitatively different from the adult's. . . . We have found these differences in every culture we have studied (Taiwan, Turkey, India, Mexico, Great Britain, Israel) occurring always in the same order" (Kohlberg, 1974, pp. 6-7).

Kohlberg then raises the question of the relation between moral development and faith development: "We have stressed so far the place of universal principles of human justice as central to moral development. . . . We need to note now that while Socrates and Martin Luther King died for principles of human justice they were also deeply religious men. What then is the relation of the development of religious faith to the development of moral principles?" (Kohlberg, 1974, p. 11).

THEORIES OF FAITH DEVELOPMENT

When activities designed to stimulate moral development are used within a religious setting, there is some hope and expectation that such development in some way parallels or stimulates increasingly more comprehensive levels of faith development. However, whether such a connection exists and how it functions is by no means clear. Kohlberg participated with educators and clergy in theorizing about parallels between moral development and faith development. Two individuals whose work in this field is prominent are James Fowler of the Faith Development Center at Emory University in Atlanta and Fritz Oser of the University of Fribourg (Switzerland). Both were in dialogue with Kohlberg over a period of many years. Their influence led Kohlberg to postulate parallels between stage development and faith development, but Kohlberg never carried out experimental studies to test these parallels.

Kohlberg's analyses and speculations about moral development and religion are brought together in Chapter 9 of his volume *The Philosophy of Moral Development* (Kohlberg, 1984), entitled "Moral Development, Religious Thinking, and the Question of Stage Seven."

It is worthy of note that Kohlberg begins this chapter by reemphasizing that it is both possible and important that moral education in the public schools of a democracy have a foundation independent of religion; that the basis of such education should be universal principles of justice, not particular religious or personal values, no matter how widely held they may be (Kohlberg, 1984, pp. 311-312). He emphasizes that the constitutional argument for the independence of public moral education from religious education has not been invalidated, despite the fact that a vocal and influential minority takes issue with this position.

Kohlberg asserts that such critics of the separation of church and state fail to distinguish between morality based on "natural law"—which holds that there are universal principles of justice that should guide all societies, and that are known to us by reason independent of specific religious revelation or faith—versus morality based on a specific creed and revelation (Kohlberg, 1984, pp. 313-314). Kohlberg calls these critics "divine command theorists" and asserts that they are correct in fearing Socratic dialogue as a danger, but as a danger to their own theories, rather than to the goals of moral education (Kohlberg, 1984, p. 314).

Socrates and Martin Luther King are Kohlberg's two great exemplar moral educators in the "natural law" mode. He identifies both as profoundly religious men, willing to die for their principles, which are partly based on their faith in reason and partly on their faith in justice which has a religious support (Kohlberg, 1984, p. 318).

Taking up the psychological question of the relationship of religious thinking to stages of moral judgment, Kohlberg notes that their primary functions are different. In Kohlberg's view, the function of moral thinking is to resolve competing claims among individuals on the basis of principle. In contrast, Kohlberg assumes that "the primary function of religious reasoning is to affirm life and morality as related to a transcendent or infinite ground or sense of the whole" (Kohlberg, 1984, p. 321). In other words, moral reasoning asks "how/why live justly?" while religious inquiry focuses on "why live?" Thus religion addresses questions that arise at the boundary of moral reasoning. They pertain to the moral domain but are not answerable in terms of moral discourse (Kohlberg, 1984, pp. 322-323).

THE SEARCH FOR A STAGE MODEL
FOR FAITH DEVELOPMENT

In their jointly-authored chapter on the exploration of moral development, religious thinking, and the question of a seventh stage (Kohlberg, 1984, pp. 311-372), Kohlberg and Clark Power integrate their experience with the stage model derived from the extensive research growing out of the refinement of the Moral Judgment Interview (MJI), with the proposed stage models of Fowler (1976) and Oser (1980). Both Fowler and Oser draw on interview material for their stage theories, but their research bases differ in scope, rigor, and extensiveness, and are only partly comparable to research on reasoning derived from the MJI. Differences in the content from which the structure of thinking is derived must also be considered. The structure of the stages of moral reasoning have been abstracted from dilemmas involving conflicts of interest among human beings in interaction. In contrast, a large proportion of the content from which faith stages have been inferred derive from the attitudes of subjects toward the nonhuman, toward belief in the supernatural. These factors underscore the tentativeness with which all hypotheses of faith development must be viewed at this point in time.

One reason Kohlberg and Power construct their own version of faith stages is that in Fowler's approach to faith no clear distinction may be drawn between one's stage of faith and one's stage of morality because each moral stage presupposes faith, even if such faith is tacit. "We believe, however, that Fowler's broad definition of faith, which does not distinguish it from moral judgment, leads to confusions—confusions that make the study of the relationship of religion and morality more difficult" (Kohlberg, 1984, p. 335).

This is not meant to deny a certain unity to the development of the valuing activity of the human personality. However, Kohlberg identifies this unity as ethical development, rather than moral or religious development (Kohlberg, 1984, p. 336).

In their chapter on "Moral Development, Religious Thinking, and the Question of a Seventh Stage," Kohlberg and Power describe a stage sequence for religious concepts that parallels the stage model for moral development and stresses evolving conceptions of a deity (Kohlberg, 1984, pp. 340-344):

At Stage 1, when children's thinking is rooted in a sense of obedience to adults, whose authority is based on their superior physical characteristics, the deity is also viewed as larger and more powerful than life; capable of making everything happen. At Stage 2, when children base their moral reasoning on a sense of fairness in concrete exchanges, they also see their relationship to God as based on fair exchange. As one child put it: "You be good to God, and he'll be good to you." God can be influenced by personal prayer and religious practice.

At Stage 3, when moral judgments are based to a great degree on a desire to meet the expectations of family, friends, and community, and when mutual trust is recognized as a primary value, God is similarly viewed as a trusted and trusting deity. Divine authority is now tempered by mercy, and the breaking of moral norms hurts God and brings shame upon the perpetrator of bad deeds.

At Stage 4, when a concern for maintaining the social system is seen as primary, the role of the deity as "law-giver" and "supreme being" overrides the personalistic view of God in the previous stages. It is no longer assumed that God will, or should, intervene in one's personal life.

Beyond the conventional stages of moral reasoning about natural and supernatural matters, it becomes increasingly more complex to try to "stage" degrees of principled religious thinking. To Kohlberg, the recognition that a "just" society must respect the rights of individuals is primary to Stage 5, and thus he sees a Stage 5 view of the deity as one who supports autonomous moral action. Stage 6 is assumed to involve a cosmic, perhaps a pantheistic, view of the universe. In speculations about the "highest" stages of a worldview that incorporates faith, Kohlberg sometimes identifies such a stage as either Stage 6 or Stage 7.

Kohlberg's claim that "religion is a conscious response to, and an expression of, the quest for ultimate meaning for moral judgment and action" (Kohlberg, 1984, p. 336) leads him to the hypothesis that moral stage development is necessary but not sufficient for development of a parallel stage of religious development. "Put in slightly different terms, the idea that development of moral principles is necessary but not sufficient for a metaphysics of morals . . . represents the idea that one moves from a better known or more certain to the more unknown or speculative" (Kohlberg, 1984, p. 337).

Identifying "moral" stages as necessary but not sufficient for parallel "religious" stages does not imply that Kohlberg visualized the postulated religious stages as "higher" or "better." A potential source of confusion about "higher" or "better" may come from the fact that Kohlberg sometimes identified the top level of the postulated faith development as Stage 6 and sometimes as a Stage 7 attached to his well-known six-stage model.

Kohlberg saw the ultimate goal of religious development as coming to terms with the meaning of life and the reasons why people should choose to live. He made no claim to certainty in his personal life or his theory building. One confirmation of the tentativeness of his theory building at the upper stages of faith and religious commitment is implicitly reflected in the fact that these concerns were not concretized in a scoring system with criterion judgments for rating subjects' responses.

THE QUESTION OF STAGE SEVEN: A SEVENTH RELIGIOUS STAGE GOING BEYOND JUSTICE PRINCIPLES

Kohlberg and Power (Kohlberg, 1984) raise this issue because they feel that while questions about moral behavior can be answered in both secular and religious ways at Stages 1 through 5, at Stage 6 universal ethical principles cannot be immediately justified by the realities of the human social order. "The religious orientation required by universal moral principles I have in the past called 'Stage 7' (Kohlberg, 1973a, 1973b) although the term is only a metaphor—used because it presupposes the conflicts and questions that arise at moral Stage 6" (Kohlberg, 1984, p. 344).

Kohlberg uses the metaphorical notion of a Stage 7 in order to seek a solution that is compatible with rational universal ethics. "The characteristics of all these Stage 7 solutions is that they involve contemplative experiences of a nondualistic variety. The logic of such experience is sometimes expressed in theistic terms of union with God, but it need not be (Kohlberg, 1984, pp. 114-115).

In religious writing, Kohlberg claims the movement to Stage 7 begins with despair. "The resolution of the despair which we have called Stage 7 represents a continuation of the process of taking a cosmic perspective whose first phase is despair" (Kohlberg, 1984, p. 345).

Marcus Aurelius' memoirs are cited as exemplars of natural law reasoning at "the metaphoric Stage 7" (Kohlberg, 1984, pp. 345-346). Another version of the striving for a cosmic perspective on morality is closer to the Greek concept of *agape* and is illustrated by quotations from a seventy-eight-year-old woman, whose philosophy could be called "responsible love" (Kohlberg, 1984, pp. 347-352). The contrast between the two examples suggests to Kohlberg that there may be somewhat different endpoints in ethical development than described in the successive stages of justice (Kohlberg, 1984, p. 354). The philosophic theories of Dewey, Kant, Spinoza, and Teilhard de Chardin are evoked and analyzed in this context (Kohlberg, 1984, pp. 356-369).

In summary, Kohlberg's view of a psychological theory of religious stages rests on metaphysical and religious assumptions consistent with, but not reducible to, rational science and morality. While Kohlberg claimed that there is a single definable structure for a sixth or highest stage of moral reasoning, a highest level of ethical or religious thinking is much less unitary and definable. Nevertheless, such speculations are essential for understanding human development (Kohlberg, 1984, pp. 371-372).

THE FAITH DEVELOPMENT STUDIES OF FOWLER AND OSER: PSYCHOLOGICAL STUDIES THAT SHARE A KOHLBERGIAN PERSPECTIVE

That religious beliefs are developmental, and can be investigated in all their dimensions, is consonant with Kohlbergian theory and research and is a significant line of inquiry for ongoing study. To date, the best-known line of inquiry has been James Fowler's theory of the stages of faith (Fowler, 1976). While Fowler bases his theory on extensive interviews, his research methodology has not had the same rigor and extensiveness as Kohlberg's Moral Judgment Interview and the criterion judgments developed and validated in the two volumes on the measurement of moral judgment (Colby, Kohlberg, et al., 1987). It is a suggestive theory, not a definitive developmental map.

Kohlberg and Fowler's dialogue about stages of faith extended over the last fifteen years of Kohlberg's life. While calling them "preliminary definitions," Kohlberg included extensive descriptions of Fowler's faith stages in his address to the National Catholic Education Association (Cleveland, 1984) and in the article, "Education, Moral Development, and Faith," which was an extended version of that address (Kohlberg, 1985).

Fowler sequences faith from the first stage, called *intuitive-projective*, to the *mythical-literal* stage, followed by a *synthetic-conventional* stage, an *individual-reflexive* stage, a *polar-dialectical* stage, and ultimately a *universalizing* stage (Fowler, 1976). Fowler believes that his conceptual scheme not only helps us to assess development in the growing child and adult but also provides the leader of a religious congregation with insights that can help him or her to foster the growth of adults individually and in interaction. In this sense, Fowler's work parallels Kohlberg's efforts during the last ten or more years of his life to connect moral development with the fostering of community (Kohlberg, 1970a, 1970b, 1970c, 1981, 1984, 1985; Power, Higgins, and Kohlberg, 1989).

How does faith development relate to moral stages? Kohlberg expected a parallel development. He felt that the critical question both psychologically and philosophically is whether moral development precedes (and causes) faith development or vise versa. Contrary to Fowler, Kohlberg's hypothesis was that moral development precedes development to the parallel faith stage. "Philosophically I incline to Kant's solution, that faith is grounded in moral reason because moral reason 'requires' faith rather than that moral reason is grounded in faith (Kohlberg, 1984, p. 124).

Fritz Oser (1980), a professor of educational psychology at the University of Fribourg who undertook postdoctoral studies with Kohlberg at the Center for Moral Education, is also at work on the construction of a stage theory for religious development. Oser's research strategies parallel Kohlberg's closely, but the content is Oser's, not Kohlberg's, as is illustrated by Oser's dilemma.

Oser created a dilemma about a medical student who—in a moment of crisis when he thinks his plane will crash—promises God that he will devote his life to the poor in Africa. To keep this promise to God means leaving his native land and breaking the promise to his fiancee to marry her. It also means saying "no" to an offer for an excellent medical practice in his own country.

Oser posits a six-stage sequence of cognitive stages of religious development, moving from a totally deterministic orientation (Stage 1), through reciprocity (Stage 2), an orientation toward volunteerism (Stage 3), an orientation on personal autonomy and a "Divine Plan" (Stage 4), self-fulfillment and intersubjectivity (Stage 5), to an orientation based on universal communication and solidarity (Stage 6) (Oser, 1980, pp. 292-307). Oser's work has considerable influence in Europe, but his contact with American psychologists also continues. Current work ties developmental theory to teaching style and teaching strategies. Mimeographed research papers are published with some frequency and are available in English as well as German and French.

KOHLBERG AS SEEN FROM THE PERSPECTIVES OF RELIGIOUS EDUCATIONISTS

In his overview of Christian religious education and moral development, James Michael Lee (Lee, 1980) attributes interest in Kohlberg's theories and research to the major position that activities designed to foster moral reasoning have in every denomination, and—not incidentally—that in an age of natural and social science many Christian educationists like to feel that they have science on their side. Also Kohlberg is highly regarded by many Christian religious educators because his views are grounded in solid provable empirical research. However, Lee is quick to point out that many Christian religious educationists focus simply on the bald stage descriptions given by Kohlberg instead of going deeper into Kohlberg's work and applying these depths to religious education. "Alas," says Lee, "those whom religious educationists would wittingly or unwittingly destroy, they first trivialize."

Lee forthrightly acknowledges that Kohlberg's view that the course of moral judgment lies in the human development process itself runs counter to the basic tenets of those who hold that theology provides the ultimate explanation and grounding for both moral development and religion teaching. "Defenders of the theological approach argue that growth in personal morality as well as in other phases of Christian living comes from an extrinsic source, typically identified as the mysterious and unfathomable action of the Holy Spirit" (Lee, 1980, p. 328).

Supporters of the theological approach to Christian education assert that empirical research such as Kohlberg's cannot measure the mysterious and unfathomable ways in which God works. "In other words, advocates of the theological approach to religious education attempt to sidestep or evade Kohlberg's data by spookifying reality" (Lee, 1980).

Lee rejects the theological position that would make God an extrinsic variable in the process of moral development. To accept Kohlberg's findings, says Lee, "is not to de-godize God. Rather, Kohlberg's findings suggest how God works in this world. Kohlberg's research data clearly imply that if God does exist, then he works in and through the process of human development, rather than by some extrinsic 'zap' of grace" (Lee, 1980, p. 329).

At the same time that Lee staunchly defends Kohlberg against theologically based religious educators who explain human understanding solely through revelation rather giving heavy weight to reasoning, Lee questions Kohlberg's claim concerning the autonomy of morality from religion. "Kohlberg operationally defines religion as religious affiliation. Thus his data do not show that morality is autonomous from religion but rather from religious affiliation" (Lee, 1980, p. 33). Furthermore, Lee points out that if Kohlberg states that activities engaged in by the self are developmental, and "religion is an activity engaged in by the self," then religion is developmental and can be investigated directly or indirectly in all its dimensions (Lee, 1980, p. 336).

One might well ask, however, how Kohlberg might have studied the influence of religious education, other than to have correlated it with the process of being religiously affiliated. To look for other causes brings us back once more to assumptions of the "extrinsic 'zap' of grace" or the secular Piagetian-Kohlbergian assertion that the developing self is the constructor of its own philosophy.

Despite the objections of supporters of the theological approach to religious education, Kohlberg's demonstration of the developmental nature of the capacity to reason about issues of justice has been cited by many religious educationists who want to move religious instruction from indoctrination to the nurturing of the human capacity toward personal autonomy within a religious framework. Thus, reason and personal choice—rather than conformity—are the features that make the Kohlbergian vision relevant to the British religious educationist Michael Grimmitt (Grimmitt, 1987, pp. 59-92). Likewise, Kohlberg's emphasis on the developmental nature of reasoning about moral issues strikes a responsive chord with the French religious educationist Didier-Jacques Piveteau and his American colleague J.T. Dillon (Piveteau and Dillon, 1977, p. 44), because it supports their position that religious education should be based on the psychological, rather than the chronological, age of the learner; a prescription previously affirmed by James Michael Lee (Lee, 1977, pp. 122-125).

Kohlberg's research has important consequences for teaching the sacraments, according to Robert Browning and his liturgist colleague Roy Reed. Since the sacraments take hold of a person according to the level of the individual's human development, Kohlberg's developmental theory has important and immediate consequences for sacramental preparation (Browning and Reed, 1985, pp. 260-263).

Religious educationists working with young people at all age levels have been influenced by Kohlbergian theory and the teaching strategies that have been extrapolated from them. Lucie Barber finds the use of dilemma discussions with elementary school children more far-reaching and organic than the values clarification approach (Barber, 1984). Don Richter stresses that religious education for youth should utilize the peer influence characteristic of adolescents at Stage 3. He believes that face-to-face relationships with significant peers heavily influence individual religious choice, much more so than television and other vicarious experiences (Wyckoff and Richter, 1982, pp. 228-232).

Kohlbergian research, especially when combined with James Fowler's research on faith development (Fowler, 1983), is an important tool for the religious educator of young adult in the view of Sharon Merriam and Trenton Ferro, who urge that young people not be "lumped together" into the single nondevelopmental category of young adults (Foltz, 1986, pp. 68-69). Similarly, James White finds that Kohlbergian developmental research has implications for adult development and for intergenerational religious education. White emphasizes that since adults are at various developmental stages they can forge links with children and youth who are at the same developmental level. Furthermore, and perhaps more importantly, intergenerational religious education can expose young people to the more developmentally advanced thinking of some older persons (White, 1988, pp. 105-130).

Kohlbergian theory has even been embraced by some administrators of religious institutions and by parish directors of religious education. Donald Bossart finds Kohlbergian theory helpful in addressing the positive role of conflict in the interpersonal relations of church administrators. Just as a certain amount of internal dissonance is involved in moving from one stage to another, so also there is a certain kind of interpersonal dissonance necessary in order for persons working together to move to new levels of cooperation and organizational achievement. Thus Kohlberg's research can lead to new basic understandings of the way in which a "corporate faith" is built (Bossart, 1980, pp. 166-171). Similarly, Donald Emler (Emler, 1989) notes that Kohlbergian research findings suggest a kind of transactional teaching style in which the religious educator weaves lessons which can enable learners to develop in the rational understanding of their religion.

Among the liberationist theorists that find Kohlberg's work highly relevant to religious education is Daniel Schipani, who feels that Kohlberg's approach inherently contains a message of liberation from restrictive patterns of moral reasoning, thus organically leading to better forms of understanding in the quest for social justice (Schipani, 1988, p. 21). From a neo-Marxist perspective, Thomas Groome sees Kohlberg's work as a developmentalist who affirms the necessity for an ongoing dialectic, within religious education, between the individual and sociopolitical forces (Groome, 1980, pp. 125-126).

In "Faith, Justice, and Kohlberg," Stephen Rowntree, a Jesuit who speaks for the liberal Catholic position that Kohlberg's work in education has something to say to the Christian concern "for a faith that does justice" (Rowntree, 1978):

Today's Church is convinced that faith, as our response to God's saving love manifested in Christ, requires action to change unjust social structures. . . . A commitment to transforming unjust social structures was not always the Church's understanding of the implications of faith, as I will show. Understanding why the Church makes this commitment today is crucial to understanding why we should be concerned with Kohlberg's theory of moral development (Rowntree, 1978, p. 230). . . .

The central element of the current Catholic understanding of the relation of faith to justice is that *faith requires action to change the unjust structures of society.* This statement of the relation of faith to justice would have puzzled St. Paul and the early Christians. We must carefully note the issue. The issue is not whether faith involves deeds of love and justice. . . . The issue is whether faith and Christian love involve action to transform social structures. Christian love relativized and rendered unimportant all social distinctions yet left them intact (Rowntree, 1978, pp. 232-234).

Since Judaism has the longest tradition of all the major Western religions, and each historical period of Jewish civilization has added nuances to the intimate relationship between religion and ethics, to ask whether a given approach to moral education is "good" Jewish education begs the question, according to Jeffrey Schein, a member of the Reconstructionist Jewish Movement. The importance of Kohlberg in Schein's view is that he has turned upside down our conception of education. "Previously, moral education has often been conceived of as a passive process; it was the values of a culture or group instilled in the individual. Kohlberg's work pointed to the active ways in which the individual constructs his or her own picture of moral reality" (Schein, *The Reconstructionist*, March 1985, p. 16).

Coming from a somewhat different perspective, Barry Chazan sets out to show that both the rabbinic and modern Jewish tradition seek to create and maintain an emotional identification with tradition that precedes the capacity to reason and a sense of affiliation he does not find in Kohlberg's primary focus on moral reasoning (Chazan, 1980).

Perhaps more importantly, Chazan sees the modern distinction between religion and morality (implicit in much of the theory and practice of contemporary education, including Kohlberg) as nonexistent and inconceivable from the classical Jewish view. Chazan quotes from Reimer: "To have asked of traditional Judaism how it conceived of the relation of religion to morality would have been to ask an incomprehensible question. 'Religion' and 'morality' did not exist for Judaism as separate categories distinct from one another: rather Judaism understands faith—the way a man stands in relation to God—to be fundamentally ethical" (Reimer, 1970, p. 1).

The uniqueness of the Jewish ethic, then, was not so much in its emphasis on the moral way but on the unification of the moral way with the godly. Justice is an obligation to God (Chazan, 1980, p. 301). Furthermore, the Jewish ethic is a practical rather than a contemplative art. Jewish ethics are formulated in specific laws, practices, parables, and tales which are all aimed at daily practice and behavior. The key means for realization of the good life is study, and study is important because of its central impact on right action (Chazan, 1980, p. 303).

Thus, Kohlberg's assertion of the primacy of justice is very "Jewish," and his lifelong preoccupation with ethical issues is very much in the Talmudic tradition. The difference lies in the fact that Kohlberg never felt he had to justify man's moral behavior to man in terms of an obligation to a deity.

Kohlberg's assumption about the autonomy of morality, which is the primary source of his appeal to some informed religious persons, is also the source of his greatest difficulty with others. Speaking for the Christian with a liberal orientation, James Lee asserts that religious education is an educational, not a theological, goal. Theological goals become important and real when they are first translated into psychological processes. Morality—and thus by implication, religious faith—is not something wholly mysterious or utterly beyond the reach of human facilitation. Subject matter and teaching procedures dynamically interact in the teaching-learning act (Munsey, 1980, pp. 326-355). For Lee, Kohlberg's theory and research illuminate some of the most basic issues in religious education (Thompson, 1982, pp. 165-177).

GUIDELINES FOR PARENTS AND EDUCATORS WHO WANT TO FOSTER RELIGIOUS AWARENESS AND COMMITMENT

Lawrence Kohlberg did not explicitly address himself to this subject in print. Thus, these suggestions are the author's but are consistent with Kohlberg's theories and convictions.

1) Support moral education programs in public school settings. The public school's effort to help children to reason about issues of fairness and justice, to take the perspective of another, to be a responsible member of the school community—these support the human developmental process. Fostering such growth enables children to reason about all issues, including religious issues, in increasingly mature ways.

2) In private and parochial school settings, use your influence to foster programs that give children a role in decision making and the creation of rules for the common good. Faith and belief should support reason and responsible behavior; faith should not be a substitute for reasoning and moral action.

3) Part-time religious education programs provide opportunities for broadening children's social perspectives. They should contribute to children's identification as members of a group but also help children to feel comfortable with people holding different beliefs.

4) No matter how young the children or how brief the program, teachers in

such programs need to help children to understand both "non-negotiable rules" and those issues where it is relevant for them to create and enforce their own rules. (For example, there may need to be some non-negotiable rules about the use and clean-up of materials that are used by various groups throughout the week. On the other hand, sharing these resources fairly during program time should be the outcome of democratic decision making.) No matter how brief a Sunday school session may be, we cannot "skip" this social foundation in favor of more religious instruction.

5) Use your influence to incorporate a social service and action component into the religious education program of your denomination.

6) Be on the lookout for children's tendency to divide the world into "we" and "they" in terms of "good" and "bad." Religious education programs have a responsibility not merely *not* to foster prejudice; they have the responsibility to counteract it actively.

PART IV

KOHLBERG FOR THE COUNSELING
AND CLINICAL PRACTITIONER

Chapter 11

Counseling and Clinical Implications of Kohlberg's Developmental Psychology

Richard L. Hayes

Counseling psychologists have long recognized the important relationship that exists between counseling and human development. Nonetheless, it was not until Lawrence Kohlberg (1969) articulated a synthesis of Mead's (1934) symbolic interactionism and Piaget's (1932/1965, 1968) genetic epistemology that a full appreciation of the developmental significance of counseling as a process of social influence was possible. Indeed, it was to "the integration of observations of the moral development of children and adolescents with their clinical diagnosis, treatment, and therapy" that Kohlberg turned his attention as a postdoctoral fellow in clinical psychology upon concluding his studies at Chicago. Nonetheless, he soon "decided that more research was needed in the field of moral development before my stage concepts could be applied to practice" (Kohlberg, unpublished manuscript, p. 10). Despite this "detour," Kohlberg left a rich legacy of ideas for clinical practice that offers the potential for extending his influence far beyond the study of moral education.

COMPETING COUNSELING TRADITIONS

Prior to Kohlberg's seminal work in moral development and his explication of the "cognitive-developmental" tradition, counselors generally accepted one or the other of two competing views of human development. In the first of these traditions, which Kohlberg called the "cultural transmission model," development is

173

viewed through the metaphor of the machine. . . . The environment is seen as "input," as information or energy more or less directly transmitted to, and accumulated in, the organism. The organism in turn emits "output" behavior. Underlying the mechanistic metaphor is the associationistic, stimulus-response or environmentalist psychological theory, which can be traced from John Locke to Thorndike to B. F. Skinner (Kohlberg and Mayer, 1972, p. 456).

The other tradition, which Kohlberg called the "romantic model," views development as a process of maturation:

The environment affects development by providing necessary nourishment for the naturally growing organism. [Both cognitive and emotional development are] believed to unfold through hereditary stages, such as the Freudian psychosexual stages, but [are] thought to be vulnerable to fixation and frustration by the environment (Kohlberg and Mayer, 1972, pp. 455-456).

Each of these psychological theories, i.e., the environmentalist and maturationist, takes a very different perspective on the notion of change, the explanation of which is at the heart of any developmental theory. For the environmentalist, development is viewed as continuous and as having no particular preferred direction. Thus age and stage are irrelevant concepts that are used as conveniences of the theorist to organize the data. For the maturationist, change is attributed to growth and differentiation. Environmental factors are recognized, but only as placing limits on individual development, not as directing its course. Maturational explanations depend upon age per se, while development is described as a continuous sequence of discontinuous stages.

As might be expected, each of these positions takes a different approach to counseling. Counselors who adopt the cultural-transmission ideology attempt to discover the environmental determinants of behavior by making baseline observations of behavior, establishing observable goals, and evaluating progress toward these goals. This empirical approach has been the dominant research tradition in counseling psychology (Hayes and Kenney, 1983). Because they believe that "cognitive development is the result of guided learning and teaching . . . [counselors who accept the cultural-transmission ideology] require a careful statement of desirable behavior patterns described in terms of specific responses" (Kohlberg and Mayer, 1972, p. 456). Because all behavior is presumed to result from learning, the general therapeutic goal is to create new conditions for learning. The result is a relativistic counseling psychology that prepares the client to adjust to the constraints of the social environment. The treatment outcome of counseling is to get along better, without anxiety and without pain, by behaving in whatever way is necessary to alleviate or endure that pain.

Counselors who adopt the romantic ideology, on the other hand, believe that what comes from within the [client] is the most important aspect of development; therefore, [counseling] should be permissive enough to allow the inner "good" (abilities and virtues) to unfold and the inner "bad" to come under control. . . . These maturationists stress the biological metaphors of "health" and "growth" in equating optimal physical development with bodily health and optimal mental development with mental health (Kohlberg and Mayer, 1972, pp. 455-456).

Maturationally oriented counselors help the client to relive earlier experiences and to work through any conflicts in an effort to allow the fullest expression of innate abilities and drives. In effect, freedom is presumed to lead to growth. This freedom is realized by removing the blocks to continued development and by providing a therapeutic environment that encourages self-discovery and promotes self-awareness. The focus is on client concerns and the alleviation of the emotional discomfort that results when needs/wants go unmet.

The maturationist's belief that development is an unfolding of innate potentialities leads to the notion that clients come into treatment at critical junctures in their own developmental histories. Client concerns are approached as if there is a *critical period* "in which the individual is especially sensitive to environmental influence in a given domain" (Kohlberg, 1969, p. 351). Treatment is reduced to crisis intervention or to the prevention of future crises.

Prior to Kohlberg, this particular explanation of development had been so omnipresent in counseling theory that many counselors assumed that maturation is synonymous with developmental theory rather than understanding it as a particular form or perspective on the nature of development. Despite the overwhelming popularity of the more behavioral approach of the environmentalists, the maturational theories have been especially useful in spelling out the *normal* or expected course of human development, especially in Western society.

The popular success of both of these approaches can be attributed, in part, to their tendency to provide simple answers to complex problems. This reductionism betrays what Kohlberg has called the "bag of virtues" strategy of the romantics and the "industrial psychology" strategy of the cultural transmissionists in taking a "value-neutral" approach to defining objectives (Kohlberg and Mayer, 1972, p. 450). As Kohlberg explained:

In the *value-free consulting model* [italics in original], the client (whether student or school) defines educational ends and the psychologist can then advise about means of education without losing his value-neutrality or imposing his values. Outside education, the value-free consulting model not only provides the basic model for counseling and psychotherapy, where the client is an individual, but also for industrial psychology, where the client is a social system. In both therapy and industrial psychology the consultant is paid by the client and the financial contract defines whose values are to be chosen (Kohlberg and Mayer, 1972, p. 464).

Although Kohlberg seems to have accepted that counselors can maintain a certain value-neutrality by virtue of having a clearly identified client, he rightly noted that "the educational psychologist, however, has more than one client" (Kohlberg and Mayer, 1972, p. 464). Indeed, the school counselor, who is a public employee, who works at the discretion of the school board, who counsels students, and who can intervene in many cases only with the parents' consent, is beset by a host of conflicting demands. As Kohlberg noted: "What the child wants, what the parents want, and what the larger community wants are often at odds with one another" (Kohlberg and Mayer, 1972, p. 464).

Kohlberg's assertions about the limitations of these approaches imply that counseling based on either romantic or cultural-transmission ideologies cannot be justified. To paraphrase his comments on education, a value-neutral counseling based on "a refusal to impose intellectual and ethical values of libertarianism, equal justice, intellectual inquiry, and social reconstruction on the [client], even though these values are held to be the most important ones," cannot be supported any more than it can be held up by the vision of the counselor as a "culture-designer, who 'educates others' to conform to culture and maintain it but not to develop the values and knowledge which would be required for culture-designing" (Kohlberg and Mayer, 1972, p. 472). Both forms of counseling lead to a certain elitism that either withholds "mental health and happiness" for fear of indoctrination or imposes "behavioral controls in the service of cultural survival" (Kohlberg and Mayer, 1972, p. 472).

As an alternative to these two streams of thought, Kohlberg offered instead the tradition of "progressivism," which encourages the nourishment of the individual's natural interaction with a developing society or environment, and a cognitive-developmental psychology to explain the nature of human development. Drawing upon the work of Piaget (1932/1965) and Dewey (Dewey, 1938/1963; Dewey and McLellan, 1964), Kohlberg discarded the dichotomy between maturation and environmentally determined learning. Instead, he argued that "mature thought emerges through a process of development that is neither direct biological maturation nor direct learning, but rather a reorganization of psychological structures resulting from organism-environment interactions" (Kohlberg and Mayer, 1972, p. 457). Taking a cognitive-developmental perspective, this "progressive ideology" holds instead that development involves "an active change in patterns of thinking brought about by experiential problem-solving situations" (Kohlberg and Mayer, 1972, p. 455).

Thus cognitive-developmental theories are interactional in that "they assume that basic mental structure is the product of the patterning of the interaction between the organism and the environment rather than directly reflecting either innate patterns in the organism or patterns of events (stimulus contingencies) in the environment" (Kohlberg, 1969, p. 350). This interactionist view of development rests on the dialectical metaphor of cognitive development as "the progression of ideas in discourse and conversation" (Kohlberg and Mayer, 1972, p. 456) and implies that counseling should stimulate development and, as such, is a moral activity. To understand fully the implications of Kohlberg's work for counseling, it is necessary to turn first to the basic structural assumptions underlying this interactionist position.

BASIC ASSUMPTIONS

Kohlberg set out initially to extend Piaget's (1932/1965) earlier line of inquiry into the cognitive processes underlying the development of children's moral reasoning. In addition, he succeeded to elaborate a social constructivist view of human functioning with far-reaching implications. Accepting Piaget's views on the cognitive development of children's thinking about the *physical* world, Kohlberg made the bold assertion that "all the basic processes involved in 'physical' cognitions, and in stimulating developmental changes in these cognitions, are also basic to social development" (Kohlberg, 1969, p. 349). Recognizing that counseling is fundamentally a social activity, Kohlberg's work does no less than call for a reconceptualization of the counseling process itself.

The primary issue in reconceptualizing counseling is that an interactionist approach characterizes development as successively more complex attempts to make meaning of the facts of one's social experience. As Kohlberg (1969) put it: "Social development is, in essence, the restructuring of 1) the concept of the self, 2) in its relationship to concepts of other people, 3) conceived as being in a common social world with social standards" (p. 349). Cognitive development is the key to understanding not only the psychology of morality but also of the processes of internalization, imitation, and identification, sex role identity, early education, the influence of culture and social experience in personality formation, social dependency and attachment, mental health, adaptation, and pathology, and virtually all of the topics in social development that have a bearing on counseling practice (see Kohlberg, 1969).

Drawing upon the collective body of Kohlberg's work, especially as represented in his classic, "Stage and Sequence: The Cognitive-Developmental Approach to Socialization" (Kohlberg, 1969), the following general principles that guided his work are offered as having direct relevance for counseling practice.

Individuals are Producers of Their Own Development

In Kohlberg's view, individuals are believed to produce their own development through the interaction of maturational, social, and physical factors that are more or less in equilibrium with one another. Inherent in human nature are certain structuring tendencies which attempt to make sense of people's experiences within themselves and of the world in which they live. The assumption is that the "basic mental structure is the result of an interaction between certain organismic structuring tendencies and the structure of the outside world" (Kohlberg, 1969, p. 352). What one knows (or rather, how one is knowing it) emerges in light of these interactions with the environment.

The client constructs reality from his or her own experience. Thus the client's reality represents a relationship between the client and the world as the client understands that world. It is not so much that clients *have* problems as that they *experience* problems, for how one understands and makes meaning of experience betrays the underlying logic of how one makes sense of one's own existence.

The implication of this self-constructive view of reality is that development is essentially the task of mastering the facts of one's existence. Interactionally oriented counselors try to understand how clients make sense of personal experience, that is, how clients make meaning. The focus of counseling is not on clients as human beings as much as it is on clients as humans being. Put in other terms, development is a verb rather than a noun in that it is an activity of self-construction that involves making meaning rather than the passive ordering of made meanings. It is to the client's struggle to understand the self and others, therefore, in the context of a shared social experience, that interactionally oriented counselors turn their attention.

Development Is Contextual

A second underlying principle to be derived from Kohlberg's work is that development takes place in a social context. Because clients actively construct their social world, the client's history is not so much a record of one's life experience as it is a living representation of one's experience of life—of one *experiencing* life. Thus, the client and the environment are not separate, nor even in interaction, but rather are inextricably linked in transactions with one another. Accepting that the counselor may be part of that environment, counseling from a Kohlbergian perspective looks more like a dialogue than a conversation. Kohlberg pointed out that "cognitive-development is a dialogue between the child's structures and the structures of the environment. . . . that the core of development is . . . cognitive change in distinctively human, general patterns of thinking about the self and the world. The child's relation to his social environment is cognitive; it involves thought and symbolic interaction" (Kohlberg and Mayer, 1972, p. 457).

The implication of this perspective is that counseling should create a context for continued development. In approaching their work from a cognitive-developmental perspective, counselors should focus on the interactions between clients and their environments. The interactionally oriented counselor attempts to provide an environment that will facilitate the client's development by acknowledging the client's reality and by supporting the client's efforts to restore some balance to the world as the client knows it.

Cognition Is an Active Relating of Events

Underlying this transactive notion of the origin of the basic mental structures is the concept of cognition. As Kohlberg explained:

> Structure refers to the general characteristics of shape, pattern, or organization of response rather than to the rate or intensity of responses or its pairing with particular stimuli. Cognitive structure refers to rules for processing or for connecting experienced events. Cognition (as most clearly reflected in thinking) means putting things together or relating events, and this relating is an active connecting process. . . . More basically, it means that the process of relating particular events depends upon prior general modes of relating developed by the organism. The most general modes of relating are termed "categories of experience" (Kohlberg, 1969, pp. 349-350).

By contrast, researchers using an environmental perspective have focused on the products of clients' cognitions rather than on the cognitive process itself. The difference between the two approaches amounts to studying what the client knows rather than how the client is knowing it.

Although cognitive-behavioral counselors (see, for example, Beck, 1967; Lazarus, 1971; Meichenbaum, 1977) have been interested in "faulty thinking," "decision-making processes," and "reasoning powers," they have tended to focus their attention on the influence of cognition on behavior. The effect has been to look at academic performance, areas of misinformation, and irrational self-talk (see Ellis, 1962) as guides to prescribing treatments that focus on changing what the client knows.

From Kohlberg's perspective, counselors should be less concerned with what their clients believe to be true, or with why they believe it, and more with how they came to believe it. Consequently, counselors should shift their attention from changing what clients believe, or from helping them to uncover the reasons why, to varying the process by which clients arrive at those beliefs.

Development Is a Qualitative Reorganization of Meaning

The idea of transactions going on between people and their environments leads to the notion of cognitive stages. Unlike the passage of phases more representative of most maturationist accounts of the life cycle, the interactionist reserves the term stage to refer to "*qualitative*" [italics in original] differences in children's modes of thinking or of solving the same problem at different ages" (Kohlberg, 1969, p. 352). Each stage is a more differentiated, comprehensive, and integrated structure than the one before it. Each succeeding stage represents the capacity to make sense of a greater variety of experiences in a more adequate way. Because "there is a hierarchical preference within the individual, i.e., a disposition to prefer a solution of a problem at the highest level available to him" (Kohlberg, 1969, p. 353), the fundamental reason for movement from one stage to the next is that a later stage is more adequate in some universal sense than an earlier stage.

The basic notion of this stage concept leads to the conceptualization of development as a movement toward greater adaptation, differentiation, and integration of distinct modes of thought in a universal, invariant, and hierarchical developmental sequence (Kohlberg, 1969). The existence of universal stages of psychological development provided the necessary theoretical framework for the earliest attempts to apply Kohlberg's work to educational intervention (Kohlberg, 1987; Kohlberg and Mayer, 1972; Mosher and Sprinthall, 1970; Sprinthall and Mosher, 1978). Although these interventions are discussed in detail elsewhere in this text, it is important to note that the work of Mosher and Sprinthall and their students represents the first systematic attempts to involve counselors as psychological educators in promoting adolescent development through the school curriculum.

Reasoning Is the Key to Understanding

A central focus on individual reasoning demands that the counselor take the client's ideas seriously. Understanding Kohlberg's work helps the counselor to speak the client's language. Instead of focusing upon the historical antecedents of present concerns or upon the nonjudgmental acceptance of the client, Kohlberg's focus upon the process of moral reasoning prompts the counselor to focus on the whole person in the process of decision making. The developmental aim of educational interventions is to provide the sort of environment that

> actively stimulates development through the presentation of resolvable but genuine problems or conflicts. For progressives, the organizing and developing force in the child's experience is the child's active thinking, and thinking is stimulated by the problematic, by cognitive conflict (Kohlberg and Mayer, 1972, p. 455).

Kohlberg's emphasis on reasoning prompts the counselor to attend to the process of decision making itself. In efforts to understand how the client came to this or that conclusion, the counselor can come to understand the client as a meaning maker, where "the acquisition of 'knowledge' as *an active change in the pattern of thinking* [italics in original] [is] brought about by experiential problem-solving situations" (Kohlberg and Mayer, 1972, p. 455). As Kohlberg (1969) argued:

> An interactional conception of stages . . . proposes that an understanding of the role of experience requires: 1) analyses of universal features of experienced objects (physical or social), 2) analysis of logical sequences of differentiation and integration in concepts of such objects, and 3) analysis of structural relations between experience-inputs and the relevant behavior organizations (p. 356).

Further, counseling should involve clients in the active practice of their own judgment.

Role-Taking Underlies Moral Development

As well, Kohlberg (1969, 1976, 1984) has helped the counselor to see the importance that attends the development of role-taking, which is "the tendency to react to the other as someone like the self and by the tendency to react to the self's behavior in the role of the other" (Kohlberg, 1969, p. 398). What is maturity but the ability increasingly to take the perspective of others in deciding what is right or fair or good?

Kohlberg (1969) argued that

> social cognition always involves *role-taking* [italics in original], i.e., awareness that the other is in some way like the self, and that the other knows or is responsive to the self in a system of complementary expectations.
> Accordingly, developmental changes in the social self reflect parallel changes in conceptions of the social world (p. 349).

Indeed, clients who come into counseling are often troubled by their failure to take the perspective of others, including themselves, fully and/or accurately. Recognizing that, for Kohlberg, "moral development is fundamentally a process of the restructuring of modes of role-taking, then the fundamental social inputs stimulating moral development may be termed 'role-taking opportunities'" (Kohlberg, 1969, p. 399). A cognitive-developmental understanding of the client's role-taking abilities helps the counselor to appreciate the limitations and the range of the client's perspective of his or her relationship to and with others.

Drawing upon the work of Baldwin (1906), Mead (1934), and Piaget (1932/1965), Kohlberg (1969) argued that "the primary meaning of the word 'social' is the distinctively human structuring of action and thought by role-taking, the tendency to react to the other as someone like the self and by the tendency to react to the self's behavior in the role of the other" (p. 398). Consistent with this cognitive-developmental view on the developmental relationships between self and society, Kohlberg's work suggests that the experience of social interaction involves a simultaneous experience between the client and the counselor, and between the client as client and the client as counselor. Consequently, the client constructs the interpersonal event of counseling in polar dimensions that may potentially be in conflict. Anything less than ideal equilibrium provides opportunities for this conflict. As Kohlberg (1969) noted: "A sense of contradiction and discrepancy at one's own stage is necessary for reorganization at the next stage" (p. 403).

Indeed, it is this sort of cognitive conflict, which arises from difficulties in making meaning of some indeterminate event, that often brings the client to counseling. Drawing upon the work of Mead (1934), Kohlberg (1969) explained that "the self needs an audience to be a self, to establish the meaning and value of its own action" (p. 418). The resolution of the conflict lies in a more stable form of self-organization on the individual level and a more stable equilibrium among the client and others with whom the client interacts.

As viewed from the perspective of the individual client, role-taking is an extensive personal experience of responsibility and choice. Therefore, counseling should be concerned with, be an examination of, and involve clients in the experience of those elements of their existence that affect the course of their own development. Counseling should involve clients in the examination of those conflicts that exist in their own lives and for which the individual client supplies the content of that experience.

The personal experiences of clients in discussing and hearing themselves in discussion will promote self-development to the extent that the experience represents some perturbation. The problem of stage change appears "to be one of presenting stimuli which are both sufficiently incongruous as to stimulate conflict in the child's existing stage schemata and sufficiently congruous as to be assimilable with some accommodative effort" (Kohlberg, 1969, p. 402). The experience of taking the role of the counselor in the presentation of one's own argument, therefore, is causally related to development. Because development requires social interaction, social interaction can be a stimulant to development. For the counselor, this argument suggests that counseling creates a social setting for the client that provides opportunities to share ideas, not only with another, but with oneself.

Development Requires Group Participation

From a Kohlbergian perspective, counseling provides the context from which ideas can grow—a sort of public forum that can serve as a healthy environment for this growth to take place. Extrapolating from Kohlberg's (1969) belief that "moral development is fundamentally a process of the restructuring of modes of role-taking" (p. 399), counselors are encouraged to help their clients to share their own thinking. This action of making one's own ideas public provides an audience to one's own reasoning, an audience made up, at least, of the client and the counselor. Recognizing that "the first prerequisite for role-taking is participation in a group or institution" (Kohlberg, 1969, p. 399), group counseling may represent a best therapeutic intervention for clients who are suffering from problems that are social in nature. Kohlberg (1969) argued that

> participation is partially a matter of sheer amount of interaction and communication in the group, since communication presupposes role-taking. In addition, the centrality of the individual in the communication and decision-making structure of the group enhances role-taking opportunities. The more the individual is responsible for the decision of the group, and for his own

actions in their consequences for the group, the more must he take the role of the others in it (p. 399).

Research into moral atmospheres and democratic schooling by Kohlberg and others (Hayes, 1980; Kohlberg, 1980; Kohlberg and Wasserman, 1980; Lickona and Paradise, 1980; Mosher, 1979; Power, Higgins, and Kohlberg, 1989; Power and Reimer, 1978; Scharf, 1973; Thompson, 1982) has underscored the importance of promoting group development as a means for influencing individual development. In contrast to the unstructured encounter group process of the romantics (see, for example, Rogers, 1970, 1983) or the highly structured techniques of the cultural-transmissionists (see, for example, Kanfer and Goldstein, 1980; Rose, 1977), Kohlberg's moral dilemma discussion approach offers clients a structured group approach that recognizes individual freedom while promoting collective responsibility.

The development of the "just community approach" to moral education (see Kohlberg, Scharf, and Hickey, 1975; Power, Higgins, and Kohlberg, 1989) may be viewed as a group counseling intervention aimed at helping clients to develop more appropriate sociomoral behavior. The "just community approach promotes character development and responsibility: a) through participation in moral discussions and exposure to new and different points of view, b) through living in an atmosphere of fairness and developing relations of loyalty and trust, and c) by taking responsibility for making and enforcing rules on oneself and other members of the group" (Kohlberg, Kauffman, Scharf and Hickey, 1974, p. 11).

The moral atmosphere of the group acts as a mediator between individual moral judgment and moral behavior. As Kohlberg explained:

> It accomplishes this through the group discussions in which [members of the group] point out to one another actions which have not been consistent with their own moral judgment and values. It attempts to develop moral action by creating a community in which people care about living up to the moral expectations of one another and in which they feel it is fair to have their own moral lapses pointed out and even disciplined because they have the right and opportunity to criticize and correct the moral behavior of other [members] (Kohlberg, Kauffman, Scharf, and Hickey, 1974, p. 36).

Rather than focus on the individual, the just community approach focuses on the community as the site for developmental intervention. The leader's "primary concern should not be with the individual, but with the meeting as a whole: its processes and its development" (Kohlberg, Kauffman, Scharf, and Hickey, 1974, p. 110). Rather than focusing on individual stage change, the group leader is encouraged to focus on the development of collective responsibility and fair decision making.

Implications of Kohlberg's Assumptions for Counseling

Despite his beginnings in clinical psychology, most of Kohlberg's writings on moral development and moral education were focused on the process of schooling and on school organization, especially as they relate to teaching. In fact, only two of Kohlberg's many articles were written to counselors directly (Kohlberg, 1975; Kohlberg and Wasserman, 1980). These articles were intended to get counselors to rethink their roles as counselors, primarily as school counselors, and suggest that "the 'just community' approach to education underlines the importance of the counselor's role as consultant and facilitator" (Kohlberg and Wasserman, 1980, p. 566).

Although Kohlberg advocated that counselors become psychological educators who bring human growth and development into the classroom, his focus was ever on the development of more morally responsive curricula. Despite recognizing that "counseling aids in the development of counselor as well as counselee because listening requires the empathy and role-taking that is important for both moral and psychological growth" (Kohlberg and Wasserman, 1980, p. 563), Kohlberg had little to say directly about reconceptualizing counseling as a process. Nonetheless, Kohlberg and his associates (see Kohlberg, Kauffman, Scharf, and Hickey, 1974) have delineated seven conditions for moral change, in which morality is used in the Deweyan sense of "pertaining to the self" (Dewey, 1960, pp. 148-151) and its development. These conditions have a clear and consistent application in the development of a program for counseling intervention.

1) Considerations of Fairness and Morality

One of the primary concerns of clients entering counseling is the rightness of their actions. Often troubled by the realities of a situation they believe to be unfair, clients wonder if they are doing the right thing in seeking help. They wonder if they have been wrong in their past behavior and if they can be experiencing all the pain associated with an inability to be a good person or the sort of good persons they would like to be.

Counseling should provide a climate in which clients are trusted and encouraged to trust themselves and others. Clients should be encouraged to consider the moral aspects of their present concerns and to examine their own thoughts and actions within the context of their past efforts at problem solving. Questions regarding personal motives, what one should or would do, and hypothesized outcomes of acts that may affect another all focus attention on the problem-solving aspects of the issues under discussion. Finally, clients should be encouraged to examine the relationship between their judgments and choices and the personal consequences that have resulted from acting on previous judgments.

2) Exposure to Cognitive Conflict

Ready access to information and freedom of expression provide clients with opportunities to engage in interpersonal communication. A discussion of the more cognitive aspects of the personal dilemmas facing clients affords them the opportunity to attempt to find solutions themselves. Such discussions create potential cognitive conflicts among client's perceptions of their individual judgments and allow for comparison between their private thoughts and their public communication. The cognitive conflicts that can arise from such discussions "exposes individuals to other viewpoints and leads them to question and rethink their own positions" (Kohlberg, Kauffman, Scharf, and Hickey, 1974, p. 31) as well as those of others.

3) Role-Taking Opportunities

The resolution of differing perspectives requires clients to comprehend their own self-conflicting viewpoints and to consider the viewpoints of others. Counseling should "provide role-taking opportunities through discussion of moral and personal issues in which each individual is encouraged to present his or her point of view to others and to understand other points of view" (Kohlberg, Kauffman, Scharf, and Hickey, 1974, p. 31). Further, clients should be encouraged to assume individual responsibility for using these discussions as opportunities for self-development.

4) Active Participation in Decision Making

Counseling not only provides opportunities for decision making but requires clients' active participation in assuming responsibility for the conduct of the sessions. Just as a romantic approach to counseling respects the rights of clients in making decisions, clients are obligated to exercise those rights in taking an active part in determining the direction of treatment. Acting in the context of a public decision-making process places responsibility on clients for the consequences of their actions. Thus, in speaking and in hearing oneself in the presence of the counselor, the client provides a meaningful direction to treatment and one to which he or she is more likely to be committed. Realization of the consequences of one's own action stimulates self-development.

5) Exposure to Higher Levels of Thinking

Kohlberg and his colleagues (Rest, Turiel, and Kohlberg, 1969) found that exposing individuals through moral discussion to the reasoning of those who were more developmentally advanced was most successful in stimulating the development of moral reasoning when the arguments were presented at a level just beyond the individual's current level of functioning. Translated to the counseling setting, this finding means that counselors should help clients by clarifying arguments and by supporting or directing attention to arguments at cognitively more complex levels. Likewise, in hearing themselves struggle with the presentation of their own thoughts, clients must attempt to clarify the meaning of their arguments for this or that alternative and, by doing so, enhance their capacity to solve their own problems.

6) Intellectual Stimulation

Problem solving is substantially an intellectual exercise that requires increasingly sophisticated thought. Research has shown that advanced intellectual ability is a necessary condition for movement to higher stages of moral reasoning (Kohlberg, 1981) and ego development (Loevinger, 1976). If counselors are to help clients fulfill their potential, provision must be made for the logical analysis of relevant information. Bibliotherapy (Schrank and Engels, 1981), use of counselor self-disclosure (Neimeyer, Banikiotes, and Winum, 1979), information giving (Biggs and Keller, 1982), and giving directives (Wright and Strong, 1982) are all techniques that, when used appropriately, can be effective in helping clients make meaning of the problems confronting them.

7) Group Counseling as Democratic Education

It was Kohlberg's contention, consistent with Dewey, that the social structure that best provides the proper context for the stimulation of development is a democracy, which Kohlberg defined as "power and participation in a social system which recognizes basic equal rights" (Kohlberg and Mayer, 1972, p. 475). Further, Kohlberg claimed to be "the first to demonstrate directly that democracy not only works, but that it also stimulates moral development" (Kohlberg, 1972, p. 16). Accepting Kohlberg's directive that "the developmental conception remains the only rationale . . . for providing the basis for a truly democratic educational process" (Kohlberg and Mayer, 1972, p. 494), the implication for counselors is that they set human development as their aim and that they become involved in the creation of intentional democratic communities to achieve this aim.

Counselors should become developmental educators who are involved in primary prevention efforts to change their clients' social environments as well as the clients themselves—an issue that is best addressed through the application of a democratic group counseling model to the reformulation of the counselor's role. Kohlberg's directive to small group leaders working in the prisons applies equally to group counselors working with their clients:

> You must consistently demonstrate your belief in the democratic process, a belief which you are trying to instill in the group members. Your authority in the unit will come from your ability to be an objective mediator, from your insistence on fairness and responsibility, from your willingness to stand up for unpopular causes and individuals for the sake of fairness, and from the appropriate recognition you give to moral development in individual community members (Kohlberg, Kauffman, Scharf, and Hickey, 1974, p. 111).

In effect, the democratic leader must be committed to the process of democracy, of letting members make decisions for themselves.

Taken together, these seven conditions make a complex agenda for reconceptualizing counseling and clinical practice from an interactionist developmental framework. Nonetheless, this agenda was not one to which Kohlberg was able to turn his attention fully before his death. Indeed, his greatest contribution may not be in moral education but rather in how much direction he left for the application of his ideas to other fields including clinical and counseling practice.

Chapter 12

Applications of Interactionist Developmental Schemes to Counseling Theory and Practice

Richard L. Hayes

PROMISING DEVELOPMENTAL SCHEMES

Kohlberg has not been alone in his efforts to bring an interactionist perspective to an understanding of human development over the past few decades. Indeed, several promising developmental schemes have been proposed that are related in one way or another to Kohlberg's scheme and have important implications for counseling practice as well.

Jane Loevinger
Accepting ego development "as the master trait in personality, as the frame that provides more specific traits with their meaning and around which the whole edifice of personality is constructed" (Blasi, 1976, p. 41), Loevinger set out to capture the developmental progress of human thought and behavior. The essence of this development, for Loevinger (1976), "is the search for coherent meanings in experience" (p. 11).

After more than twenty-five years of research using a sentence completion questionnaire (Loevinger and Wessler, 1970), Loevinger provided a blueprint for the sequential development of conceptions of self, having derived a sequence of milestones for ego development. Like Kohlberg's work in moral development, Loevinger's (1976) theory of ego development is an application of Piaget's (1932/1965) structural stage model of development: Stages of ego development form an invariant sequence of hierarchical transformations, which are structured wholes. For Loevinger, each stage is a characterology within an age cohort that presents an abstraction, the actions of which can be described but which cannot itself be observed directly. Loevinger has described seven stages and two transitions between stages that form a continuum that closely parallels Kohlberg's stage sequence (Lambert, 1972), although Kohlberg and she disagreed about whether moral development is separate from or merely subsumed by ego development (Kohlberg, 1984, pp. 397-401; Loevinger, 1976, p. 441).

Unlike, Kohlberg, Loevinger was not a clinician nor did she have any direct interest in applying her theory to educational or counseling practice. Nonetheless, practitioners have been very interested in applying her findings in clinical settings. For example, counseling research has suggested that empathy is the most powerful factor in bringing about positive change (Carkhuff, 1969; Rogers, 1961). Recognizing that empathy, by definition, involves understanding another person by taking that person's frame of reference, an interactionist perspective would argue for empathy as a particular form of role-taking. Indeed, Kohlberg asserted that "the child's whole social life is based on 'empathy,' i.e., on the awareness of other selves with thoughts and feelings like the self" (Kohlberg, 1969, pp. 393-394).

Further, Kohlberg believed that empathy is a primary phenomenon and that "what development and socialization achieve is the organization of empathic phenomena into consistent sympathetic and moral concerns, not the creation of empathy as such" (Kohlberg, 1969, p. 394). Thus, increasing levels of both ego and moral development would be expected to be related to changes in the form or conditions under which an empathic response might be generated rather than the content of the response itself. Not surprisingly, ego development has been shown to be related positively to the ability to be empathic (Kagan and Schneider, 1977).

Extending the notion that the organization of empathic phenomena develop in concert with moral judgment, Swensen (1980) has suggested that clients should be matched by ego stage with counselors who are one stage above them for therapy to be maximally effective, a practice reminiscent of the "plus one" convention used in stimulating moral development through classroom discussions (see, for example, Blatt and Kohlberg, 1973). This matching allows the counselor to serve as a *pacer* (Dember, 1965) for the client, who attempts to master the complexity presented by the counselor's novel behavior, thus enhancing the client's own complexity (see D'Andrea, 1984).

Further, Swenson (1980) has proposed that there may be a decreasing influence of environmental factors on personal decision making as individuals advance to higher levels of ego development. Thus organic and manipulative therapies may be more effective at higher levels. Young-Eisendrath (1985) proposed that the relative success of behaviorally oriented therapies with children and the mentally retarded and the success of psychoanalysis with the wealthier and better educated clients may be due, in part, to a proper matching of the therapy with the appropriate client by ego level. Extrapolating from Kohlberg's notion of ego development as "the awareness of new meanings in life" (Snarey, Kohlberg, and Noam, 1983, p. 303), this research suggests that, as clients move to higher stages of moral and ego development, different therapies may be necessitated to help clients make new meanings of their past experience and become capable of making still newer meanings of those experiences of which they are just becoming aware.

Robert Selman

Following the open-ended clinical method first used by Piaget and later applied by Kohlberg, one of Kohlberg's Harvard colleagues, Robert Selman (1980), has studied the development of interpersonal understanding. In particular, his research has focused "on the ability to take the perspective of another (social role-taking), and on the relation of this ability to theoretically parallel stages in the development of moral thought" (Selman, 1976, p. 300). Rather than view progression in role-taking as resulting from the accumulation of social knowledge, as in most behavioral accounts, Selman took an interactional approach that searched for qualitative changes in the process by which children structure their understandings of the relation between the perspective of self and others.

Selman's model of social cognition has been verified empirically (Selman, 1980) using a set of interpersonal dilemma stories followed by a semi-structured interview. The resulting model consists of five stages that satisfy the Piagetian criteria of a universal, invariant, hierarchical sequence of structured wholes and that appear to have the same necessary-but-not-sufficient relationship to Kohlberg's moral stages that the moral stages have to Piaget's cognitive stages (Selman, 1971, 1976).

Specifically, "the child's cognitive stage indicates his level of understanding of physical and logical problems, while his role-taking stage indicates his level of understanding of the nature of social relations, and his moral judgment stage indicates the manner in which he decides how to resolve social conflicts between people with different points of view" (Selman, 1976, p. 307). Not surprisingly, Selman has also suggested that logical parallels exist between his stages of social cognition and Loevinger's ego stages (1980, pp. 304-307).

Selman's theoretical approach "construes ego development as consisting of various conceptual domains, each with its own set of interrelated stages, together defining an ego-development grid" of "content categories to be understood and acted upon by the child" and "a developmental sequence of stages for each of the content areas" (1976, pp. 311, 316). Commenting upon the importance of this model for his own work, Kohlberg wrote that Selman's work suggested that:

The equivalent Piagetian stage of physical cognition is a necessary prior achievement for, but is not sufficient to ensure the attainment of, the parallel level of social cognition, and that both of these, in turn, are necessary but not sufficient for the development of the equivalent Kohlbergian level of socio-moral reasoning, which in turn is a necessary but not sufficient condition for the attainment of the parallel level of ego development. In this sense, Selman's domain of social cognition is a crucial link in our structural subdomain theory of ego development (Snarey, Kohlberg, and Noam, 1983, p. 313).

Consistent with Kohlberg's view, Selman believes that cognitive-developmental theory can enrich clinicians' understandings of the social and emotional development of their clients and can provide guidelines for selecting developmentally appropriate interventions. Recently, Selman has been interested in the study of interpersonal negotiation strategies whereby adolescents and children "*think* [italics in original] about strategies for social conflict resolution across different interpersonal contexts (Selman and Schultz, 1988, p. 208). In particular, he has been interested in understanding the relationship between verbalized competence and actual performance—the difference between thought and action—as a means to evaluating a client's developmental status and for creating an integrated framework for developmental diagnosis.

As well, Selman has attempted to integrate a view of the role interpersonal context plays in social thought as a function of the interaction between persons. As an example, he has found that relationships between adolescent peers vis-à-vis those of adolescents and adults provide for greater "reciprocity of complement" such that "adolescents may more readily develop reciprocal or collaborative strategies in the context of their interactions with peers, and then perhaps transfer these skills to negotiations with adults" (Selman and Schultz, 1988, p. 222). The implication for clinical practice is that counseling, at least with adolescents, may be facilitated best by using peer helpers *prior to* involvement with adult counselors.

Further, Selman has proposed that, despite the relationship between developmental strands and the sequentiality of developmental progression, individuals do not necessarily proceed through these stages in a wholistic fashion. Rather, Selman has suggested that psychopathology may be, in part, a reflection of the failure of clients to integrate thought and action in different social contexts. Selman has proposed a three-dimensional model for integrating thought and action in social cognition such that structural level, functional skills, and interpersonal orientation or style are really the same phenomenon being studied by different methods.

At the highest levels of development these different views are integrated (similar to Kohlberg's own notions about the relationship between thought and action) such that there is an increasing rapprochement between the client's ideal thoughts and actual behavior. Research using this "model of integrated thought and action suggests that it is the interaction between a) level of competence and b) the *gap* [italics in original] between competence and performance that provides extremely useful information in individual assessment for clinical purposes" (Selman and Schultz, 1988, p. 237).

Selman believes that counseling provides a context that is both natural and ideal for the study of clients' self-reported recollections of their own strategies for interpersonal negotiation. In counseling, "individuals are constantly retelling their versions of interpersonal conflicts" (Selman and Schultz, 1988, p. 233). Further, Selman suggests that the assessment of variations in actual behavior should be done across different times so that the client may be observed in interaction with significant others over a broad variety of social contacts. "Interpersonal performance is not simply determined by with whom the individual is interacting but also by all the other emotional and motivational factors that make a particular context unique" (Selman and Schultz, 1988, p. 238).

The shift in Selman's work from an earlier emphasis on the study of social-cognitive competence to his current emphasis on social interaction has brought the study of emotion within the realm of an interactionist approach that is more than cognitive-developmental. Apparently, the greater the gap between thought and action, the greater the imbalance between the expression of emotions characterized by an active relating to the environment and those emotions characterized by helpless distress. Recalling the implications of Kohlberg's work for a conceptualization of group counseling as providing a context for development, it is important to note that Selman has argued that

> children's affective difficulties must be treated in real contexts, where the affect can safely arise, rather than only in hypothetical practice sessions or contexts involving temporally distant reflection on past interpersonal events. Such treatment requires a therapeutic context that provides positive social interactions and a feeling of safety, allowing negative, unpleasant, or frightening affect to emerge and offering opportunities for learning that these feelings can be sufficiently controlled, dealt with, and managed. A treatment setting with these features increases the probability of achieving profound developmental change, change not only in the structure of thought (insight) but in the structure of action (and even basic personality) as well (Selman and Schultz, 1988, p. 243).

The implications of Selman's approach is that counselors not only must understand their clients but also must understand their clients' social interactions over many contexts, over many interactions, over a long period of time. Then, by formulating interventions "one level above the frame of mind in which an individual is functioning at any given moment" the counselor can "speak to the structural level of an individual's negotiation as well as the manifest (or even latent) content of his concerns" (Selman and Schultz, 1988, p. 245). More than anything else, Selman's developmental therapy points to the necessity to extend a Kohlbergian approach to include social context as a variable in the diagnosis and treatment of developmental psychopathology.

William Perry

Based on interviews with college undergraduates over a fourteen-year period, Perry and his associates (Perry, 1970) identified changes in students' intellectual and ethical development during the college years. Although he had originally considered "the variety in students' response to the impact of intellectual and moral relativism . . . as a manifestation of differences in 'personality,' . . . it had not yet occurred to us that it might be more fruitful, at least for our purpose, to consider such differences primarily as expressions of stages in the very developments we were setting out to explore" (Perry, 1970, p. 7). Despite his modest intentions to "illustrate" this variety in response, he succeeded not only in refocusing Piaget's work in epistemological inquiry but also in adding an advance that describes individual's attempts to make commitments in response to existential theorizing about ultimate concerns.

Each of the nine positions in Perry's scheme represents a mode of intellectual development in a cognitive-developmental sequence of stages that moves from a simplistic/categorical to a complex/pluralistic view of knowledge and values. The nine positions may be grouped into three general categories: dualism, relativism, and commitment.

Perhaps because Perry is a clinician who developed his theory in an attempt to capture his own observations, his scheme has found a ready audience among counselors, especially in higher education. For example, students who think dualistically classify all things into right and wrong. Right Answers exist in the Absolute and are known to Authority, whose job it is to give the Answer to the student. In counseling, the dualistic person may accept that certain areas like feelings or advice on child management are areas where nobody really knows the answers although career guidance may be viewed as based on "scientific information" (Young-Eisendrath, 1985, p. 8).

Similarly, with development to a relativistic position uncertainty becomes legitimate, and everyone is recognized as having a right to an opinion. Clients at this stage are likely to question the counselor's authority vis-à-vis the authority of other more scientific helpers such as physicians or possibly psychiatrists. With further development to commitment, relativism is accepted, but the student gradually accepts the responsibility to live in a pluralistic world. Clients at this level recognize that different counseling treatments arise out of different contexts and that the counselor's authority derives from training and experience in matching the client to the appropriate treatment.

Although Perry's scheme has required some adjustment to correct for the discontinuity between earlier and later stages (see Kitchener and King, 1981), his theory has had a broad impact on curriculum development in higher education (Mentkowski, 1988; Mentkowski, Moeser, and Strait, 1983), career development (Knefelkamp and Slepitza, 1976), and the stimulation of intellectual and ethical development among college students (Stephenson and Hunt, 1980). In counseling, Young-Eisendrath (1985) has used Perry's scheme to anticipate authority issues in the counselor-client relationship. Clearly, Perry's work has much to offer those who are interested in the application of a cognitive-developmental approach to the epistemology of ultimate questions, of how one comes to understand the origins, nature, and limits of knowledge, especially within social contexts such as education and counseling.

Robert Kegan

A former student of both Kohlberg and Perry, Kegan has been interested in the study of the self in transformation over time. Kegan (1984) accepted Piaget's "conceptions about the mental organization of inanimate objects" (p. 7) and Kohlberg's application of this theory to "the mental organization of 'people objects' " (p. 8), to create a framework for understanding differences in the construction of meaning by different persons under similar life experiences over the lifespan.

Kegan's (1982) developmental scheme presents six stages of ego development, each of which represents an *evolutionary truce in the natural emergency of the self.* His is a lifespan developmental approach to the study of object relations, which he views as relations to that which some motion has made separate from the self. This motion involves the construction of meaning itself through an evolutionary process whereby objects are differentiated from the self and integrated with the self simultaneously. Thus ego development involves the setting and resetting of boundaries between self and other in a way that subsumes the theoretical perspectives of other interactionists. Although he has claimed that Kohlberg's "works as a whole [represent] the single most original and potentiating contribution to the understanding of the ego since Sigmund Freud" (Kegan, in press, p. 1), Kegan's own theory is an attempt to unify "the person's construction of the physical (Piaget), moral (Kohlberg), interpersonal (Selman), self-reflective (Perry), [and] theoretical (Fowler) worlds" (Kegan, 1979) as separate strands of a more basic activity.

For Kegan, the activity of being a person is the activity of meaning-making. "The most fundamental thing that we do with what happens to us is organize it. We literally make sense" (Kegan, 1982, p. 11). For counselors who want to understand their clients, cognition must be recognized as more than what the client knows, however irrational or misinformed that may appear. To understand a client is to enter into that region *"between* an event and a reaction to it—the place where it actually *becomes* an event for that person" (Kegan, 1982, p. 2). It is in this zone of mediation that counselors will help clients better to make meaning of their experience.

In Kegan's view, counseling provides a second-best means of support for a system in which the *natural* facilitation of development has broken down. Because he has focused on the transition points in development as points of disequilibration, Kegan views psychopathology as a period of crisis that occurs after the old balance in ways of knowing has fallen away and a new balance has yet to be established. If, as Kegan suggests, personality development is essentially the universal, ongoing process of meaning-making, then the developmental counselor should focus not so much on stages of development, as in the Kohlberg dilemma discussion interventions, as on the process and experience of developmental crisis by the client. For Kegan, counseling provides a holding environment for the client's efforts to make meaning in the face of crisis, which *is* the transformation of meaning and a movement toward growth. Thus, the process of counseling itself, like development, can be viewed as involving the loss of the old self and "the dying of a way to know the world which no longer works . . . [from which emerges] a *new* balance . . . a new integration, a new direction" (Kegan, 1982, p. 267).

For the present, Kegan's theory represents the best attempt to define a structured unity to the processes of the ego and its development from an interactionist perspective. Kegan rejected Kohlberg's argument "that the ego compromises relatively circumscribed subdomains that stand in asymmetrical relation to each other . . . [and that] development in a logically prior subdomain appears to be necessary but not sufficient for the parallel level of development in another subdomain" (Snarey, Kohlberg, and Noam, 1983, p. 308). Instead he has argued for the exploration of "the inner world of 'domain dysynchronies,' e.g., and the processes that work toward their integration" (Kegan, in press, p. 30). Nonetheless, it is important to note that Kegan's approach has been to argue for a view of the ego as a unified structure that attempts to make meaning of experience in a more or less wholistic fashion.

Gil Noam

Rather than attempt the direct application of Piagetian theory to clinical practice, "a theory already in question in the very field, developmental psychology, [from which researchers and clinicians bridging clinical and developmental ideas] most heavily draw," Noam has argued for "an intertwining of clinical and developmental theory [through] empirical observation and therapeutic application" (Noam, 1988a, p. 274). A former student and collaborator of Kohlberg's (see Kohlberg and Noam, unpublished manuscript; Noam, Kohlberg, and Snarey, 1983), Noam (1988a) has been very critical of those theorists who "have adopted hard-stage principles of structural wholeness, sequentiality, and hierarchical integration, as if they were dealing with the development of cognitive operations, and . . . directly applied the principles of logical operations to self and life by way of a method of analogy" (p. 279).

In particular, Noam has questioned whether a given stage change successfully transforms and integrates all aspects of the self as these various theorists have claimed. Noting that higher stages of moral and ego development don't lead necessarily to greater mental health and that clients appear both to function and to test at different stages simultaneously, Noam has proposed that the most mature aspect of the self may not be the same as *the* overall self. Rather than accept that development represents a transformation of earlier stages, thus locating psychopathology in the most mature stage of which a person is capable of functioning, Noam (1988a) concluded that "global extensions of Piaget's structural principles of cognitive development [including Kohlberg's,] into the arena of personality are insufficient for the study of the self and psychopathology" (p. 281). Instead, Noam believes that it is the relationship between the most recent developmental advances and all earlier developmental positions that is responsible for the self's activities and, in particular, psychopathology.

Nonetheless, Noam has proposed a framework of "stages of internal and interpersonal self-perspectives." Unlike the clinical interviews used by his predecessors, however, Noam's method of empirically evaluating these self-positions assumes that "a) this system captures only the most mature aspect of a person's development, and b) the self can have reached different levels within different relationship domains" (Noam, 1988a, p. 286). The outcome is a profile of developmental perspectives rather than assignment to a single stage. For counselors, the most significant implication of this approach is that clients may be assessed as functioning at a most mature perspective while simultaneously being influenced by processes that reflect more primitive perspectives. These more primitive perspectives owe their origin to the resistance of earlier experiences to integration into a higher order system. These products, which Noam (1988a) calls "encapsulations, . . . persist in the form of themes and attributions about the self and important relationships . . . as a living part of the self's internal and interpersonal life" (p. 289).

Importantly, these encapsulations have their own logic—it is the logic of the most mature stage at which the client was functioning at the time of the encapsulation. Thus an understanding of the self-logic underlying the client's current most mature level of functioning, coupled with an understanding of the self-logic underlying the client's encapsulation(s), will help the counselor not only to recognize the early self-organizations but also to address them in treatment. Although such treatment remains experimental and investigative at this time, the general approach is one of understanding the system of relationships between the contents of one's lived experience, encapsulations as forms of living biography, and the more mature structures with which they co-exist. This "biographical and transformational" approach leads to a notion of counseling as a reconstructive process whereby earlier, more primitive modes of functioning are transformed and integrated with later, more mature structures.

PROSPECTS FOR THE FUTURE

Just as two decades of research have shown the efficacy of a cognitive-developmental approach to education in school settings, the decades ahead are likely to see extensions of this interactionist approach into clinical and counseling settings as well. Unlike the school applications, which offered development as the aim of education, clinical applications are more likely to seek other aims for counseling. Kohlberg's original terminology for this approach as "cognitive-developmental, interactionist" is giving way to names like "structural," "transactive," and "constructivist." Whatever the name, such an approach to human functioning, more than anything else, depathologizes client concerns. Rather than invoking an image of a conflicted or maladjusted client, a Kohlbergian view of the client focuses on the mismatch between the client's current level of functioning and selected dimensions of the surrounding social environment.

Rather than focusing upon the stimulation of development, an interactional developmental counseling psychology is more likely to concentrate on helping clients with their efforts toward integration. As Noam (1988b) argued: "The ultimate definition for mental health is not the person who can love and work, but the person who can continue to develop through life . . . The aim of therapy is the person who can create ever new meaning in work and love by taking constructively the hurdles and opportunities, as well as disappointments, created by life" (pp. 118-119).

While counselors await a unifying theory of counseling, the near future is likely to offer more integrations of Piagetian and Kohlbergian schemes with existing therapies (see Block, 1982; Carlsen, 1988; Cowan, 1988; Hayes, 1984; Ivey, 1986; Kohut, 1977; Malerstein and Ahern, 1982; Noam, 1988a, 1988b; Rosen, 1985) in attempts to reconceptualize psychopathology. In the meantime, counselors who begin to look at the world through a Kohlbergian lens will find they must take even everyday experiences as challenges to moral growth. What Kohlberg has advocated is a new kind of counselor—one who is an applied developmental psychologist who expects research to change the way social institutions do their work and who gets involved in the process of change.

PART V

THE KOHLBERG LEGACY FOR
THE HELPING PROFESSIONS

Chapter 13

Kohlberg in Perspective:
A Backward and a Forward Look

James Rest

Practically every psychology text published since 1970 makes mention of Lawrence Kohlberg and his six-stage model for the development of moral judgment. In this brief chapter on the influence of Kohlberg on his time and on times to come, I want to cast a backward and forward look at 1) how psychologists' perceptions of moral development have been influenced by Kohlberg, 2) how the stage concept has been linked to cognitive moral development and to the role of moral education in the schools, 3) why reaction to Kohlberg's theories have sharpened and extended psychologists' views about the role of other processes, variables, and key concepts besides Kohlberg's focus on moral judgment, and 4) how Kohlberg's theories on school interventions have clarified and extended our perception of the role of the school in moral development.

In the 1950s, when Kohlberg was doing his dissertation research, it was widely accepted that moral development was something you essentially absorbed from your culture. It was assumed that researchers need not worry about the individual's subjective interpretation or understanding of moral norms. In contrast, Kohlberg was convinced that the individual's understanding of social situations was critical to the study of morality. While Skinner claimed that the study of inner cognitions was superfluous, Kohlberg made cognition his primary target.

At that time, Piaget's work was virtually unknown to Americans. To Kohlberg, Piaget's abstract-logical models of cognitive functioning seemed to be the most robust model for explaining moral, as well as general, cognitive reasoning. Much of Kohlberg's energy during the 1960s was devoted to arguing the usefulness of Piaget's approach and to extend Piaget's approach into the domain of social and personality development. In Kohlberg's chapter in the Goslin Handbook (1969) for example, he reinterprets the entire field of social and personality development from a cognitive-developmental point of view.

Kohlberg and his colleagues argued for an even harder stage concept in the area of moral judgment than Piaget did. In the 1983 SCRD Monograph that Kohlberg co-authored with Ann Colby, John Gibbs, and Marcus Lieberman, the results of the twenty-year longitudinal study of moral judgment were presented as the strongest possible defense of the stage concept.

I would suggest that Kohlberg's attraction to Piaget's model of cognitive functioning was due in part to his interest in driving as big and sharp a contrast as was possible between content and structure. One reason Kohlberg wanted to argue for as big a contrast between content and structure as possible was that he wanted to emphasize that his brand of moral education was constitutionally defensible and was not a violation of the separation between church and state. He argued that moral education in the schools need not involve the teaching of religion or any specific doctrine. Moral education should facilitate the development of naturally emerging improvements in understanding the social world, through focus on the development of basic problem-solving strategies. Dilemma discussions were educational strategies for developing such problem-solving capacities.

Important as Kohlberg's stage concept has been, I would suggest that it has not been his most important contribution to the psychology of moral development. What is more important is his emphasis on the cognitive construction of social reality. The conviction that morality must take account of the ways people understand society and social relationships, and that this involves a process of inner cognitive construction, is fundamental to Kohlberg's approach.

There is an irony in the history of the stage concept; the irony has to do with the role the stage concept played in the debates between behaviorists and cognitive psychologists in the 1950s and 1960s. Behaviorists argued that all phenomena of behavior could be accounted for in terms of functional relationship with the environment and that it was unnecessary to postulate inner, unobservable, cognitive processes. Cognitive psychologists argued that it was necessary to postulate cognitions because without them one could not explain phenomena like 1) consistencies in organizational patterns across situations, 2) abrupt changes that occur system-wide in certain behavioral domains, and 3) regular, step-wide progressions in behavioral change over time. The line of argument was that you had to believe in the value of studying cognition because stage-like phenomena could not be explained otherwise.

The irony is that today almost all psychologists accept the value of studying cognitions, but many psychologists have great difficulty in accepting the claim that stage-like phenomena actually exist! And so the end-point is widely accepted, but the arguments used to support the end-point are less accepted.

While Piaget's impact on psychology is and has been tremendous, doubts have been raised both about his stage concept and his use of logical formalism to model cognitive processes. Were Kohlberg alive today, he might well be open to altered views of cognitive development. Kohlberg embraced Piaget because Piaget's theory was the most profound and defensible theory of the human mind available at the time. If we find new theories of learning and cognitions that are more profound and defensible, we should adapt these new approaches. That is what Kohlberg would do in our place. At one APA conference, Kohlberg said that the stage concept was like a leaky boat—he was busy patching up the stage concept trying to keep it afloat, but if any more sea-worthy boat came along he would not mind jumping ship.

It is possible that Kohlberg attempted to define the fundamental structures of moral thinking at too formal a level of abstraction. Perhaps "content" and "structure" are not the only possible cognitive elements; perhaps it is also helpful to think in terms of schema, scripts, and other frames of reference.

By now everyone realizes that there's more to the psychology of morality than Kohlberg's six stages of moral judgment. Additional variables, such as moral sensitivity, moral identity, moral motivation, or moral character may have to be taken into account. Orientations other than moral judgment may have to be taken into account; some have proposed care or response as the key concept, some have proposed filial piety or obedience to God. I propose that we be as bold and imaginative in articulating new theory as Kohlberg was, but then follow the bold theory with solid research as he did.

If one reads the literature of the 1970s and early 1980s that is critical of Kohlberg, one finds him taken to task for making bold claims of universality based in good part on an initial research base of fifty boys from Chicago. Why did Kohlberg claim that he could generalize sequential stage development for all people from an initial research base limited to fifty boys from Chicago?

A colleague tells a story that may help to explain Kohlberg's boldness. Having just finished his doctoral dissertation, Kohlberg presented his findings at the next APA convention. There he properly hedged and qualified his findings and gave due respect to the limitations of his dissertation. The audience reaction was zero. Kohlberg was turning morality research on its head, but it was as if he had said nothing. After this experience, he decided that he had to be bolder; and the Kohlberg of the 1960s and 1970s was very bold indeed and was successful in getting heard.

During the 1970s, when Kohlberg was making bold claims that went way beyond his published data, psychologists challenged him for not having a reliable scoring system that others could replicate and for not having valid data that produced the age trends predicted by his theory. At the same time, Kohlberg was under attack from philosophers regarding the conceptual adequacy of his theory and under attack from educators who wanted him to demonstrate how his ideas could be implemented in school settings.

Kohlberg responded to his critics by working and reworking his scoring system until he had a final version that demonstrated amazing reliability. His twenty-year longitudinal study showed amazing confirmation of the trends predicted by the theory. Other longitudinal studies, with both males and females, in the USA and other countries, replicated the results of the Chicago sample of boys as well. Kohlberg did not leave the issue of the validity and usefulness of his six-stage theory in the air. He did not make his case merely by quoting a handful of anecdotes or by making broad-brush observations about the human condition. He did the conceptual, empirical, and applied work to give substance to his claims.

Not the least of Kohlberg's legacy to a new generation was his personal involvement with the major educational interventions described in other chapters of this volume. In contrast to his focus on individual assessment, in school interventions designed to foster moral development Kohlberg focuses his attention on interaction within the group. The key question for moral education in the schools should be: How do you build a sense of community and how do you maintain community?

This emphasis on community is not the same as the conventional concept of civic education, nor is it synonymous with thinking of the school as a happy family. In school, the child must come to realize that there is more to morality than being friendly with your friends; that there is more to morality than showing love to those who think you are lovable; that there is more to morality than being generous with those who turn you on. In school the child should learn to relate to communities that for the most part consist of strangers. In school the child should learn how to build and participate in wider communities, how to construct social institutions and social organizations that can accomplish what small groups of friends cannot accomplish.

Because the major Kohlberg interventions took place in schools with large numbers of deprived and/or disengaged teenagers, much community building had to focus on compensatory activities to develop trust and care. If and when the "just community" model is extended to other populations, learning to build and participate in ever-widening communities will be seen as a primary task for moral education in adolescence and young adulthood; one in which Kohlberg helped to show the way.

Chapter 14

Kohlberg and His Circle of Friends

Lisa Kuhmerker

While countless theoreticians and practitioners have been influenced by Kohlberg's publications, the major contributions to moral development theory and education have been made by individuals whose work brought them into personal contact with Kohlberg. Of this group, a substantial proportion met Kohlberg in the context of their graduate and postgraduate work, and many of the excerpts in the following pages are from people to whom Kohlberg had been either a formal or informal dissertation adviser. A small but not insignificant number of people met Kohlberg through students they had in common. Some became colleagues through school intervention projects. The smallest number, like myself, had no strong "academic claim" for requesting an appointment with Kohlberg, but persevered against considerable odds.

As the founder of the Association for Moral Education, I persuaded Larry to come to one of the early meetings of the fledgling group, and from that point on he was always "first among equals" in our hearts. When the membership honored me by creating a Kuhmerker Award for service to the association, it was the most natural thing in the world for Larry to be the first recipient of the award. How best to honor a man like Kohlberg? A plaque was appropriate but insufficient. We peeked into Larry's address file and solicited letters from a remarkably long list of close colleagues, collected them, and read liberally from the contributions at the award dinner.

It was a joyous occasion, and when I remember Larry I think of two occasions: the first time I met him and the evening he received the Kuhmerker Award. So, within the space limits of my contribution to this volume, I want to share part of both sets of memories.

I don't remember exactly what year I met Larry Kohlberg; it could have been 1969 or 1970. I know it was in the "old days," when correspondence disappeared into a bottomless pit, and the hapless individual who was drafted to answer the Center's telephone claimed to be taking messages but was powerless to make appointments.

It was at that point that I decided to take three days out of my life and literally sit on the doorstep of Larry's office until he fell across me. At that time, Larry had a small office in Larsen Hall at Harvard. It was filled to the ceiling with books and papers. It seemed to me that there were a great many young men at work in various cubicles. Every so often, when the secretary was quite positive that Larry would not be appearing within the next hour, I made a quick foray into one of those offices. Bob Selman's office is one that stays in my mind. We had no sooner begun to talk when one young man after another filed into the office and conversation got better and better. Suddenly, without preamble, they rose as one . . . and announced that they were off to play basketball! One might say that the subsequent creation of the Association for Moral Education is no more or less than a creative way to assure that there would be some time each year when women interested in moral development theory and practice could be sure that their male counterparts would not cut short a good conversation by retreating to the locker room.

I resumed my vigil on Larry's doorsill. Somewhere toward the end of the second afternoon, he appeared. He answered my specific questions but merely whetted my curiosity. Since I was staying another day, I asked if I could borrow something to read overnight. Larry rummaged in the pile on the desk and pulled out a manuscript. "This is the only copy I have," he said, "you really have to promise to bring it back."

I remember returning to my motel room early in the evening, climbing into bed, and starting the manuscript. It was *From Is to Ought*. I had had no idea what to expect, and I was enthralled. All my ideas clicked into place in a new way. It was surprising; it was exhilarating. It was absolutely the only time in my life when I had a peak experience alone in a motel room.

Year after year I revisited the Center. Several times I attended scoring workshops and informal consortiums. If there was no "event," I simply came to attend one of the weekly open sessions in Room 313. Moral development theory changed the way I thought about learning and teaching. If I haven't suffered from "teacher burnout" I owe it to Larry; to his ideas and to the people I met who were working—or waiting—for Larry Kohlberg.

Making a selection from the letters is no easy task. Perhaps a good way to begin is by quoting from the reminiscences of Liam Grimley, a professor at Indiana State University, who was one of Kohlberg's earliest friends and colleagues. In recalling their experiences together, Grimley decided that four words best described Kohlberg: lovable, courageous, exciting, and dedicated.

The word "lovable" is not a term we often think of using to describe an eminent psychologist, educator, writer, and scholar. But in your case, it's the very first word that comes to mind. You not only have the quality of being lovable, but you also have a remarkable ability to insure this characteristic in those who work with you. Over the years there has gathered around you—at Harvard and elsewhere—an extraordinary group of lovable people, faculty and students alike. This group does not operate like a professional organization but more like a club of good-humored, lovable people, all of whom have not only a peculiarly fanatical interest in the study of moral development but also a deep personal affection for Lawrence Kohlberg, the man.

Robert Kegan—a colleague at Harvard who has integrated Kohlbergian theory into his thinking so thoroughly that he has created a developmental clinical theory that sees what is commonly accepted as mental "breakdown" as actually a failure of developmental "breakthrough"—remembers taking his life in his hands as a passenger in Kohlberg's car.

We piled into the front seat, you behind the wheel, me on your right. The car was in the Larsen lot, facing a yard-high brick wall. You turned on the engine, put the car in gear and rammed right into the wall, the car flying back to its original position. You and it rested a moment. Then you started the engine up again, put it in gear, and you and I and the car flew once again smack into the wall, once again bouncing back to our starting point. I remember thinking, "This is a novel approach to exiting a parking lot. But what persistence!" This is a note of admiration and affection for your persistence, Larry—and of appreciation for what it has wrought.

Kegan's reminiscence moves from literally smacking into a brick wall to the struggle of the "young upstarts" who called themselves "clinical developmentalists" to bring developmental and clinical psychology together. The task seemed at times as wearying and apparently ill-fated as the ride in the Larsen parking lot.

Isn't it remarkable, I thought. For twenty-five years this man has kept faith with an idea. And what struck me was not so much that the idea is as important as it ever was or that it is the foundation for so much other work now getting attention—although I think these things are also true. What struck me was how much we all derive from your continuing example that an idea can be compelling enough, and an individual devoted enough, for the two to spend twenty-five years together in a relationship as fresh and combustible today as when it began. . . . I have been changed by your quiet and persistent faithfulness, a stubbornness on behalf of everyone's development. . . . The wall in the Larsen lot is still standing but a lot of other walls are not.

Gil Noam, on the staff of McLean Hospital and Harvard's Department of Psychiatry, recalls the first time he invited Kohlberg to dinner:

I had just arrived in this country . . . and had only the barest of furnishings acquired from fourth-hand stores. You probably did not notice that the chair you sat on was dangerous, the bowl you ate from was cracked and the table you sat at was a desk covered with a sheet. In fact, it became clear that you could be at home almost anyplace as long as important dialogue was possible.

The experience of that first evening has been the core of our relationship. Your questions and our dialogue have contributed greatly toward integrating myself, theories, our relationship, a new sense of history and biography, and a new vision of development. All this with two main tools: "why" and respect.

In making contact with the children of students and colleagues to whose houses Kohlberg was invited for dinner, he often drew on his youthful skill as a magician. Tom Lickona, professor at SUNY Cortland, has a son, Mark, who was an aspiring magician at the age of eleven, when he and Kohlberg took turns entertaining guests. But Mark learned more than some new tricks from Kohlberg. Shortly thereafter, he wrote the following fantasy:

I accept the nomination for election for the President of the International Brotherhood of Magicians. I have always had a dream of becoming a great magician. I shall take all responsibility and make sure that all our meetings are properly organized. What's more, I shall always maintain a fair and cooperative mood toward my fellow magicians.

Most "Kohlbergians" came "under the influence" during their mentor's years at Harvard. Jim Rest was one of the small number who began to work with Kohlberg when they were at the University of Chicago. Rest remembers meeting Larry when the latter was a not very well-known assistant professor. As Rest was moving through the clinical psychology sequence, friends suggested he take Kohlberg's course.

They said that the course was very stimulating, although the instructor was totally unfair in loading up the reading assignments and course requirements. Indeed, for only three lousy credits, Larry assigned about 2000 pages of reading, required a term paper and a research project, and a midterm exam and a final. The course was great but it just about killed everybody who took it. After working your head off for Larry's introductory course, it seemed only a small step to make developmental psychology your life's work.

At Chicago, Larry's courses drew the largest crowds of students and at one point he advised almost a dozen dissertations per year. His manner was low-key but his enthusiasm and his brilliance attracted more interest and more students than the staffing in developmental psychology could handle. The other faculty . . . believed that the future of psychology was in biopsychology . . .

and thought that developmental psychology would soon fade away. Hence Larry was lured to Harvard.

After collecting my dissertation data in Chicago, I moved to Harvard to join Larry as a post-doc. I look upon those days as the Camelot era. At the Center for Moral Education there was a sense of being at the right place at the right time, that terribly new and important breakthroughs were just around the corner . . . that granting agencies and foundations were eager to fund projects, that questions of social justice were on everyone's mind, and we thought we had the answers—or nearly had the answers.

It was at this point that the scoring of moral dilemmas began to take on monumental proportions. Kohlberg became convinced that his 1958 scoring system ought to be revised, and he wasn't going to settle for just a little tidying up. As Rest recalls:

> If I remember correctly, the first revision of the 1958 scoring system required a scorer to cross-classify a moral judgment simultaneously along eight dimensions, and there were over two and a half million possible combinations. . . . Larry's assistants at the Center (of which I was one) began to complain and drag our feet. Larry's tactic in response was to call a national conference and invite one hundred people. . . . Although Larry said the scoring workshop was to enable other psychologists to use his scoring system, I think the real purpose was to whip his assistants into line. . . . Later on I also suspected that Larry would call another scoring workshop whenever he felt his assistants were working less than eighty hours a week.

Despite his rueful recollection of the innumerable items scorers of Moral Judgment Interviews were expected to categorize, Rest took the occasion of the Association for Moral Education's honoring of Lawrence Kohlberg to share with the group his belief that Kohlberg's distinctive role in psychology has often been misperceived:

> Foremost he is a visionary, a discoverer of new phenomena and new connections, a proposer of new approaches, one who works on the big picture and keeps the major questions in focus. This sort of psychologist is rare among American psychologists . . . but also, being so rare, Larry's role is all the more important in American psychology, for otherwise many of us would not have identified the important questions, would not have a conceptual framework for designing our own work, or would not have become interested in psychology at all.

In the first letter I quoted, Liam Grimley calls Kohlberg, "lovable, courageous, exciting and dedicated." I hope that the lovable, exciting, and dedicated dimensions of Kohlberg's personality have leaped out from these pages. If so, it is fitting to close with excerpts from a letter that highlights the fourth of these dimensions. Norman Sprinthall, a professor at the University of North Carolina, recalls:

> While at the Harvard Graduate School of Education, I learned many things like the importance of theoretical relativism and similar games of sophistry. . . . Also I learned the difference between such breath-taking rhetoric and action. It was during the infamous Nixon-Kissinger "incursion" into some parts of Laos-Cambodia called the Parrots Beak when I came of age on that score.

> The faculty, at that time, seemed righteously outraged at this latest attempt to win South East Asia by destroying the countries. I too was certainly caught up in the immorality of such an adventure and found myself the author of a formal proposal to the faculty to take a stand on the question.

> After due reverence was paid to the necessities of academic freedom . . . a resolution was struck. The votes counted. We had won. The faculty for the first time had authorized a document proclaiming that the administration of the country was in error on moral grounds. I was feeling triumphant.

> At that moment the Dean queried, "Well, who will take the position paper to Washington?" Since I had been standing up a good deal of the time debating the issues, I naturally felt some obligation to offer. After accepting, I then asked, "And who will help me?"

> It would be difficult to describe in the light of passing years, just how silent the meeting became. It was just like a sailing ship in the doldrums. Motionless. Eerily quiet. These giants of education who daily proclaimed the virtues of equality, of human rights, of democratic citizenship, and who had themselves just voted overwhelmingly in favor of the resolution, now sat in perfect repose, looking at their shoes.

> Numbed and dazzled by this educational experience, I finally did notice one lone figure, somewhat unkempt in attire, standing next to me. Although I had met him on a number of prior occasions, that was the time I really met Larry.

Bibliography

Ahmed, R.A., Gielen, U.P., and Avellani, J. (1987). Perceptions of parental behavior and the development of moral reasoning in Sudanese students. In C. Kagitcibasi (Ed.). *Growth and progress in cross-cultural psychology.* Lisse, Holland: Swets and Zeitlinger.

Anderson, C.S. (1982). The search for school climate: A review of the search. *Review of Educational Research,* 52:368-420.

Armon, C. (1984). Ideals of the good life and moral judgment: Ethical reasoning across the lifespan. In M. Commons, F. Richards, and C. Armon (Eds.), *Beyond formal operations: Late adolescent and adult cognitive development.* New York: Praeger.

Baldwin, J.M. (1906). *Social and ethical interpretations in mental development.* New York: Macmillan.

Barber, L. (1984). *Teaching Christian Values.* Birmingham, AL: Religious Education Press.

Beck, A. (1967). *Depression: Causes and treatment.* Englewood Cliffs, NJ: Prentice Hall.

Berkowitz, M.W. and Gibbs, J.C. (1983). Measuring the developmental features of moral discussion. *Merrill-Parker Quarterly,* 29:399-410.

Berkowitz, M.W., Gibbs, J.C., and Broughton, J.M. (1980). The relation of moral judgment stage disparity to developmental effects of peer dialogues. *Merrill-Palmer Quarterly,* 26:341-57.

Blasi, A. (1976). Concept of development in personality theory. In J. Loevinger (Ed.), *Ego development* (pp. 29-53). San Francisco: Josey-Bass.

Blasi, A. (1980). Bridging moral cognition and moral action: A critical review of the literature. *Psychological Bulletin,* 88:1-45.

Blatt, M. (1969). The effects of classroom discussion programs upon children's level of moral development. PhD dissertation, University of Chicago.

Blatt, M. and Kohlberg, L. (1975). The effects of classroom moral discussion upon children's moral judgment. *Journal of Moral Education,* 4:129-61.

Block, J. (1982). Assimilation, accommodation, and the dynamics of personality development. *Child Development, 53*, 281-295.

Bossart, D.E. (1980). *Creative conflict in religious education and church administration.* Birmingham, AL: Religious Education Press.

Browning, R.L. and Reed, R. (1985). *The sacraments in religious education and liturgy.* Birmingham, AL: Religious Education Press.

Carkhuff, R. (1969). *Helping and human relations.* Vol 2. New York: Holt, Rinehart and Winston.

Carlsen, M. (1988). *Meaning-making: Therapeutic process in adult development.* New York: Norton.

Chazan, B. (1985). Jewish education and moral development. In B. Munsey (Ed.), *Moral Development, Moral Education, and Kohlberg.* Birmingham, AL: Religious Education Press.

Cheng, S.W. (1990). Characteristics of moral judgment among college students in Taiwan, examined in the light of Kohlberg's stage scheme of moral judgment. In Chinese Culture University, *Proceedings of CCU-ICP International Conference. Moral Values and Moral Reasoning in Chinese Societies* (pp. 339-377). Chinese Culture University, Taipei (Taiwan).

Chesbrough, L. and Conrad T. (1981). Creating a "just community": Planning, process, and participation. *Moral Education Forum,* 6-4:8-13.

Codding, J. and Arenella, A. (1981). Creating a "just community": The transformation of an alternative school. *Moral Education Forum,* 6-4:2-7.

Codding, J. with Arenella, A. (1981). Supporting moral development with a curriculum of ethical decision making. *Moral Education Forum,* 6-4:14-23.

Colby, A. (1978). Evolution of a moral-developmental theory. In W. Damon (Ed.), *New Directions for Child Development: Moral Development.* Vol. 2. San Francisco: Jossey-Bass.

Colby, A. and Kohlberg, L. (1987). *The measurement of moral judgment. Vol. 1: Theoretical foundations and research validation.* New York: Cambridge University Press.

Colby, A., Kohlberg, L., Speicher, B., Hewer, A., Candee, D., Gibbs, C., and Power, C. (1987). *The Measurement of Moral Judgment. Vol.2: Standard Issue Scoring Manual.* New York: Cambridge University Press.

Colby, A., Kohlberg, L., Fenton, E., Speicher-Dubin, B., and Lieberman, M. (1977). Secondary school moral discussion programmes led by social studies teachers. *Journal of Moral Education,* 6:90-111.

Colby, A., Kohlberg, L., Gibbs, J., and Lieberman, M. (1983). A longitudinal study of moral judgment. *Monograph of the Society for Research in Child Development, vol.48, no.4.*

Commons, M. Richards F. and Armon, C. (Eds.). (1984) *Beyond formal operations: Cognitive development in late adolescence and adulthood.*

New York: Praeger.

Cowan, P. (1988). Developmental psychopathology; A nine-cell map of the territory. In E. Nannis and P. Cowan (Eds.), *New directions for child development: Developmental psychopathology and its treatment* (pp. 5-29). San Francisco: Jossey-Bass.

Damon, W. (1977). *The Social World of the Child.* San Francisco: Jossey-Bass.

D'Andrea, M. (1984, February). The counselor as pacer. *Counseling and Human Development, 16,* 1-15.

Dember, W. (1965). The new look in motivation. *American Scientist, 53,* 409-427.

DeVries, R. with Kohlberg, L. (1987). *Programs of Early Education: The Constructivist View.* New York: Longman.

Dewey, J. (1916/1966). *Democracy and Education.* New York: Macmillan.

Dewey, J. (1938/1963). *Experience and Education.* New York: Macmillan.

Dewey, J. (1960). *Theory of the moral life.* New York: Holt, Rinehart and Winston.

Dewy, J. and McLellan, J. (1964). The psychology of number. In R. Archamebault (Ed.), *John Dewey on education: Selected writings.* (pp. 207-208). New York: Random House.

Dien, D.S.F. (1982). A Chinese perspective on Kohlberg's theory of moral development. *Developmental Review, 2:* 331-341.

Durkheim, E. (1925/1973). *Moral education: A study in the theory and application of the sociology of education.* New York: Free Press.

Edwards, C.P. (1981). The comparative study of the development of moral judgment and reasoning. In R.H. Munroe, R.L. Munroe, and B.B. Whiting (Eds.), *Handbook of cross-cultural human development.* New York: Garland.

Edwards, C.P. (1986). Cross-cultural research on Kohlberg's stages: The basis for concensus. In S. Mogdil and C. Mogdil (Eds.), *Lawrence Kohlberg: Concensus and controversy.* London: Falmer Press.

Ellis, A. (1962). *Reason and emotion in psychotherapy.* New York: Lyle Stuart.

Emler, D.G. (1989). *Revisioning the DRE.* Birmingham, AL: Religious Education Press.

Fenton, E. (1976). The cognitive-developmental approach to moral education. *Social Education, 40* (April) 4.

Fenton, E. (1977). The implication of Lawrence Kohlberg's research for civic education. In B.F. Brown, *Education for Responsible Citizenship: The Report of the National Task Force on Citizenship Education.* New York: McGraw-Hill.

Fenton, E. (1980). The role of dilemma discussion in education. In S.H. Gomberg, D.K. Cameron, E. Fenton, J. Purtek, and C.L. Hill, *Leading Dilemma Discussions: A Workshop,* pp. 153-161. Pittsburgh: Carnegie

Mellon University.

Fenton E. and Wasserman, E. (1985). *A Leader's Guide to Improving School Climate Through Implementing the Fairness Committee: A Manual for Students and Teachers; A Community Approach to Resolving Grievances.* (A revision of the 1976 Fairness Manual by Wasserman) Cambridge, MA Schools, Manuscript, 42 pp.

Fowler, J. (1981). *Stages of faith: The psychology of human development and the quest for meaning.* San Francisco: Harper & Row.

Fowler, J. (1987). Varieties of presence in stages of faith. *Moral Education Forum,* 12,1,4-14.

Frankena, W.K. (1973). *Ethics.* Second edition. Englewood Cliffs, NJ: Prentice Hall.

Freud, S. (1933). *New introductory lectures on psychoanalysis.* New York: Norton.

Galbraith, R.E. and Jones, T. (1976). *Moral reasoning: A teaching handbook for adapting Kohlberg to the classroom.* Anoka, MN: Greenhaven Press.

Gates, B. (1985). ME + RE = Kohlberg with a difference. In S. and C. Mogdil (Eds.), *Lawrence Kohlberg: Consensus and Controversy.* Philadelphia: Falmer International.

Gibbs, J.C., Arnold, K.D., and Burkhart, J. (1984). Sex differences in the expression of moral judgment. *Child Development, 55,* 1040-1043.

Gibbs, J.C., Arnold, K.D., Morgan, R.L., Schwarz, E.S., Gavaghan, M.P., and Tappan, M.B. (1984). Construction and validation of a multiple-choice measure of moral reasoning. *Child Development, 55,* 527-536.

Gibbs, J.C., Basinger, K.S. and Fuller, R.L. (in press). *Moral maturity: Measuring the development of sociomoral reflection.* Hillsdale, N.J.: L. Erlbaum.

Gibbs, J.C. and Wideman, K.F. (1982). *Social intelligence: Measuring the development of sociomoral reflection.* Englewood Cliffs, NJ: Prentice Hall.

Gielen, U.P. (1986). Moral reasoning in radical and non-radical German students. *Behavior Science Research, 20* (1-4), 71-109.

Gielen, U.P. (1990). Some recent work on moral values, reasoning and education in Chinese societies. *Moral Education Forum,* 15, (1), 3-22.

Gielen, U.P., Miao, E., and Avellani, J. (1990). Perceived parental behavior and the development of moral reasoning in students from Taiwan. In Chinese Culture University, *Proceedings of CCU-ICP International Conference. Moral Values and moral reasoning in Chinese Societies* (pp. 464-506). Chinese Culture University, Taipei (Taiwan).

Gilligan, C. (1982). *In a different voice.* Cambridge, MA: Harvard University Press.

Gilligan, C. and Attanucci, J. (1988). Two moral orientations: Gender differences and similarities. *Merrill-Palmer Quarterly, 34*, 223-237.

Gilligan, C., Langdale, S., Lyons, N., and Murphy, J.M. (1982). *The contribution of women's thought to developmental theory: The elimination of sex bias in moral development research and education.* Unpublished manuscript, Cambridge, MA: Harvard University.

Gilligan, C., Ward, J., and Taylor J. (Eds.) (1980). *Mapping the moral domain: A contribution of women's thinking to psychology and education.* Cambridge, MA: Harvard University Press.

Gomberg, S.H., Cameron, D.K., Fenton, E., Purtek, J., and Hill, C.L. (1980). *Leading Dilemma Discussions: A Workshop.* Pittsburgh: Carnegie Mellon University.

Grimmet, M. (1987). *Religious education and human development.* Great Wakering, England: McCrimmons.

Groome, T.H. (1980). *Christian religious education.* San Francisco: Harper & Row.

Haan, N., Smith, B., and Block, J. (1968). Political, family and personality correlates of adolescent moral judgment. *Journal of Personality and Social Psychology, 10,* 183-201.

Harkness, S., Edwards, C.P., and Sper, C.M. (1981). Social rules and moral reasoning: A case study in a rural African community. *Developmental Psychology, 17,* 595-603.

Hartshorne, H. and May, M.A. (1928/1930). *Studies in the Nature of Character. Vol 1: Studies in Deceit; Vol. 2: Studies in Service and Self-Control; Vol. 3: Studies in the Organization of Character.* New York: Macmillan.

Hayes, R. (1980). *The democratic classroom: A program in moral education for adolescents.* PhD dissertation, Boston University.

Hayes, R. (1984). Making meaning: Expanding the "C" in "BASIC ID." *Journal of Humanistic Education and Development, 23,* 146-145.

Hayes, R. and Kenny, J. (1983). Search for a system: Developmental paradigms, counseling research, and the Journal of Counseling Psychology. *Journal of Counseling Psychology, 30,* 438-442.

Hickey, J. (1972). *The effects of guided moral discussion upon youthful offenders' moral judgment.* PhD dissertation, Boston University.

Hickey, J. and Scharf, P. (1980). *Towards a just correctional system.* San Francisco: Jossey-Bass.

Higgins, A. (1980). Research and measurement issues in moral education interventions. In R. Mosher (Ed.), *Moral Education: A First Generation of Research and Development.* New York: Praeger.

Higgins, A. (in press). The just community approach to moral education: Evolution of the idea and recent findings. In W. Kurtines and J. Gewirtz (Eds.), *Moral Behavior and Development: Advances in Theory, Research and Application.* Hillsdale, N.J.: Lawrence Erlbaum Associates.

Higgins, A., Power, C., and Kohlberg, L. (1984). The relationship of moral judgment to judgments of responsibility. In J. Gewirtz and W. Kurtines (Eds.), *Morality, Moral Development, and Moral Behavior: Basic Issues in Theory and Research.* New York: Wiley.

Ivey, A. (1986). *Developmental therapy.* San Francisco: Jossey-Bass.

Jennings, W. (1979). *The juvenile delinquent as a moral philosopher: The effects of rehabilitation programs on the moral reasoning and behavior of male youthful offenders.* PhD dissertation, Harvard University.

Jennings, W., Kilkenny, R., and Kohlberg, L. (1983). Moral development theory and practice for youthful and adult offenders. In W.S. Laufer and J. M. Day (Eds.), *Personality theory, moral development and criminal behavior.* Lexington, MA: Lexington Books.

Jennings, W. and Kohlberg, L. (1983). Effects of just community programs on the moral development of youthful offenders. *Journal of Moral Education*, vol.2, no.1.

Kanfer, F., and Goldstein, A. (Eds.) (1980). *Helping people change.* New York: Pergamon Press.

Kegan, R. (1979). *A neo-Piagetian approach to object relations.* Paper presented at the meeting of the Center for Pyschological Studies, Chicago.

Kegan, R. (1982). *The evolving self: Problem and process in human development.* Cambridge, MA: Harvard University Press.

Kegan, R. (1986). Kohlberg and the psychology of ego development: A predominantly positive evaluation. In S. Mogdil and C. Mogdil (Eds.), *Lawrence Kohlberg: Consensus and controversy.* (pp. 163-182). Philadelphia: Falmer Press.

Kenney, R. (1983). *The creation of a democratic high school: A psychological approach.* PhD dissertation, Boston University.

Kitchener, K., and King, P. (1981). Concepts of justification and their relationship to age and education. *Journal of Applied Developmental Psychology, 2,* 89-116.

Knefelkamp, L., and Slepitza, R. (1976). A cognitive-developmental model of career development: An adaptation of the Perry scheme. *The Counseling Psychologist, 6,* 53-58.

Kober, W. (1980/1981). Living in a "just community": A student perspective. *Moral Education Forum*, vol. 5-2; reprinted in vol. 6-4.

Kohlberg, L. (1958) *The development of modes of thinking and choices in the years from 10 to 16.* PhD dissertation, University of Chicago.

Kohlberg, L. (1963). Moral development and identification. In H. Stevenson (Ed.), *Child Psychology. 62nd Yearbook of the National Society for the Study of Education* (pp. 277-332). University of Chicago Press.

Kohlberg, L. (1964). The development of moral character and ideology. In M.L. Hoffman and L.W. Hoffman (Eds.), *Review of child development research*, vol. 1 (pp. 383-431). New York: Russel Sage Foundation.

Kohlberg, L. (1967). Moral and religious education in the public schools: A developmental view. In N. and T. Sizer (Eds.), *Religion and public education*. Boston: Houghton Mifflin.

Kohlberg, L. (1969). Moral education in the school. *School Review,* 74:1-30.

Kohlberg, L. (1969). Stage and sequence: The cognitive-developmental approach to socialization. In D. Goslin (Ed.), *Handbook of socialization theory and research*. Chicago: Rand McNally.

Kohlberg, L. (1970a). Education for justice: A modern statement of the platonic view. In N. and T. Sizer (Eds.), *Moral education: Five lectures.* Cambridge, MA: Harvard University Press.

Kohlberg, L. (1970b). The moral atmosphere of the school. In N. Overley (Ed.), *The Unstudied Curriculum.* Washington, D.C.: Association for Supervision and Curriculum Development.

Kohlberg, L. (1971a). Cognitive-developmental theory and the practice of collective moral education. In M. Wolins and M. Gottesman (Eds.), *Group Care: The Israeli Approach.* New York: Gordon and Breach.

Kohlberg, L. (1971b). From is to ought: How to commit the naturalistic fallacy and get away with it in the study of moral development. In T. Michel (Ed.), *Cognitive development and epistemology.* New York: Academic Press.

Kohlberg, L. (1971c). Indoctrination versus relativity in value education. *Zygon,* 6:285-310.

Kohlberg, L. (1971d). Moral education, psychological view of. *International Encyclopedia of Education,* Vol. 6. New York: Macmillan and Free Press.

Kohlberg, L. (1971e). Stages of moral development as a basis for moral education. In C. Beck, B. Crittendon, and E. Sullivan (Eds.), *Moral education: Interdisciplinary approaches.* Toronto: University of Toronto Press.

Kohlberg, L. (1971f). *Structural issue scoring manual.* Unpublished manuscript, Harvard University, Center for Moral Education.

Kohlberg, L. (1972). A cognitive-developmental approach to moral education. *The Humanist, 32,* 13-16.

Kohlberg, L. (1974). Education, moral development and faith. *Moral Education Forum,* 4,1.

Kohlberg, L. (1975). Counseling and counselor education: A developmental approach. *Counselor Education and Supervision, 14,* 250-256.

Kohlberg, L. (1976). Moral stages and moralization: The cognitive-developmental approach. In T. Lickona (Ed.), *Moral development and behavior: Theory, research and social Issues.* New York: Holt, Rinehart and Winston.

Kohlberg, L. (1978). Preface. In P. Scharf (Ed.), *Readings in moral education.* Minneapolis: Winston.

Kohlberg, L. (1980). High school democracy and educating for a just society.

In R. Mosher (Ed.), *Moral Education: A First Generation of Research and Development.* New York: Praeger.

Kohlberg, L. (1981). *Essays on moral development, Vol. I: The philosophy of moral development.* New York: Harper & Row.

Kohlberg, L. (1984). *Essays on moral development, Vol. II: The psychology of moral development.* New York: Harper & Row.

Kohlberg, L. (1985). A just community approach to moral education in theory and practice. In M. Berkowitz and F. Oser (Eds.), *Moral Education: Theory and Practice.* Hillsdale, NJ: Lawrence Erlbaum.

Kohlberg, L. (1986). My personal search for universal morality. *Moral Education Forum,* 11-1:4-10.

Kohlberg, L. and Candee, D. (1984). The relation of moral judgment to moral action. In W. Kurtines and J. Gewirtz (Eds.), *Morality, Moral Behavior, and Moral Development.* New York: Wiley.

Kohlberg, L. with DeVries, R., Fein, G., Hart, D., Mayer, R., Noam, G., Snarey, J., and Wertsch, J. (1987). *Child Psychology and Childhood Education: A Cognitive Developmental View.* New York: Longman.

Kohlberg, L., Kaufman, K., Scharf, P., and Hickey, J. (1974). *The just community approach to corrections: A manual, Part I.* Cambridge, MA: Moral Education Research Foundation.

Kohlberg, L., Lieberman, M., Power, C., and Higgins, A. (1981). Evaluating Scarsdale's "Just Community School" and its curriculum: Implications for the future. *Moral Education Forum, 6-4,* 31-42.

Kohlberg, L., and Mayer, R. (1972). Development as the aim of education. *Harvard Educational Review,* 42:449-96.

Kohlberg, L., and Noam, G. Theories of the lifespan. In L. Kohlberg (Ed.), *Ethical Stages through the lifecycle.* Unpublished manuscript. Cambridge, MA: Harvard University.

Kohlberg, L. and Turiel, E. (1971). Moral development and moral education. In G. Lesser (Ed.), *Psychology and educational practice.* Glenview, IL: Scott Foresman.

Kohlberg, L., and Wasserman, E. (1980). The cognitive-developmental approach and the practicing counselor: An opportunity for counselors to rethink their roles. *Personnel and Guidance Journal, 58,* 559-567.

Kohut, H. (1977). *The restoration of the self.* New York: International University Press.

Kuhmerker, L., Mentkowski, M., and Erickson, L. (1980). *Evaluating moral development and evaluating educational programs that have a value dimension.* Schenectady, N.Y.: Character Education Press.

Kuhmerker, L. (Ed.) (1981). Facing history and ourselves. *Moral Education Forum,* 6-2, 68.

Kuhmerker, L. (Ed.) (1981). Creating a just community. *Moral Education Forum, 6-4,* 64.

Kurtines, W.M. and Gewirtz, J.L. (Eds.), (1984). *Morality, moral behavior and moral development: Basic issues in theory and research.* New York: Wiley.

Kurtines, W.M. and Gewirtz, J.L. (Eds.), (1987). *Social Development and Social Interaction.* New York: Wiley.

Lambert, H. (1972). *A comparison of Jane Loevinger's theory of ego development and Lawrence Kohlberg's theory of moral development.* PhD dissertation, University of Chicago.

Lazarus, A. (1971). *Behavior therapy and beyond.* New York: McGraw-Hill.

Lee, B. (1973). *A cognitive-developmental approach to filial development.* Master's thesis. University of Chicago.

Lee, J.M. (1977). *The religious education we need.* Birmingham, AL: Religious Education Press.

Lee, J.M. (1980). Christian religious education and moral development. In B. Munsey (Ed.), *Moral development, moral education, and Kohlberg.* Birmingham, AL: Religious Education Press.

Lee, J.M. (1982). The authentic source of religious instruction. In Thompson, N.H. (Ed.) *Religious education and theology.* Birmingham, AL: Religious Education Press.

Lei, T. (1990). A longitudinal study of Chinese character change with special reference to young adulthood. In: Chinese Culture University, *Proceedings of CCU-ICP International Conference. Moral Values and Moral Reasoning in Chinese Societies* (pp. 250-276). Chinese Culture University, Taipei (Taiwan).

Leming, J.S. (1973). *Adolescent moral judgment and deliberation of classical and practical moral dilemmas.* PhD dissertation, University of Wisconsin.

Leming, J.S. (1983a). *Contemporary approaches to moral education: An annotated bibliography and guide to research.* New York: Garland.

Leming, J.S. (1983b). *Foundations of Moral Education: An annotated bibliography.* Westport, CT: Greenwood Press.

Leming, J.S. (1985). Kohlbergian programmes in moral education: A practical review and assessment. In S. and C. Mogdil (Eds.), *Lawrence Kohlberg: Consensus and controversy.* Philadelphia: Falmer International.

Lickona, T. (Ed.), (1976). *Moral development and behavior: Theory, research and social issues.* New York: Holt, Rinehart and Winston.

Lickona, T. (1980). Beyond justice: A curriculum of cooperation. In C. Cochrane and M. Manley-Casimir (Eds.), *Development of moral reasoning.* New York: Praeger.

Lickona, T. (1983). *Raising good children.* New York: Bantam Books.

Lickona, T. and Paradise, M. (1980). Democracy in the elementary school. In R. Mosher (Ed.), *Moral education: A first generation of research.* New York: Praeger.

Lieberman, M. (1981). Facing history and ourselves: A project evaluation. *Moral Education Forum*, 6-4, 36-41.

Lind, G., Grocholweska, K., and Langer, J. (1987). Haben Frauen eine andere Moral? Eine empirische Untersuchung bei Studentinnen and Studenten in Österreich, der Bundesrepublick Deutschland und Poland. (Do women have a different morality? An empirical study by female and male students in Austria, Germany, and Poland.) in L. Unterkirchner and I. Wagner (Eds.) *Die andere Hälfte der Gesellschaft* (The other half of society.) (pp. 394-406). Vienna, Austria: Verlag des österreichischen Gewerksschafts-bundes.

Lind, G., Hartman, H., and Wakenhut, R. (Eds.), (1985). *Moral development and the social environment: Studies in the psychology and the philosophy of moral judgment and education.* Chicago: Precedent Publishing.

Lockwood, A. and Harris, D. (1985) *Reasoning with democratic values,* Vols. 1 & 2. New York: Teachers College, Columbia University.

Loevinger, J. (1966). The meaning and measurement of ego development. *American Psychologist, 21,* 195-206.

Loevinger, J. (1976). *Ego development.* San Francisco: Jossey-Bass.

Loevinger, J. and Wessler, R. (1970). *Measuring ego development I: Construction and use of a sentence completion test.* San Francisco: Josey-Bass.

Lyons, N.P. (1983). Two perspectives: On self, relationships and morality. *Harvard Educational Review, 53,* 125-145.

McNamee, S. (1978). Moral behavior, moral development and motivation. *Journal of Moral Education, 7,* 27-32.

Malerstein, A., and Ahern, M. (1982). *A Piagetian model of character structure.* New York: Human Sciences Press.

Markoulis, D. (1989). *Postformal and postconventional reasoning in educationally advanced adults.* Unpublished paper. University of Thessalonika, Greece.

Meichenbaum, D. (1977). *Cognitive behavior therapy.* New York: Plenum.

Mentkowski, M. (1988). Paths to integrity: Educating for personal growth and professional performance. In S. Srivasta and Associates, *Executive integrity: The search for high human values in organizational life* (pp. 89-121). San Francisco: Jossey-Bass.

Mentkowski, M., Moeser, M., and Strait, M. (1983). Using the Perry scheme of intellectual and ethical development as a college outcomes measure: A process and criteria for judging student performance (Vols. 1 and 2). Milwaukee: Alverno Productions.

Merriam, S. and Ferro, T. (1986). Working with young adults. In N.T. Foltz, (Ed.) *Handbook of adult religious education.* Birmingham, AL: Religious Education Press.

Mogdil, S. and Mogdil, C. (1986). *Lawrence Kohlberg: Consensus and controversy.* London: The Falmer Press.

Moon, Y.L. (1986). A review of cross-cultural studies on moral judgment development using the Defining Issues Test. *Behavior Science Research, 20* (1-4), 147-177.

Mosher, R.L. (1978). A democratic high school: Damn it, your feet are always in the water. In N. Sprinthall and R. Mosher (Eds.), *Value Development . . . as an Aim of Education.* Schenectady, NY: Character Education Press.

Mosher, R.L. (1979). *Adolescents' Development and Education: A Janus Knot.* Berkeley: McCutchan.

Mosher, R.L. (1980). A democratic school: Coming of age. In R. Mosher (Ed.), *Moral Education: A First Generation of Research and Development.* New York: Praeger.

Mosher, R.L., and Sprinthall, N. (1970). Psychological education in the secondary schools: A program to promote individual and human development. *American Psychologist, 25,* 911-924.

Mosher, R.L. and Sullivan, P. (1976). A curriculum in moral education for adolescents. In D. Purpel and K. Ryan (Eds.), *Moral Education: It goes with the territory.* Berkeley: McCutchan.

Nisan, M. and Kohlberg, L. (1982). Universality and cross-cultural variation in moral development: A longitudinal and cross-cultural study in Turkey. *Child Development, 53,* 865-876.

Noam, G. (1985). Stage, phase, and style: The developmental dynamics of the self. In M. Berkowitz and F. Oser (Eds.), *Moral education: Theory and application.* Hillsdale, NJ: Erlbaum.

Noam, G. (1986). The theory of biography and transformation and the borderline personality disorders: A developmental typology. *McLean Hospital Journal, 11,* 79-105.

Noam, G. (1988). The theory of biography and transformation: Foundation for a clinical-developmental therapy. In S. Shirk (Ed.), *Cognitive development and child psychotherapy* (pp. 273-317). New York: Plenum.

Noam, G. (1988b). A constructivist approach to developmental psychopathology. In E. Nannis and P. Cowan (Eds.), *New directions for child development: Developmental psychopathology and its treatment* (pp. 91-121). San Francisco: Jossey-Bass.

Noam, G., Kohlberg, L., and Snarey, J. (1983). Steps toward a model for the self. In B. Lee and G. Noam (Eds.), *Developmental approaches to the self* (pp. 59-134). New York: Plenum.

Noia, B. (1983). Cheating and truancy: Discipline and locus of control in a "just community" school. *Moral Education Forum,* 8-3:1-9.

Nunner-Winkler, G. (1984). Two moralities? A critical discussion of an ethic of care and responsibility versus an ethic of rights and justice. In J.L. Gewirtz and W. Kurtines (Eds.), *Morality, moral behavior and moral development.* New York: Wiley.

Oser, F. (1980). Stages of religious judgment. In C. Brussel (Ed.), *Toward moral and religious maturity.* Morristown, NJ: Silver Burdett.

Paolitto, D. (1975). *Role-taking opportunities for early adolescents: A program in moral education.* PhD dissertation, Boston University.

Perry, W. (1970). *Forms of intellectual and ethical development in the college years.* New York: Holt, Rinehart and Winston.

Piaget, J. (1932/1965). *The Moral Judgment of the Child.* Glencoe, IL: Free Press.

Piveteau, D.J. and Dillon, J.T. (1977) *Resurgence of religious instruction.* Birmingham, AL: Religious Education Press.

Power, C. (1979a). *The moral atmosphere of a just community high school: A four-year longitudinal study.* PhD dissertation, Harvard University.

Power, C. (1979b). The moral atmosphere of the school. Part 1 & 2. *Moral Education Forum, 4-1:9-14 and 4-2:20-26.*

Power, C. (1985). Democratic education in a large high school: A case study. In M. Berkowitz and F. Oser (Eds.), *Moral Education: Theory and Application.* Hillsdale, NJ: Lawrence Erlbaum.

Power, C. (1988). *The moral atmosphere of the school.* Manuscript.

Power, C., Higgins, A., and Kohlberg, L. (1989). *Lawrence Kohlberg's Approach to Moral Education.* New York: Columbia University Press.

Power, C. and Reimer, J. (1978). Moral atmosphere: An educational bridge between moral judgment and action. In W. Damon (Ed.), *New directions for child development.* Vol. 2. San Francisco: Jossey-Bass.

Pratt, M.W., Golding, G., and Hunter, W.J. (1984). Does morality have a gender? Sex, sex role, and moral judgment relationships across the adult life span. *Merrill-Palmer Quarterly, 30,* 321-340.

Puka, B. (1988). *Caring, concern and just regard: Different voices or separate realities?* Mosaic Monograph No. 4, University of Bath, England.

Reimer, J. (1977). A study in the moral development of kibbutz adolescents. PhD dissertation, Harvard University.

Reimer, J., Paolitto, D., and Hersch, R. (1983). *Promoting moral growth: From Piaget to Kohlberg.* 2nd ed. New York: Longman.

Reimer, J. and Power, C. (1980). Educating for democratic community: Some unresolved dilemmas. In R. Mosher, (Ed.), *Moral Education: A First Generation of Research.* New York: Praeger.

Rest, J. (1968). *Developmental hierarchy in preference and comprehension of moral judgment.* PhD dissertation, University of Chicago.

Rest, J. (1979). *Development in judging moral issues.* Minneapolis: University of Minnesota Press.

Rest, J. (1983). Morality. In P. Mussen (Ed.), *Handbook of child psychology,* Vol. 3, 4th ed. (pp. 556-629). New York: Wiley.

Rest, J. (1986a). *Moral development: Advances in research and theory.* New York: Praeger.

Rest, J. (1986b) *Manual for the Defining Issues Test: An objective test of moral judgment development.* 3rd ed., Minneapolis, Minnesota Research Projects.

Rest, J.R. (1986c). Moral research methodology. In S. and C. Mogdil (Eds.) *Lawrence Kohlberg: Consensus and Controversy.* (pp. 455-469). Philadelphia: The Falmer Press.

Richter, D. (1982). The creative process in adolescent development. In D.C. Wyckoff and D. Richer (Eds.), *Religious education ministry with youth.* Birmingham, AL: Religious Education Press.

Roetz, H. (1990). *Kohlberg and Chinese morality: A philosophical perspective.* Unpublished paper, J.W. Goethe Universität, Frankfurt, Germany.

Rogers, C. (1961). *On becoming a person.* Boston: Houghton Mifflin.

Rogers, C. (1970). *Carl Rogers on encounter groups.* New York: Harper & Row.

Rose, S. (1977). *Group therapy: A behavioral approach.* Englewood Cliffs, NJ: Prentice Hall.

Rosen, H. (1985). *Piagetian dimensions of clinical relevance.* New York: Columbia University Press.

Rowntree, S., S.J. (1978). Faith and justice and Kohlberg: A Catholic perspective. In P. Scharf (Ed.), *Readings in moral education.* Minneapolis: Winston.

Sachs, D. and Prusnovsky, V. (1981). Supporting the "just community" concept: Sharing moral development theory and practice with teachers. *Moral Education Forum,* 6-4:24-30.

Salzman, F. (1981). *A discussion of Sharon's dilemma.* Manuscript.

Scharf, P. (1973). *Moral atmosphere and intervention in the prison.* PhD dissertation, Harvard University.

Scharf, P. (1987). *Readings in moral education.* Minneapolis: Winston.

Schein, J.L. (1985). Moral education in Jewish schools. *Reconstructionist,* Part I - March 15-19; Part II - December 9-13.

Schipani, D.S. (1988). *Religious education encounters liberation theology.* Birmingham, AL: Religious Education Press.

Schlafli, A.J., Rest, J., and Thoma, S. (1985) Does moral education improve moral judgment?: A meta-analysis of intervention studies using the DIT. *Review of Educational Research,* 55:319-52.

Schwarz, E. (1983). Moral development: A practical guide for Jewish teachers. Denver: Alternatives in Religious Education.

Selman, R. (1971). The relation of role-taking to the development of moral judgment in children. *Child Development, 42,* 72-91.

Selman, R. (1976). Social-cognitive understanding. In T. Lickona (Ed.), *Moral development and behavior* (pp. 299-316). New York: Holt, Rinehart and Winston.

Selman, R. (1980). *The growth of interpersonal understanding: Clinical and developmental analyses.* New York: Academic Press.

Selman, R., and Schultz, L. (1988). Interpersonal thought and action in the case of a troubled early adolescent: Toward a developmental model of the gap. In S. Shirk (Ed.), *Cognitive development and child psychotherapy* (pp. 207-246). New York: Plenum.

Shaheen, J. and Kuhmerker, L. (1991). *Our book of big ideas: A program for kindergarten to grade three.* Manhattan, KS: Master Teacher.

Smith, M. (1985). Religious education. In S. and C. Mogdil (Eds.), *Lawrence Kohlberg: Consensus and controversy.* Philadelphia: Falmer International.

Snarey, J., Kohlberg, L., and Noam, G. (1983). Ego development in perspective: Structural stage, functional phase, and cultural-age periods models. *Developmental Review, 3,* 303-338.

Snarey, J., Reimer, J., and Kohlberg, L. (1984). The sociomoral development of kibbutz adolescents: A longitudinal, cross-cultural study. *Developmental Psychology, 21,* 3-17.

Speicher-Dubin, B. (1982). *Relationships between parent moral judgment and family interaction: A correlational study.* PhD dissertation, Harvard University.

Sprinthall, N., and Mosher, R. (Eds.) (1978). *Value development as the aim of education.* Schenectady, NY: Character Education Press.

Stephenson, B., and Hunt, C. (1980). Intellectual and ethical development: A dualistic curriculum intervention for college students. In V.L. Erickson and J.M. Whitely (Eds.), *Developmental counseling and teaching* (pp. 208-28). Monterey, CA: Brooks/Cole.

Stern-Strom, M. and Parsons, W. (1982). *Facing history and ourselves: Holocaust and human behavior.* Watertown, MA. Intentional Educations Inc.

Thoma, S.J. (1986). Estimating gender differences in the comprehension and preference of moral issues. *Developmental Review, 6,* 165-80.

Thompson, L. (1982). *Training elementary school teachers to create a democratic classroom.* PhD dissertation, Boston University.

Turiel, E. (1983). *The Development of social knowledge, morality and convention.* New York: Cambridge University Press.

Vasudev, J. and Hummel, R.C. (1987). Moral stage sequence and principled reasoning in an Indian sample. *Human Development, 30,* 105-118.

Vine, I. (1986). Moral maturity in sociocultural perspective: Are Kohlberg's stages universal? In S. Mogdil and C. Mogdil (Eds.), *Lawrence Kohlberg: Concensus and controversy.* London: The Falmer Press.

Walker, L.J. (1980). Cognitive and perspective-taking prerequisites for moral development. *Child Development,* 51:131-39.

Walker, L.J. (1984). Sex differences in the development of moral reasoning: A critical review. *Child Development, 55,* 677-691.

Walker, L.J. The development of moral reasoning. Annals of Child Development, 5, 33-78.

Walker, L.J. (in press). Sex differences in moral reasoning. In W.M. Kurtines
and J.L. Gewirtz (Eds.), *Moral behavior and development: Advances in theory, research and application.* Vol. 2 Hillsdale, New York: Erlbaum.

Wasserman, E. (1975). Implementing Kohlberg's "just community" in an alternative high school. *Social Education,* 40:203-7.

Wasserman, E. (1977). The development of an alternative high school based on Kohlberg's just community approach to education. PhD dissertation, Boston University.

Wasserman, E. et al. (1982). *The Teacher Advisory Program (TAP): A Multicultural Approach to High School Orientation and Support for Ninth Grade Students; A Teacher Guide.* Cambridge, MA Schools, Manuscript; 123pp., A validated Title IV-C Project.

Wasserman, E. and Garrod, A. (1983). The application of Kohlberg's theory to curricula and democratic schools. *Educational Analysis,* 5, 17-36.

White, C.B. (1986). Moral reasoning in Bahamian and United States adults and children: A cross-cultural examination of Kohlberg's stages. *Behavior Science Research, 20* (1-4), 47-70.

White, J.W. (1988). *Intergenerational religious education.* Birmingham, AL: Religious Education Press.

Wyckoff, D.C. and Richter, D. (1982). *Religious Education Ministry with Youth.* Birmingham, AL: Religious Education Press.

Young-Eisendrath, P. (1985, January). Making use of human development theories in counseling. *Counseling and Human Development, 17,* 1-12.

Zalaznick, E. (1980/1981). The just community school: A student perspective. *Moral Education Forum,* 5-2:27-35.

Acknowledgments

We thank the many members of the Association for Moral Education with whom we brainstormed about the focus and content of this volume. Special thanks are due to Ann Higgins and Ralph Mosher who read all or most of our manuscript.

It would not have been possible to give a comprehensive overview of the final years of Kohlberg and colleagues in the New York City school programs without drawing extensively from *Lawrence Kohlberg's Approach to Moral Education* (1989) co-authored by Clark Power, Ann Higgins, and Kohlberg and completed by the first two authors after Kohlberg's death. Grateful acknowledgment is made to Columbia University Press, for permission to quote from Power, C., Higgins, A., and Kohlberg, L. (1989), *Lawrence Kohlberg's Approach to Moral Education*, from pages 53, 54, 57, 64, 69, 99, 100, 121-2, and 137.

Grateful acknowledgement is made for permission to publish excerpted and condensed material from James Rest's First Annual Lawrence Kohlberg Memorial Lecture, sponsored by the Association for Moral Education, Pittsburgh, PA, November 11, 1988, and published in whole by *The Journal For Moral Education* (1989), v.18-2.

Grateful acknowledgement is made to Lawrence Erlbaum Press, for permission to reprint "The Kohlberg Legacy to Friends" from Kurtines, W. and J. Gewirtz (in press), *Moral Behavior and Development*, Vol. I, pp. 15-20.

Grateful acknowledgment is made to Cambridge University Press for permission to quote from Colby, A. and Kohlberg, L. (1987). *The Measurement of Moral Judgment*, Vol. I, pp. 12, 167, 229-23, and Vol. II, p. 28.

Grateful acknowledgement is made to Harper & Row Press for permission to quote from Lawrence Kohlberg (1984), *Essays on Moral Development, Volume I, The Philosophy of Moral Education*, p. 30 and Volume II, *The Psychology of Moral Development*, pp. XIII, IVX, 9, 14 and 537.

Grateful acknowledgement is made to John Wiley Press for permission to quote from Kurtines, W. and J. Gewirtz, (1987), *Social Development and Social Interaction,* pp. 80, 106 and 128, and from Paul Mussen (Ed.) (1983). *Handbook of Child Psychology,* Vol. IV, p. 588.

Grateful acknowledgment is made to Thomas Lickona for permission to reproduce the table in *Moral Behavior: Theory, Research and Social Issues.* (1976) published by Holt, Rinehart and Winston.

The following material was first published in the *Moral Education Forum:*
Lawrence Kohlberg—My Personal Search for Universal Morality. MEF (1986) v.12-1, pp. 4-10.
William Kolber—Living in a "Just Community": A Student Perspective. MEF (1981) v.6-4, pp. 43-46.
Edward Zalaznick—The Just Community School: A Student Perspective, and Dialog: Lawrence Kohlberg Talks with Edward Zalaznick. MEF (1980) v.5-2, reprinted in v. 6-4 (1981), pp. 47-56.
Beverly Noia—Cheating and Truancy: Discipline and Locus of Control in a Just Community School. MEF (1983) v.8-3, pp. 56-64.

Index of Names

Index of Subjects

232